THE
MARINE AQUARIUM HANDBOOK

Beginner to Breeder

Martin A. Moe, Jr.

Green Turtle Publications
P.O. Box 17925
Plantation, Florida 33318

Green Turtle Publications
P.O. Box 17925
Plantation, FL 33318

Library of Congress Cataloging-in-Publication data.

Moe, Martin A.
The marine aquarium handbook : beginner to breeder /
Martin A. Moe, Jr. — New ed.
     p.   cm.
Includes bibliographical references and index.
ISBN 0-939960-07-9 (acid-free)
   1. Marine aquariums.   I. Title.
SF457. 1, M63   1992
639.3'42—dc20   92-4908
                                                         CIP

First printing, April 1982
    22 printings
New edition, January 1992

10 9 8 7 6 5 4 3

Printed in the United States of America

Cover photo: A pair of common clownfish, *Amphiprion ocellaris*, watch over their eggs that are attached to a rock near the base of their anemone.

Contents

To my parents, Martin and Clara,

Whose support and encouragement were neverfailing.

Preface

So you want to go marine. The lure of those brilliant gems of life from far off tropical seas is beginning to get to you. But a good marine aquarium set up is a bit expensive, and you have heard that the failure rate of new marine aquarists is frighteningly high, and even though freshwater aquaria hold no fears for you, the big step to saltwater gives you the trembles. Well, you are not alone and your fears are not without some justification. Most of the failures with marine aquaria are due to lack of knowledge of the biological processes that occur in the aquarium.

The marine aquarium is a miniature ecosystem; the interactions of living organisms are what makes it work, and the living balance of the aquarium is as delicate as life itself. Although it is these same processes that keep a freshwater aquarium in good health, the "balance" of a marine aquarium has a narrow edge and requires at least a basic understanding of the factors that create a healthy marine aquarium. Many people have asked me in the last few years how to go about setting up a marine tank, and I have been happy to give them what advice I could in 30 minutes or so of conversation. This is usually inadequate, however, because one often does not remember everything that is said, and one seldom remembers to say everything.

The intent of this book is to present in simple, basic language the information necessary to develop a successful marine aquarium, and to know why it is successful. And those who want to try their hand at breeding marine fish will find all they need to know to spawn and rear some of the most popular marine aquarium fish in a home environment. It is not designed to be an expensive picture book or a dry laboratory manual. It is an information book, a hobbyist's handbook that is enjoyable to read and provides basic understandings and working techniques as well.

Preface to the second edition

The original preface is still accurate. The only change I might make is to put less stress on the "narrow edge" and "delicate balance" of a marine aquarium. It seems that now in the 90's more wholesalers, retailers, and hobbyists have a better knowledge of how a marine aquarium works, know better how to care for marine fish and invertebrates, and are able to avoid or cure most parasitic infestations. Better equipment for professionals and hobbyists is now available, and fish and invertebrates seem to reach the aquarist in better condition. For all these reasons, the failure rate of new marine aquarists seems to have greatly declined. One can now become a marine aquarist with relatively little fear of failure if the project is undertaken with a reasonable amount of research, care, and effort. There are now many books and several good magazines for the marine aquarist that provide information on all facets of the hobby. And of course, the new edition of the *Handbook* is also now available.

The *Handbook* has changed in two ways. First, we carefully went through the old text and, with the advantage of new computer technology (spelling checkers) and the editing wisdom acquired over the last few years, edited and updated the old text. We added a lot of new information and set off the major new additions with bold brackets [....]. Thus the reader has the original text, improved by editing and revisions, and a complementary, updated guide to the important, recent developments in the hobby, integrated in one volume. The hobbyist can then make decisions between working with the old "tried and true" techniques or going with the new "bigger and better" methods, based on what works best with the budget, space, and time that the aquarist wishes to devote to the hobby.

Introduction

Most of the Earth is ocean, and of the aquatic environments of the world, coral reefs are among the most environmentally stable and biologically dynamic. Coral reefs only occur within about 30 degrees of latitude from the equator. They can only live and grow where average annual water temperatures are 73 to 77°F; salinity is constant and high; sunlight strongly penetrates the shallow, clear oceanic water; and dissolved nutrients are very low. The environment changes little from season to season, year to year; but the animals and plants endlessly war for food and space.

These elements of existence have created a wonderland of form, color, and behavior—a wonderland that we can capture, in small measure, in our home aquarium. The romance and mystery of tropic seas can be reflected in a small simulated coral reef snug in one's living room while winter winds pile snow against the door. Not so long ago, 30 years or so, a successful marine aquarist was regarded with awe and wonder as one favored by Neptune himself, and thus privy to the secrets of the deep. Now we know that those pioneering individuals were not specially favored, but only had the courage to persist, despite failures, and the tenacity to stick with methods that worked for them. Now we know why certain methods and techniques work and why others fail, and although maintaining a marine aquarium is not as easy as keeping a freshwater tank, most of the questions now have answers, and with a little effort, the average fish fancier can be a successful marine aquarist.

Three very important, relatively recent developments have put a marine aquarium within reach of most aquarists. These are the development and commercial availability of the all glass tank, wide distribution of synthetic sea salts, and the understanding of the biological functions of the undergravel filter. These basic developments have made possible the rapid and extensive growth of the marine segment of the tropical fish hobby.

[Now, 10 years later, the marine sector of the aquarium hobby has grown greatly, and major advances have been achieved in the technology of keeping home marine aquaria. New philosophies of filtration, new concepts of lighting, new books, more widely dispersed working knowledge, and most important, new hardware and equipment are now available that allow the novice marine enthusiast to achieve beautiful and successful displays with almost certain success. One still has to do one's homework, however, but there is now far less uncertainty in the wonderful world of keeping marine aquaria. A good aquarium shop and your local aquarium society are excellent sources of help and information. An aquarium shop will usually know of the nearest aquarium society with a marine interest and steer you in the right direction. Society members will be glad to keep you from major error and support you in your efforts to become a successful marine aquarist.

Even though all the new technology—trickle filters, protein skimmers, high intensity lighting, pH controllers, ion-exchange resins, etc.—makes things quite easy, although more expensive, for marine aquarists; it is important to note that the "old" technology—undergravel filters, activated carbon filtration, air lift pumps, standard fluorescent lighting, etc.—still works quite well. The establishment and maintenance of a marine aquarium with the "old" or "traditional" technology was, and is, a major part of this book. This is because the traditional technology, even though limited, allows an aquarist to establish and keep a marine aquarium (even to the point of breeding some marine fish) with a minimum of expense—a very important consideration to many novice marine aquarists. The "old" techniques also allow an aquarist with one or two expensive, beautiful reef and fish systems to keep a few less expensive, smaller aquariums as quarantine tanks or specialty tanks. The "old" undergravel technology will never die (although it may fade a bit), and the basic information on these techniques will always be of value.

In this new edition, I mention and describe much of the "new" technology, usually in a comparision with the old, to inform the aquarist of what is now available. Make no mistake, the new technology, still under explosive development, greatly broadens the horizons of the marine aquarist, and creates a better, more stable marine aquarium environment with less required filter-cleaning maintenance than the old techniques. *However, as long as the aquarist understands and accepts the limitations of the "old" technology, a very interesting, successful, educational, entertaining, and inexpensive marine aquarium can be established and maintained.*

This new edition of the *Handbook* provides the marine aquarist with the basics of the old and the new technology. Both "tried and true" and "new and improved" techniques can be used to create the marine aquarium system that best accommodates each individual suitation. Chapter 1 has been expanded to include all the basic types of small marine aquarium systems that a marine aquarist may now buy or build. My other book, *The Marine Aquarium Reference : Systems and Invertebrates*, is more advanced and describes modern marine aquarium techniques and technology in great detail. It will be useful to any aquarist interested in keeping marine invertebrates or in establishing a reef tank or other type of advanced marine system.]

The major innovation yet to flower, but now waiting in the wings, is the commercial propagation of many species of marine tropical fish. When this occurs, the marine aquarium hobby, and control and preservation of the tropical fish resources of coral reefs, will truly come of age. It is now possible for the home aquarist to spawn and rear certain species of marine fish. Certainly it is more difficult to breed marine fish than it is to rear guppies and goldfish, but the knowledgeable and determined home hobbyist can achieve some success in this area, and I write here from actual experience.

[Ten years later, we are closer to the goal of "commercial propagation of many species of marine tropical fish", but unfortunately, we are still waiting. There are now quite a number of hobbyists that have successfully spawned and reared marine tropical fish, mostly clownfish and gobies, and a few of these have even been able to supply small numbers of marine fish to commercial outlets. To my knowledge, however, there is still only one large commercial hatchery for marine tropical fish, clownfish and gobies, and this is Aqualife Research Corporation on Walker's Cay in the northern Bahamas. There are now a few other small marine fish hatcheries (the Florida Keys, Illinois, and England); and a number of hobbyists have also been successfully rearing a few marine tropical fish. It is still not an easy task to spawn and rear marine fish, but the stimulus to do so is ever increasing, and technology and techniques are constantly developing. I think we will soon see some very interesting and astounding developments in breeding and propagating marine aquarium fish and invertebrates.

Also in the next few years, we **must** see the elimination of fish collection with cyanide! Use of this poison to collect fish for aquariums and food destroys the coral reef environment and fish populations, and casts a very dark shadow on the future of the industry and the hobby.]

A trouble free, entertaining, and rewarding display is the goal of most marine aquarists, and I hope this book will continue to contribute to that end. I have directed it toward those who need an accurate, easily understood guide to the basics of marine aquarium keeping. The emphasis is on simple techniques that work, low cost methods, and the how and why of what happens in a marine aquarium. It discusses topics as basic as tank set up and as advanced as breeding, and thus should be useful to the old hand as well as the beginning marine aquarist.

Chapter 1

THE AQUARIUM

Size, Shape, Style, and Construction

The first decision you make after you decide to become a marine aquarist usually concerns the container that will house your own private little parcel of ocean bottom. This basic choice of a tank will have a great effect on your future success and on the type and size of fish and invertebrates you can maintain. [Note that now, in the 1990's, selection of an aquarium involves much more than size and dollars. The decision includes lighting, type of filtration, and even serious consideration about the kinds of marine organisms one wishes to keep. Although expense is still a major factor, the same dollar can purchase systems quite different in design, function, and purpose. See the last section of this chapter for basic information on the types of marine aquarium systems now available to marine aquarists.]

If this is your first marine aquarium, you should ask yourself some basic questions about your plans and intentions before you buy or build a tank. Here are a few good questions for starters:

How much money do I want to spend?

Do I want to start with a large tank (because large tanks are more biologically stable) and work with it until I know what I'm doing?

Or do I want to start with a small tank of 20 gallons or less (because the investment is much less), and then get a large tank when I do know what I'm doing?

Do I want to work with an undergravel filter in a traditional type marine aquarium system (because it's easier and cheaper), or do I want to set up a marine aquarium system with a trickle filter even though it is more costly (because it provides a much better aquatic environment for fish and invertebrates)?

Do I want to keep exotic tropical marine fish or just local critters?

Should I build my own tank and filter to save money or should I buy commercially made equipment?

How much space, money, and time do I have to devote to a marine aquarium?

These are all good questions and you're the only one who has the answers. But before you make these decisions, it makes sense to get as much information as possible. Read everything you can find and talk to good dealers and successful aquarists. Don't automatically believe everything you read and hear, because there is a lot of inaccurate information around as well as experimentally verified facts. Good marine hobbyists always think, and experiment to find the techniques that work best for them. [This is even more important now than it was 10 years ago. Now there are many more techniques and types of equipment to consider when setting up a marine aquarium system. The new section at the end of this chapter details these options.]

Contrary to some existing opinions, a marine aquarium can be maintained in a 10 gallon tank, a 5 gallon tank, and even a 1 gallon jar, if one so desires. The same biological systems will work in one gallon as well as 300 gallons, but the smaller the system, the easier it is to overcrowd, and there is less "reserve" filtration capacity. I would recommend a 20 gallon tank to a beginner, because this is large enough to keep an interesting number and variety of fish with adequate filtration capacity, and is still small enough to be manageable and economical. Also, if you do graduate to a larger tank, the 20 gallon makes a good second tank for treatment or quarantine. Another thing to consider on the size of your tank is weight. This may seem curious, but if you overlook it you could be in a peck of trouble. One gallon of seawater weighs 8.5 pounds, which isn't an awful lot, but 50 of them together weigh 425 pounds, and 100 gallons weighs 850 pounds. It may be a little disquieting to come home after a rough day at work and find your new 100 gallon marine tank in the apartment underneath yours, which, I have heard, has happened before.

The shape of a marine tank is important because it can affect the filtering capacity of the tank. The more surface area in the filter, which covers the bottom of the tank, the greater the number of fish that the tank can safely support. Therefore, a low flat tank with an undergravel filter has a slightly greater filtering capacity than a high sided tank of the same gallonage. If you really want a high style tank because the fish have greater depth to swim, or because it fits the planned placement of the tank, or because you just like that style better, go ahead and get it. Few marine aquarists will notice any difference in filtering capacity between well maintained high and low tanks. A marine tank can be any shape you wish providing that the filter is large enough to carry the biological load residing in the tank. You can even have an inverted pyramid if you wish, but better plan on a filter outside the tank if this is the case. [Now that trickle filters are available, a tank can be any configuration one wishes, since the filter can easily be located outside the tank. The typical low and wide configuration, however, still provides the best ratio of surface area to volume for good gas exchange and ease of maintenance.]

Selecting an aquarium

Unless you want an exceptionally large tank or a very unusual shape, the only way to go is with an all glass aquarium. Avoid any tanks with metal or exposed concrete or wood. There are many companies that manufacture all glass tanks, and one should shop for price and quality as with any other purchase. Because of the fragile nature of a glass box, it is always wise to inspect it carefully before you truck it home. Watch for cracks, of course, but also be aware of more subtle defects. Are the edges of the tank chipped, and if so, did the chips break through or damage the silicone seals? If it is a large tank, is the bottom piece made from glass a size thicker than the sides? Is the reinforcement about the top and bottom well made, totally plastic, and firmly attached? Is the silicone seal evenly distributed along all seams? Check for disruptions of the seal by viewing each edge through the overlapping side. Numerous air bubbles and channels through the seal may indicate potential leaks and glass cuts that are not perfectly square. If the glass is not cut square, cracks and leaks will probably occur, especially in large tanks. Buy your tank from a good dealer, one recommended by other aquarists, and you will get a good tank and good advice.

[In the early 80's, acrylic plastic tanks were just starting to pop up here and there. Some were made from flat sheets of ½ to 1 inch Plexiglas® or Lucite® glued together like a glass tank, and some were molded into rectangular, round, and even bubble shapes. Nowadays, acrylic tanks are truly spectacular. A large acrylic reef tank in a custom cabinet with all the right lighting and filtration is a marvel to behold—an expensive marvel, but a marvel nonetheless. Acrylic tanks are a bit difficult to build, since the plastic must be worked with great precision, especially large tanks, so that all edges are exactly right and will weld together perfectly. Holes must be drilled with special bits and cuts made with special saws to prevent the plastic from melting and chipping. Even though the plastic is more easily worked than glass (once you know how), it still requires development of special skills to work acrylic with care and precision. Acrylic tanks are also more prone to scratching and marring than glass, and one must be very careful when cleaning the inside and outside surfaces. If acrylic surfaces do get marred, it is possible to polish out shallow scratches and restore acrylic to a perfect luster, but this can be a major project. Note that acrylic tanks also take space travel very well, especially the bubble formed tanks. Captain Picard has one aboard the *Enterprise*, and as far as I know, he hasn't had a speck of trouble with it. He has noted, however, that lionfish sometimes lose their appetite at warp speed.]

Constructing an all glass tank

You may, if you're a handy sort of person, decide that to save money and to fulfill a creative urge you should build your own tank. If you plan to charge for your time and trouble, forget it and buy a tank. Building your own tank, however, does have some advantages: first, you will save money (not much, but some); second, you can build any size or shape you wish to fit any placement you desire; and third, it adds a unique and creative dimension to the hobby. Since I have built most of my own tanks, I can give you a few tips on construction.

Working with glass

It doesn't pay to build your own tank unless you use ¼ inch *salvage* plate glass. This is glass that has been salvaged from windows and showcases and is generally worn and a little scratched, but still satisfactory for an aquarium. Turn the scratched side inward, and when water fills the scratches they will disappear. Give the glass shop the *exact* measurements for each piece of glass you need, specify salvage plate glass, and tell them that all pieces must be cut square and exact to measurements because they are to be part of an aquarium. If you use new ¼ inch plate glass or build a tank as large as 50 gallons or more and need glass thicker than ¼ inch, the cost may equal or exceed a commercially available tank.

Cutting glass

[If you're looking for an even greater challenge, you can cut the glass for the tank out of scrap ¼ inch plate glass yourself. This is an art in itself, and glass cutting requires a lot of practice before one becomes proficient, or even reasonably successful. Start with a new glass cutter (a couple of dollars at most hardware stores), some scrap glass, and a carpet or towel covered sturdy table. Make sure that the glass is squeaky clean before attempting the cut. Any grubbiness on the glass at the point of the score will prevent a smooth, even score. Keep the glass cutter in a can of kerosene or paint thinner to provide lubrication and prevent rust. Use a strong, very straight guide for the glass cutter. It must be thick enough to prevent the glass cutter from riding up over the edge of the straight edge and messing up the score. A hard, straight one by two is much better than a thin, flimsy yardstick. Measure the cut carefully, use a fine point felt marker (not a grease pencil, the grease can gum up the glass cutter) to mark the beginning and end point of the score. Place the marks about ¹⁄₁₆ inch under the actual measure to allow for the extra width of the glass cutter.

Hold the straight edge **firmly** on the glass and draw the glass cutter from one end of the glass to the other with a strong, straight, even, unbroken stroke—pressing the cutter strongly into the glass. The resulting score on the glass must be straight, it must score the glass deeply and evenly along the entire length of the glass (edge to very edge), and it must be accomplished in only one stroke. It the cutter skips a section of the score and you have to try again to make the score complete, the chances for a wandering break are very high. If you are cutting to exact measurements, you can't flub up; the score has to be right the first time.

The moment of truth comes once the score is on the glass. Then the glass must be broken evenly and smoothly along the score. There are two ways that I know of to do this. There is a little ball on the end of the metal glass cutter that is used to tap the glass on the score and then, in the best of all worlds, the glass cracks and breaks right along the score in a perfect cut from one end to the other. Sometimes the break goes only partway along the glass and another tap or two is required to drive the break all the way along the score. This works best on thinner glass, 1/16 to 1/8 inch thick. Sometimes, especially in thicker glass, if the score is not perfect, the break wanders from the score, and the 20 gallon tank that was planned, suddenly becomes a 10 gallon tank.

The other way to break the glass along the score usually results in a better break. Make sure that the carpet or towel extends over the edge of the table. Carefully line up the score with the edge of the table and lay the glass flat on the table with the short end extending off the table. Pick up the end of the glass that extends out over the table so that the glass is tilted up off the edge of the table about 4 to 6 inches. Then bring the glass sharply down to the edge of the table, impacting the glass on the table edge right along the scored line. **Wear gloves and eye protection!** The glass should then break evenly right along the scored line. It is also possible to place a dowel rod under the padding, line up the score along the top of the dowel, and pop the glass on the dowel top rather than along the edge of the table.

Drilling holes

Now I'll give you some real good advice on drilling a hole in the bottom glass of the tank. First of all, if at all possible, drill the hole in the bottom piece before the tank is assembled. Drilling a hole in an assembled or factory made tank is quite possible, but if the bottom or side breaks, the tank is ruined, whereas it is much easier to just cut another piece of glass to the right size if the hole is attempted in only a bottom piece. Note that drilling a hole will probably also void any warranty on the tank. Second, carefully measure the center point where the hole is to be drilled and mark it with a felt marker. Third, take the bottom piece to professional glass worker and ask them to drill the size hole you need at the proper place. That's the good advice.

Now if you still really want to drill your own holes in the glass, you probably have a lot of spare time, a lot of technical expertise, and probably even wind your own armatures for pump motors. One can drill (actually grind is a more accurate term) holes in glass with a professional glass drilling machine, a drill press, a drill press unit that rigidly mounts a hand held electric drill, or even free hand with a hand held electric drill. Small holes (like for air line) can be drilled with a small, brass spear point drill, but large holes, ½ to 2 inches (for drains and pipes), must be done with a tube drill. Some tube drills are edged with diamond dust, but most are brass tubes made expressly for drilling holes in glass. Make sure that the glass is not chipped, cracked, or scratched in the area where the hole is to be drilled.

Build a small dam about ½ inch high with clay all around the prospective hole. Put about a teaspoon of silicon carbide grit and a tablespoon or two of water into the dam. Small spear point drills need only cutting oil, no carbide cutting grit is needed. Start the drill, run it on slow speed, and let the weight of the drill grind the bit through the glass. Extra pressure on the drill only increases the chances of chipping and cracking. Support the glass well on the underside with cardboard or styrofoam. Hold the drill very steady and go slowly to avoid chipping and breaking, especially near the end when the drill begins to break through the glass. You may want to turn the glass over and finish the cut from the other side, especially with a spear point drill. Practice lots before drilling a hole in that three by six foot piece of half inch glass, and good luck.]

Building the tank

Your tank will be glued together with a silicone rubber sealer available in aquarium shops and hardware stores. Dow Corning and General Electric both make a good silicone sealer. Some types of these silicone sealers are manufactured for use on boats and in bathrooms and have a mildewcide incorporated in the sealer. If you make your tank with a silicone rubber sealer that has been so treated, there will be much weeping and wailing and gnashing of teeth. The safest course is to use only a product that specifies itself as an aquarium sealer on the label. Working with this silicone rubber sealer is quite an experience. I can only describe the uncured texture as a mixture of library paste and chewing gum scraped up off a hot sidewalk. It sticks to your fingers, to the glass, to your pants, your face, and the table; it gets on the glass where you don't want it and never quite

Figure 1 The completed 20 gallon tank. This one has been in hatchery use for 10 years and is still very serviceable. Note the patches on the bottom. Chips and cracks can be easily and permanently repaired by cementing a small piece of glass directly over the break with silicone sealer. Make sure that the sealer is spread all around the piece of patch glass so that water cannot seep under the patch. See Figure 2.

gets all over every edge where it must be. It is great fun, however, to peel it off your hands in long, thin strips when you finish. It's good stuff to have around even if you don't build your own tank, because it fixes leaks very well and repairs numerous household items. I advise you to practice working with the silicone sealer before starting, especially if you want a neat, professional tank when you finish. Wetting your fingers with a mix of vinegar and water also helps to keep the sealer in its place.

Now, if you still want to build your own tank, here are the dimensions and construction instructions for a 20 gallon tank of convenient shape as shown in Figure 1. I prefer to have the sides rest on top of the bottom piece, although I have seen many aquariums done in the European fashion with the sides surrounding the bottom.

Materials and Measurements

3 pieces, 30" x 12½"
(bottom, front and back sides)

2 pieces, 12" x 12½"
(left and right sides)

1 piece, 12" x 3"
(center brace, optional)
One 3 oz tube, silicone rubber sealer

All glass pieces are ¼ inch plate glass with seamed edges. The edges are seamed with a special grinding machine in a professional glass shop to remove the razor sharp edges of cut plate glass. You can do the same thing with fine sandpaper or a fine cut file and reduce the cost of the glass. Unless the sandpaper or file is very fine, you may create small chips along the edge. Fine chips won't cause leaks, but they do not enhance the appearance of the tank. The edges are razor sharp before they are seamed, so be very careful.

Procedure

Note that the bottom, front, and back sides are all the same dimensions. Pick the best piece for the front side and the worst piece for the bottom. Clean all the pieces with a commercial glass cleaner, wipe them clean and dry, and lay them out on a table with the sides surrounding the bottom, next to the edge where they will stand. Be sure to put a drop cloth or newspaper under the work, so that the sealer doesn't get all over the new marble table top and the woman or man in your life will not have cause to verbally abuse you.

This aquarium will be 30" long and 12¾" high. The sides will stand on top of the bottom and the ends will fit inside the front and back sides. It is easier to apply the silicone sealer to the edges of the side to be applied rather than to the bottom and the existing sides. Building the aquarium should be done all at one time so that you get a continuous seal from the sealer. You have five to ten minutes to put the whole thing together, and after it's done, **leave it alone until the silicone cures**. The more you push and wiggle it, the more problems you create. Try to set each piece into place with a minimum of adjustment. If, perchance, your glass was not cut perfectly square, you may notice that every time you push the front piece square with the left side, the front then separates from the right side. If this is the case, let one side stay a bit off, and add a little extra silicone sealer to fill in the gap. Although it may not look perfect, the tank will still function very well. It is far better to fill in a little gap than to mess up all the sides trying to force the glass into an impossible perfect fit. A bead of silicone between the side joints is actually good. Large all glass tanks in Europe are often built with a ⅛ inch gap between the sides that is filled with a bead of silicone. The silicone is flexible and this reduces the stress of glass on glass when a large tank is filled.

The first piece to set in place is the back side. Run a thin bead of sealer along the bottom edge and carefully place the side on the back edge of the bottom piece. Now you've got a problem. You can't let go of the back side or it will fall over, but you have to let go to add one of the ends to the tank. This is why it pays to think ahead. The best thing to do is to have someone hold the back side upright in position while you continue with an end. It is possible, however, to place a heavy object close to the back side so that it leans against the object slightly and does not fall over. This is the most delicate part of the whole operation.

Once the back is securely held or supported, run a thin bead of sealer along the bottom and back edge of one end, and carefully and gently press it into place. Take care that you don't push the back side off the bottom during this second step. As the end attaches to the back side and bottom piece, the two upright sides will support each other, and bracing or holding is no longer necessary. Masking tape is often recommended to help hold the sides to the bottom and to each other, but unless the tank is quite large or the glass is not cut perfectly square, I find that it is not worth the bother to use tape or other supports.

The other end is the next piece to attach. Once again run a thin bead of sealer along the bottom and back edge of the end piece and carefully and gently press it into place. Take care once again that you do not push the back side off the bottom piece. Now the only piece left is the front side. Run a thin bead of sealer along the edges of the upright ends and along the bottom edge of the front side. Hold the front side at an angle so that you can first place the bottom of the side on the edge of the aquarium bottom and then carefully push the front piece into place against the upright ends. Some of the sealer will squeeze out from between the glass on the inside and outside of the tank. This is the point where you find out if the glass was not cut perfectly square. If gaps in the seals occur, settle for the best fit you can with a minimum of movement. If the ends do not fit square against the back and front sides, just make sure that the space is completely filled with silicone sealer, smooth the seam a bit, and let it cure hard.

Don't fiddle with the sealer on the outside until after it cures, and then use a razor blade to cut it off cleanly with the edge of the outside glass. Don't pull it off, because this may cause leaks. The sealer on the inside can also be cut off after curing; this gives the tank a neat professional appearance. However, I prefer to use a small wooden or metal spreader and carefully train the inside bead into a thin wedge along every inside corner of the tank. This must be done within a few minutes of application, before the sealer forms a surface skin. If this is done carefully, the appearance of the tank is not affected and insurance against leakage is obtained. A piece of raw potato can be cut to the shape of the wedge required and then drawn along the inside corner to form the wedge. The sealer does not adhere to the raw potato and, with practice, this makes a neater job.

The brace is the last piece to be added. This tank does not really need a brace, but I usually put one in the center for additional strength, which is needed in a commercial situation. Wait about 24 hours until the tank has cured before attaching the brace. The brace extends from the top center of the front side to the top center of the back side and is designed to fit in-between the sides and flush with the top edge of the tank. The brace could be cut a half inch longer and be placed on the top of the sides, but then covers would not fit flush with the tank top. The tank can be placed on its side to apply the brace so it won't slip down while curing, or the brace can be supported from the bottom while it cures.

This same general procedure can be used to construct tanks to your own size specifications. You can use a little imagination and custom design tanks in many different shapes. It is even possible to make a tank within a tank and have freshwater fish in one compartment and marine fish in another, or even build a terrarium inside the fish tank.

[I've heard aquarists say, "Yeah, Moe tells you how to build a tank, chuckle, chuckle. Like you really need to build a tank these days." Okay, okay, so small, all glass tanks are not very expensive these days, and building your own is a holdover from the 60's when all glass tanks were scarce, almost as scarce as a little extra money was back then. Still, it adds an interesting dimension to the hobby, so I'll leave this section intact and even expand it a little.

Note that the same basic procedures can be used to custom build all glass tanks of different sizes for different purposes: a thin, high tank 4 inches wide for photography; or a tall, square tank for rearing larval fish; or a special size to fit under a tank table as a sump tank for a homemade trickle filter. If you do build a thin tank for photography, get an extra piece of glass that will just fit between the sides and also extend up and out of the tank by a couple of inches. This extra piece can then be inserted into the tank at an angle to form a transparent wedge to hold the specimen in place above the bottom of the tank for photographic purposes. The wedge glass should be clear and clean without any scratches, and cut so that there is only about an eighth of an inch between the edge of the glass and the sides of the tank. The glass can then move back and forth to adjust the size of the wedge to allow for the size and mobility of the specimen. Water can flow between the front and back of the wedge glass, but specimens must remain in the front of the glass. Various color backgrounds are easily made by placing colored construction paper behind the photography tank. The paper is far enough behind the specimen to be out of focus, but the color comes through as a clear and clean, smooth color background in the photograph.]

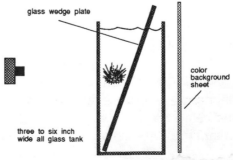

glass wedge plate

color background sheet

three to six inch wide all glass tank

Photography tank

Repairing tanks

[A little knowledge of glass working often comes in handy for a marine aquarist. All glass tanks, especially older ones, may suffer cracks or chips when moved or stored or filled without being properly supported on the bottom. These tanks can be easily repaired with a few pieces of scrap glass and ample silicone sealer. Suppose a 50 gallon tank has suffered a crack part way across the bottom of the tank. The first thing to do is to complete the crack. Tap the end of the crack and make it run all the way to another edge. If this is not done, water pressure will force the crack to continue to run through the glass when the tank is refilled, and it will leak, and you will have to do the whole job over again. There can be no blind cracks in the glass of any tank that is repaired. The crack must be forced out to an edge.

Cut or break pieces of glass of the same thickness as the bottom in widths of about two inches, so that they can be arranged along the entire crack with about one inch extending out on each side of the crack. The wider the repair piece, the stronger the repair. Cut any inside wedge of silicone sealer away from the sides of the tank where the crack meets the edge, to accommodate placement of the repair piece against the side. Cut or break the repair pieces so that they fit properly and arrange them so that they completely cover the crack from one edge of the tank to the other. Be sure that all the glass is clean.

Remove the repair pieces, but keep them in the proper order. Use an ample amount of silicone sealer along the crack and nearby areas and place each repair piece into its place (Figure 2). Make sure that the silicone completely fills the area between the tank bottom and the repair piece. Push the repair pieces hard against the bottom to squeeze excess sealer out from between the repair piece and the tank bottom. After all repair pieces are properly positioned and sealed into place, run a bead of silicone sealer along all exposed edges of each repair piece, including filling the areas near the side of the tank. Wait two or three days before

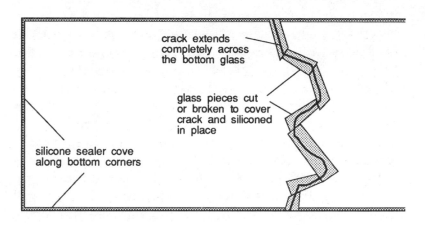

Figure 2 Repair of a cracked tank bottom. Glass pieces cut to overlap the crack and fit from one end of the crack to the other. The silicone cove at the bottom corner is cut away to allow the repair piece to butt against the tank side.

filling the tank to make sure that all the silicone sealer has cured. Such a patch is not pretty, but it can save a tank, and often the patch can be covered by the filter, a bottom substrate, or some other internal tank structure. This same technique can also be used to cover a drain hole in the bottom of an all glass tank. In this case, the patch glass and silicone sealer can always be removed if the drain hole is needed again in the future.]

Breeding marine fish requires a separate tank for the pelagic larval stage of marine fish. The tank described above was used as a juvenile tank to hold and grow small clownfish after they had passed through the larval stage. A good larval tank should have a high side design to provide a tall water column for the pelagic (free swimming) larval fish. A 36 gallon tank with the general dimensions of 18" wide by 26" long by 18" high works well to rear up to a couple hundred anemonefish through the larval stage.

Types of Marine Aquarium Systems

[When I first wrote this book in the late 1970's and early 80's, there was only one basic type of home marine aquarium system. Sure, there were some hobbyists that experimented with various types of external filter systems, and there were some multi-tank systems with trickle filters around; but basically, a marine aquarium system consisted of an undergravel filter, bleached white coral, some type of auxiliary "hang on the back of the tank" filter, and air lift tubes that moved water through the undergravel filter. Lighting was mostly a spin-off from freshwater tanks and usually consisted of one or two, 20 to 40 watt fluorescent bulbs with a red or orange tint. This was the basic setup for tanks of all sizes, and the aquatic world of most marine aquarists was limited by available equipment, and by the basic idea of a marine aquarium that almost everyone held.

Then, in the mid 80's, everything began to open up. Aquatic biologists and marine aquaculturists had been talking and writing for some years about the importance of natural spectrum, high intensity lighting, and now suddenly everyone was increasing light levels on marine tanks. Powerhead pumps became available, water flows through undergravel filters were increased, and strong water movement inside the tank was found to be very beneficial to fish and invertebrates. Aquarists also discovered and became very interested in the ecological relationships between the fish, algae, invertebrates, and bacteria within their tanks.

The coral reef tank created in the basement of the Smithsonian Institution and George Smit's series of articles in Freshwater and Marine Aquarium Magazine on European wet/dry trickle filters, found a responsive audience in American marine aquarists. Aquarium manufacturers began producing new equipment and, with the dawning of the light (full spectrum with a blue peak, high intensity light, of course), many marine aquarists were satisfied with nothing less than a real coral reef in their living rooms.

Even though all these techniques and technologies "new" to the marine aquarium hobby have rather suddenly become available, the majority of marine aquarists have stayed with the old tried and true, traditional undergravel techniques. And this is fine, because, **within limits**, this type of system allows one to keep a very nice marine aquarium, and this book provides a guide to this technology. A hobbyist should know what else is possible, however, and so I have included a thumbnail sketch of the five basic marine aquarium systems (in my opinion). Each of these categories is based on a particular technical philosophy of keeping a marine aquarium. The entire structure of each type of system—the lighting, the filtration, the water flows, the captive organisms—represents a certain "school of thought", and an aquarist who follows that philosophy of marine aquarium keeping will usually build a system containing most of the elements of that system as described below. Most marine aquarists, however, are pragmatic individualists, and will go with what strikes their fancy, their space, their interests, their budget, and with what works for them, and so a lot of variety has crept into the structure of marine aquarium systems over the last few years.

The following descriptions of the basic systems may be helpful in that they will give you some idea of the purpose, structure, and function of most of the elements of the various categories of modern marine aquarium systems (at least as I see them), and you can mix and match to suit your own ideas. Note that a detailed explanation of the structure, function, and operation of the various components of these marine aquarium systems can be found in *The Marine Aquarium Reference : Systems and Invertebrates* and in some of the more recent books listed in the selected references. **Also, if you don't know anything at all about marine aquarium systems, it may be a good idea to return to this section after reading Chapters 2 through 6, which will provide a little more basic background in the structure and function of marine systems.**

Categories of small marine aquarium systems

1. The traditional or standard undergravel setup.

2. The "Low-tech" reef, fish, or algae system.

3. The "High-tech" coral reef system.

   A. A shallow water coral reef system.
   B. A deep water coral reef system.

4. The "natural" live rock based reef system.

5. The "natural" algae based fish or reef system.

The traditional or standard marine aquarium system

The traditional undergravel biofilter tank is the foundation of the marine aquarium hobby and the primary concern of this book. The undergravel filter efficiently transforms nitrogenous and organic waste (proteins, carbohydrates, fats, ammonia, and nitrite) into nitrate and other basic nutrients (a process known as mineralization, see Chapter 2), and makes it possible to keep marine fish and other animals in a relatively small glass box. These nutrients, however, are trapped in the tightly closed filtration cycle—accumulate within the system—and the life support capability of the system is limited to relatively hardy marine fish and invertebrates. Intense, full spectrum lighting enhances the life support capabilities of this basic system, but even with very light biological loads, nutrients still rapidly accumulate and micro red, blue-green, and hair algae grow wild with intense light and high nutrient levels. Note that nutrients are good in balanced diets and in gardening, but generally bad when dissolved in marine aquarium system water. Excess nutrients stimulate excess growth of hair, slime algae and bacteria, things that are not welcome in marine aquariums.

Figure 3 illustrates a typical traditional marine aquarium set up. The water is slowly circulated down through the layer of gravel above the filter plate, through the slotted, porous filter plate, and then up the airlift tubes and back

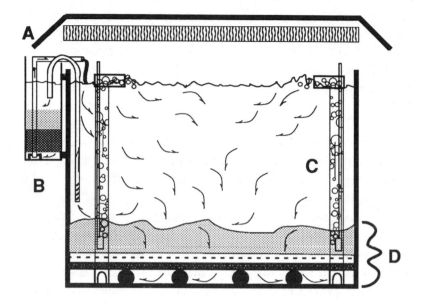

A. Lighting. Shop light with two, 2 or 4 foot fluorescent bulbs or a standard aquarium light hood.

B. Auxiliary filter. A small external filter with floss for mechanical filtration and activiated carbon for chemical filtration.

C. Air lift assembly. One inch diameter lift tube powered by air stone or powerhead pump.

D. Undergravel filter. One to two inches of filter media held above the filter plate with a fine screen. The filter plate is supported above the bottom by marbles or other solid supports.

Figure 3 The basic structure of a traditional type marine aquarium system. Biological filtration is provided by an undergravel filter.

into the tank. A reverse flow filter pushes water down under the filter plate where it flows upward through the filter bed. Reverse flow filters are more efficient, providing that water flows are evenly dispersed through the entire bed. A hanging auxiliary filter is usually added on the back or side to provide additional mechanical and usually chemical filtration. Other types of filtration components can be added to the system, most with positive results that expand the life support capability of the system, but the basic function of the system is set by the undergravel filter. The undergravel filter is a simple, inexpensive technique that provides the immediate, high volume biological filtration required to maintain a relatively large number of marine fish in a small container—the goal of most novice marine aquarists. If you want to keep large, beautiful growths of macroalgae, hard and soft corals, or delicate marine fish and invertebrates that cannot withstand the accumulation of nutrients, then it is wise to invest in a different type of marine system.

The "Low-tech" reef, fish, or algae system

One of the basic concepts in the new marine aquarium technology is the abandonment of the undergravel filter in favor of an external "wet/dry" and/or "trickle" filter. The wet/dry and trickle filter are not the same thing, although the distinction between the two is a bit fuzzy. The wet/dry filter consists of several trays that usually contain a calcareous gravel. Water drips through the trays first (the "dry" section), and then flows through a submerged section of gravel or other biomedia (the "wet" section).

This design, Figure 4, was one of the first external drip type filters and combined the trickle concept with a submerged biological filter. It works well and gives the system water an exceptional amount of biological filtration and, usually, adequate gas exchange (removal of carbon dioxide and replacement of oxygen), but it also traps and cycles nutrients and fosters a build up of nutrients in the water. It is an improvement over the undergravel filter but has some of the same drawbacks. The trickle filter consists of the distribution of water over the top of a container of filter media through either a drip plate (a plate with numerous holes) or a rotating spray bar. The water drips through the filter media (usually past a counter current of air forced upward through the filter media), and gas exchange and biological filtration is accomplished. The filter media is usually an open, non-toxic plastic structure. This type of filter (see Figure 4) traps and cycles little in the way of nutrients, performs adequate biofiltration, and affords good gas exchange. Note that although a trickle filter efficiently adds oxygen to the water and somewhat less efficiently removes carbon dioxide, it is not at all effective in stripping ammonia gas from the water. A trickle filter "ammonia scrubber" would have to be 10 or 12 feet tall and have a great quantity of air forced through it to effectively "blow out" dissolved ammonia. A trickle filter removes ammonia from the water through bacterial biofiltration. As a biological filter, it functions in the same way as an undergravel filter except that it supports few decay bacteria that break down complex organic compounds, while still supporting large enough colonies of nitrifying bacteria to transform all ammonia and nitrite into nitrate. It is the key filter element in most advanced modern marine aquarium systems. It traps little detritus and is not an efficient "nutrient sink" as is an undergravel filter, but it does cycle some nutrients and can work to maintain a low level of dissolved nutrients in some reef systems.

A "low-tech" marine aquarium system, see Figure 5, consists of an efficient mechanical prefilter that takes water from a surface overflow, usually a protein skimmer, a trickle filter, a chemical filter compartment with activated carbon and/or an ion exchange resin, a sump tank, and a pump to return the water to the tank. The water return to the tank may be at the surface or the bottom or a combination of both. There is usually a surface spray hole or a small return just under the surface to break the siphon effect that develops if the pump should happen to shut off. This prevents the sump tank from overflowing and pouring water all over the living room floor and dripping down into the apartment below. (Although this may be a good way to finally meet the cute redhead that lives in that apartment. Well, maybe not.)

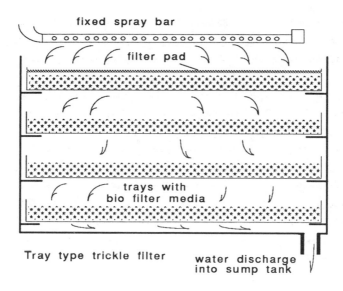

Tray type trickle filter

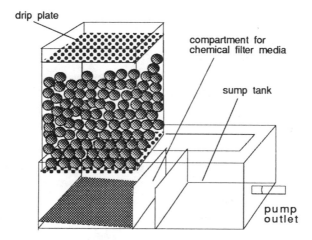

Tower type trickle filter with
ball media and drip plate

Figure 4 The wet/dry filter (above) consists of a series of trays
exposed to air ("dry") that contain filter media through which the
water trickles down to a submerged bio filter ("wet"). The trickle
filter (below) consists of a tower type structure that contains an
open (high void space) filter media. Water is dispersed over the top
of the filter media, and biological filtration and gas exchange occurs
as the water trickles through the filter media.

A protein skimmer is a very important part of this and most other modern marine aquarium systems. A protein skimmer mixes fine air bubbles and saltwater in a tubular container and creates a foam that rises to the top and is trapped in a cup. The foam contains the dissolved organic compounds that attached to the bubbles and were then carried out of the system with the foam. It is an effective and efficient way to remove organics from the system before they break down into basic nutrient compounds.

The lighting on a low-tech system is usually based on fluorescent lights, at least four, 40 watt bulbs, and maybe even six bulbs, or even high output (HO) or very high output (VHO) bulbs **(both of which require a special ballast)** depending on the system. Metal halide bulbs can also be used, but they are usually a bit expensive for a low-tech system.

Live rock is usually an important part of a low-tech system, but even without live rock, a low-tech system functions better than a standard undergravel system. Live rock consists of baseball to football sized, porous, usually calcareous rock that has been taken from the sea with its microscopic life, and often some of the larger invertebrate and algal growths, still alive and functioning. Once all the mud and silt and excess organic growth is removed from the rock (a process known as seeding and/or curing), the natural aerobic (with oxygen) bacteria on and near the surface of the rock and the anaerobic (without oxygen) bacteria deep within the rock function in the aquarium system to oxidize nitrogenous wastes to nitrate and, respectively, to reduce nitrate to nitrogen gas which then passes out of the system into the atmosphere. So live rock is the physical base for a captive reef, a functional biofilter system, and the support, and often the source, for living organisms of the coral reef community. If a low-tech system does not have a live rock reef, then the tank usually has a very thin sand or gravel substrate on the bottom, or some other bottom cover, unless it is simply a holding or experimental system.

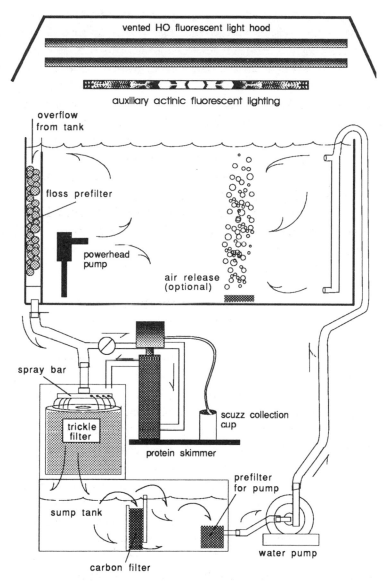

Elements of the low-tech reef tank

Figure 5 The basic structure of a "low-tech" marine aquarium system. Biological filtration is provided by a trickle filter and, usually, a live rock reef.

Nutrient control in a low-tech system is much easier than in a standard undergravel system, but unless the animal bioload is very low, and very careful nutrient control is practiced by the aquarist, some nutrients will be cycled, and it will be difficult to run a nutrient poor, dedicated coral culture tank. With a low-tech reef tank system, however, it is relatively easy to run a spectacular and healthy fish tank, a fantastic macro algae tank, or a hardy coral reef tank.

The difference between a low-tech and a high-tech system gets a bit fuzzy when one considers the elements of a "high-tech, low-tech" system contrasted with a "low-tech, high-tech" system (anybody still with me here?). What I'm trying to say is that the high end of one and the low end of the other sort of blend together. The high-tech system controls and manipulates about everything that can be controlled and manipulated, as discussed below, while the low-tech system, with expense a consideration, uses fluorescent, high intensity lighting; trickle filtration; and protein skimming to provide just the basics of reef tank technology.

Nutrient control can be a problem in a low-tech system, especially if hard and soft corals are maintained, and a true coral reef tank aquarist has to be on the ball to keep delicate corals in a low-tech system. An aquarist setting up a first reef tank in low-tech mode is best advised to go slow and work with hardy animals. Some of the hardiest soft corals are the mushroom anemones, leather corals, gorgonians, *Xenia* waving hand corals, the zoanthids, and star polyps. Hardy hard corals are the bubble corals, plate coral, hammer coral, octobubble coral, open brain coral, and elegance coral. Marine fish suitable for a reef tank with corals include clownfish, dwarf basslets, royal grammas, mandarin fish, some species of tangs, gobies, blennies, hawkfish, pygmy angels, firefish, and jawfish. **Actually, when it comes to keeping corals, or even marine fish, the skill and knowledge of the aquarist is more important then the complexity and expense of the equipment.**

The High-tech coral reef system

Figure 6 illustrates a basic high-tech marine reef system. An in-depth discussion of all the elements of such a system is beyond the scope of this book. *The Marine Aquarium Reference* and other books, videos, and computer programs listed in the reference section at the end of the book will provide the serious reef tank hobbyist with detailed information on the equipment and techniques of high-tech reef tank establishment and maintenance. A high-tech reef tank system is designed to create the high quality, marine environment necessary to maintain and even culture hard and soft corals and other delicate marine organisms. There are also other ways that this can be done, but the "high-tech" system gives the aquarist the most detailed information on, and greatest control over, the fundamental environmental conditions within the system.

The high-tech type of reef system is broken down into two categories, the shallow reef system and the deep reef system. There are great differences in the natural environment and in the organisms that inhabit tropical shallow and deep reefs. Shallow reefs, 10 to about 40 feet deep, receive strong sunlight with a good bit of low energy red, orange, and yellow light; sustain a lot of strong water movement in the form of wave surge and tidal and oceanic currents; usually experience substantial seasonal temperature fluctuations; and experience variable amounts of plankton, silt loading, and nutrients in the water. Deep reefs (I arbitrarily define deep reefs for the purpose of this discussion as about 50 to 120 feet deep) receive no red and very little orange and yellow light, the spectrum is mostly blue and violet with a little green, and light intensity is much diminished. Wave surge seldom reaches deep reefs, and although oceanic currents may be strong in some deep areas at some times, water movement is usually gentle. Temperature fluctuations occur, but are not as great as those experienced by shallow reefs, and plankton, silt, and nutrient loads are usually consistently less than those over shallow reefs. Some species of coral, sponge, and algae live in both shallow and deep environments, and many species are found only on shallow or deep reefs. Those that are found in both environments are individually adapted to the particular depth where they were taken. In corals, the structure of the hard skeleton, the soft tissues, and the amount of *zooxanthellae* (the symbiotic algal cells in the soft tissue of the coral) are adapted to the light, temperature, and pressure of the depth where the coral lived. A deep water coral can usually adapt to a shallow reef tank, but it takes time, and the specimen should be placed deep in the tank and in a shaded area.

Most reef tanks are designed to be shallow reef systems. Lighting is intense and, of course, pressure is minimal; algal growth is often moderate to heavy; and the organisms are usually taken from shallow reef environments. A reef tank designed to simulate a deep reef has mostly blue light of much lower intensity; is (or should be) much cooler, 70 to 75 °F or so; contains little or no algae; and has deep water corals such as *Dendronephyta*, some sponges, and a few deep water fish such as cuban hogfish and black cap basslets. A reef system designed to be a deep reef should be carefully planned in both structure and organisms. Lighting, temperature, and internal water flows are the most significant differences between the shallow and deep reef tank systems.

Figure 6 illustrates the various elements of a high-tech reef tank and about where they fit into the system. Note that there are various opinions about the absolute necessity of each of these elements, and how, where, if, and when they should be used. The following list refers to each of the elements of a high-tech reef tank that are diagramed in Figure 6, and provides a brief description of their function. Refer to other reef tank books and videos for more detailed information.

1. Metal halide lighting   A shallow reef tank generally does well with lighting that has a surface level intensity of 10,000 to 15,000 lux, a color temperature of 5000 to 5500 °K, and CRI (Color Rendering Index) of about 90. Metal halide

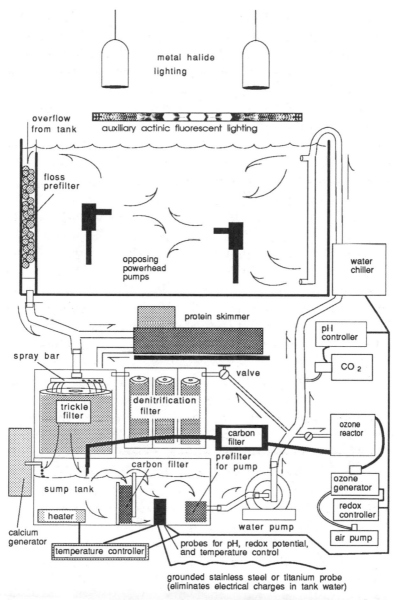

metal halide lighting

overflow from tank

auxiliary actinic fluorescent lighting

floss prefilter

opposing powerhead pumps

water chiller

protein skimmer

pH controller

CO$_2$

spray bar

valve

trickle filter

denitrification filter

ozone reactor

carbon filter

prefilter for pump

ozone generator

carbon filter

redox controller

sump tank

calcium generator

heater

water pump

air pump

temperature controller

probes for pH, redox potential, and temperature control

grounded stainless steel or titanium probe (eliminates electrical charges in tank water)

Elements of the high-tech reef tank

Figure 6 The structure of a "high-tech" marine aquarium system. Biological filtration is provided by a trickle filter and a live rock reef.

lighting designed for marine aquarium systems best provides this quality of light, although a variety and abundance
of fluorescent lights are also adequate. Note that the size
and depth of the tank are important considerations in choos-
ing lighting for a reef tank.

2. Auxiliary actinic or blue fluorescent lighting Most
corals, and their resident *zooxanthellae*, require light in the
blue end of the spectrum for photosynthesis. An auxiliary
Actinic 03 or Radiant Blue fluorescent light helps to provide
this type of light for shallow and deep corals.

3. Overflow prefilter Water leaves the tank from the
surface (surface skimming) and enters a mechanical prefilter. The floss in this prefilter traps particles of detritus, bits
of algae, and other macro and microscopic particles before
they can enter the trickle filter. It is very important in a reef
tank holding corals to replace the prefilter floss frequently.
Bacteria quickly begin to grow in the floss, and the trapped
particles are soon broken down into basic nutrients. The
organic particles that are the source of these nutrients can be
removed from the system if the floss is changed frequently
(at least weekly).

4. Protein skimmer This is a very important part of any
reef system since it removes dissolved organic compounds
and microscopic particles from the aquarium water. A protein skimmer is most efficient when it draws water directly
from the tank before any other type of filtration, except
perhaps a floss prefilter.

5. Trickle filter This is an efficient filter system that
provides biological filtration and gas exchange for all types
of marine aquarium systems.

6. Calcium generator Calcium, strontium, and molybdenum are of great importance in the coral reef tank since
corals require all three of these minerals for sustenance and
growth. Most tanks require regular additions of these elements to replace what is lost to biological activity within the
system. Calcium levels should be maintained at about 420
ppm. A calcium generator gradually adds a calcium solu-

tion, usually calcium hydroxide (limewater or *kalkwasser*) or calcium chloride or calcium oxide, on an automated basis with a small peristaltic pump or other delivery system.

7. Sump tank An external trickle filter requires an open sump tank to catch the unpressurized flow from the filter. This sump tank must be large enough to hold all "free" water in the system that may drain back to the sump if the pump fails or is shut off. It is also a good location for various probes, heaters, chemical filter chambers, etc.

8. Heaters A large reef tank system may require up to 250 watts of heating capacity. Two heaters are usually best, for then if one fails, the other can keep the tank in a survivable range for corals and tropical marine fish until the other heater is replaced.

9. Temperature controller An electronic temperature controller may be set up when both a heater and chiller are in the system. Such a temperature controller balances the operation of the heater and the chiller to maintain system temperature within a very narrow range.

10. Carbon and/or resin filter chamber A section of the sump tank is often set up for a chemical filter media. The chamber is best designed to direct a flow of water through the filter media. Simply placing a bag of carbon and/or resin in the sump tank is not nearly as effective as actively flowing water through the media.

11. Sensing probes A section of the sump tank can be reserved for sensing probes for temperature, pH, and redox potential. These probes sense the condition of the water and send the information to their controllers, which then operate the equipment that changes that water quality parameter.

12. Electrical ground probe The more electrical equipment that is attached to a marine aquarium system, the greater the chance of stray electrical charges in the saltwater. Sometimes an electrical charge is great enough to give the aquarist a small (hopefully) electric shock when the water is touched, but often the aquarist may not notice the charge in the water. A small charge, however, may adversely affect fish and invertebrates, causing stress and abnormal behavior. There is even some anecdotal evidence linking a stray electrical charge with lateral line erosion in some marine fish. Stray electrical charges can be eliminated by placing a stainless steel or titanium probe in the system water and grounding this probe to a solid ground such as the ground in a electrical outlet or a metal plumbing pipe. This is a good precaution for both reef and fish tanks.

13. Pump prefilter One never knows what could wind up in a sump tank—maybe even a parakeet or a roach. A prefilter on the intake for the pump is a good safeguard.

14. The water pump A good water pump is critical. Don't skimp on this piece of equipment. Most reef systems require a pump that will give between 4 and 6 tank volume exchanges per hour. It is best to get a pump that has a capacity greater than the minimum requirement since back-pressure on the pump created by filter elements and the height of the pump line to the tank reduces the flow that is delivered to the tank. Be sure to measure flow through the system at the point of delivery into the tank.

15. Ozone and/or oxygen generator and reactor An ozone and/or oxygen reactor is a closed filter unit in which water flows thinly over a media with a large surface area. Air within the unit is at a slightly higher (2 to 4 psi) pressure than ambient atmospheric pressure and has a normal oxygen content, or may be ozonized. The slight pressure and great surface area per water volume within the unit causes the water to become supersaturated with oxygen or ozone, and this greatly increases the positive effect of these gasses.

16. Ozone generator Ozone, the unstable, triatomic form of oxygen (O_3), is usually generated by passing air over an active electrical spark. Ozone breaks down rapidly but lasts long enough to become dissolved in water and to break down most complex organic compounds in the water. It is added to the water in an ozone reactor.

17. Ozone carbon filter Ozone in the water is harmful to most organisms in reef tanks and must be removed before the water is cycled back to the tank. An activated carbon filter will remove ozone from the water, and this filter should be in the return line from the ozone reactor. The return from the ozone reactor should not go into the trickle filter, since it may adversely affect nitrifying bacteria.

18. Denitrification filter Some species of bacteria are able to live in oxygen free or very oxygen poor environments by utilizing oxygen tied up in nitrate molecules (NO_3). The oxygen is used by the bacteria, and the nitrogen is eventually released as nitrogen gas. This process can be controlled in a sealed filter chamber by providing a substrate for the bacteria colonies, a source of carbohydrate food for the bacteria, and by allowing water to flow so slowly through the filter that the oxygen in the water is quickly exhausted, and the bacteria must become anaerobic in all but the first section of the filter. A well designed, well maintained denitrifying filter can maintain nitrate levels in a marine aquarium system at near zero, but operation of such a filter requires constant attention to keep it balanced with the fluctuating nitrate levels in the system.

19. pH controller The pH of a marine tank is controlled/affected by the accumulation of organic matter in the water, the intrinsic buffer system of saltwater, the activity of algae in the system, and the amount of carbon dioxide in the water. Carbon dioxide (CO_2) dissolved in seawater creates carbonic acid which lowers the pH of the water. Thus, addition of CO_2 lowers the pH of the system and removal of CO_2 increases pH. Algae use carbon dioxide during photosynthesis, and in a tank rich in algae, enough carbon dioxide can be taken from the water to cause the pH to rise. A rise in pH can be counteracted by the injection of CO_2 into the water. In an automated system, a controller is usually set at a low pH of about 8.0, and when the pH rises a bit above that point, CO_2 is released into the system. The pH then drops, and when it reaches the set point of 8.0, CO_2 release is shut off, photosynthesis in the tank continues to use CO_2, and the pH drops until the controller again releases CO_2.

20. Water chiller Pumps and lights on modern reef systems create a lot of heat, and some systems become too warm during the summer months or even too warm for the optimum temperature (76 °F) of a reef system during much of the year. Several brands of chillers are now available that cool aquarium water. They are rather expensive and are usually found only on high-tech systems.

21. Opposing powerhead pumps or surge generators A passive flow of water into and out of the tank is not good for reef systems. Most corals and anemones need active water movement for tissue stimulation and feeding activity. A constant, unidirectional flow over the specimen is helpful, but frequent flow reversal is much better. Powerhead pumps can be set up to either revolve or change flow direction periodically, or to go on and off in coincident with other pumps. This type of activity creates changes in flow patterns that better stimulate corals, sponges, and anemones.

The natural live rock based reef system

European marine aquarists and now some American aquarists prefer to operate coral reef tanks with dependence only on a loosely constructed live rock reef (with ample water flow through the reef); a very effective protein skimmer; a little activated carbon filtration; a heater and/or chiller as required; metal halide or intense fluorescent lighting; calcium, strontium, iodine, and molybdenum supplements; and great attention to elimination of excess nutrients. Very remarkable results have been achieved in growth and maintenance of hard and soft corals with this type of system, illustrated by the diagram in Figure 7.

In a typical marine fish system, fish and other animals produce a lot of metabolic waste—ammonia and organics—that must be processed by an extensive population of nitrifying bacteria grown in an undergravel, wet/dry, or trickle type biological filter installation. In a coral and/or algae reef system, the animal and plant metabolisms are in a better "balance", since the bioload of animal and plant tissue is

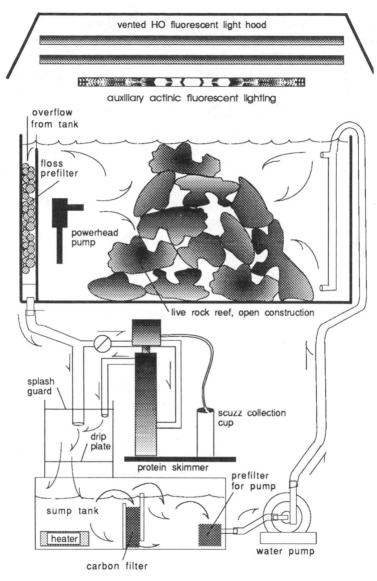

vented HO fluorescent light hood

auxiliary actinic fluorescent lighting

overflow from tank

floss prefilter

powerhead pump

live rock reef, open construction

splash guard

scuzz collection cup

drip plate

protein skimmer

prefilter for pump

sump tank

heater

carbon filter

water pump

Essential elements of the live rock, natural reef tank

Figure 7 The structure of a live rock, reef system. Biological filtration is provided only by the presence of an extensive and loosely constructed live rock reef.

more equal. The plants can quickly use the ammonia and nitrate produced by animals and bacteria, and these animal metabolic products are produced in the immediate vicinity of the plants (within the same organism in the case of corals and their *zooxanthellae*), which enhances the tight cycle of available nutrients, just as in the natural coral reef environment. The live rock, which functions as an aerobic and anaerobic biological filter, is also right on the site of nutrient exchange and "mops up" any nitrogen compounds that may escape the plant/animal nutrient exchange.

The frequently changed prefilter and the protein skimmer function to remove detritus particles and dissolved organics from the system **before** bacteria can break them down into nutrients that would stimulate growth of unwanted algae. The absence of a large biological filter (an undergravel or trickle filter) prevents the rapid transformation of ammonia and nitrite into nitrate, the concomitant liberation of other nutrients, e. g. phosphate, from the breakdown of complex organic compounds, allows these organic compounds to be **rapidly removed** through protein skimming, and thus enhances nutrient removal. Freshwater, used as make up water for evaporation losses and to mix artificial saltwater for water exchange, must also be as nutrient free as possible, and so freshwater for these marine systems is often produced with reverse osmosis and/or a deionization process. Activated carbon filtration also removes some nutrients and keeps the water crystal clear by removing organic dyes.

These systems require attentive and knowledgeable aquarists (as do all marine aquaria), but this effort is well rewarded with beautiful and healthy corals. Two recent references to this technology are Sprung, J. and C. Delbeek (1990) New Trends in Reef Keeping, FAMA (Freshwater and Marine Aquarium Magazine): Vol, 13, No. 12. pp. 8, 9, 11, 12, 14, 16, 19-22, 180, 182, 184; and Nilsen, A. (1991) Coral Reefs and Reef Aquariums—Part I, Aquarium Fish Magazine: Vol. 3, No. 12: pp 18, and Part II, Vol. 4, No. 1: pp 18.

The natural algae based fish or reef system

Just as nitrifying bacteria process animal metabolic waste and function as a biological filter, algae can also do very much the same thing. An algae based natural marine

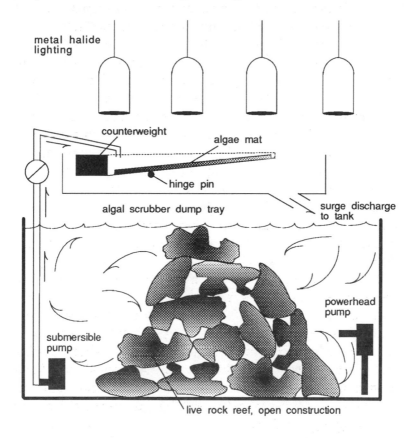

metal halide lighting

counterweight

algae mat

hinge pin

algal scrubber dump tray

surge discharge to tank

powerhead pump

submersible pump

live rock reef, open construction

Essential elements of the algal filter based, natural reef tank

Figure 8 The structure of the algal filter based, natural marine reef system. Biological filtration is provided by the presence of a live rock reef and an auxiliary algal scrubber device.

aquarium system is similar to the live rock based system except that it also includes an algal scrubber positioned outside the tank, usually as a dump tray that returns water back to the tank, Figure 8. The algal growths directly under the intense metal halide or florescent lighting remove nutrients from the water, and the live rocks in the tank also act as a biological filter through their resident colonies of nitrifying bacteria. A protein skimmer and carbon filtration can also be used with this type of system to enhance water clarity and reduce dissolved organics, although a properly established, maintained, and harvested algal turf scrubber creates a natural plant/animal balance in this type of marine system. Dr. Walter Adey, the developer of the simulated coral reef in the basement of the Smithsonian Institution, and Karen Loveland describe this type of system, and other advanced natural system techniques, in their recent book, *Dynamic Aquaria*.

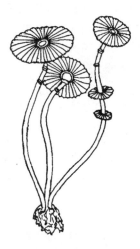

Mermaid's cup
Acetabularia crenulata

Chapter 2

THE WATER

Composition, Collection, and Manufacture

Natural Seawater

Should one use natural or synthetic seawater in a marine aquarium? This question is almost always sure to spark a lively discussion. Cries of POLLUTION! BACTERIA! and ORGANIC OVERLOAD! arise from one corner and are met by shouts of NATURAL COMPOSITION! COMPLETE TRACE ELEMENTS! and ESSENTIAL ORGANIC COMPOUNDS! reverberating from the other.

[There is much less contention these days on the relative merits of synthetic seawater versus natural seawater. Synthetic seawater, the better brands, has proven to be every bit as capable as natural seawater in supporting life (including delicate invertebrates) in large and small marine aquarium systems. Assuming a pollution and parasite free source of natural seawater, cost and convenience are now the most important factors in the choice between natural and artificial or synthetic seawater.]

Composition of natural seawater

Let's take a look at the composition of natural seawater, and this will give us some clues on how to use it in a marine aquarium. Seawater is an extremely complex and dynamic fluid when all of its inorganic and organic constituents are considered. Fortunately you don't have to have a degree in marine chemistry to be able to set up and maintain a marine aquarium, but it is helpful to know what kinds of things make up natural seawater, especially if you plan to use Mother Nature's formula. The components of natural seawater can be put into four broad classifications.

The first of these is **pure water**, the ultimate solvent. Water represents about 96% of all the stuff in a bucket of seawater. This is the part that evaporates off, causes rain, and leaves everything else behind in the form of a white, crusty residue. Obviously it is the stuff left behind in the bucket that makes seawater so different from freshwater.

The second component of seawater goes under the broad term of **inorganic solids and gases**. All the dissolved salts, trace elements, inorganic pollutants, and dissolved gases belong in this category, which, except for the gases, usually make up over 99% of the crusty white stuff at the bottom of the bucket. Only seven kinds of salts (sodium chloride, magnesium chloride, magnesium sulphate, calcium sulfate, potassium sulfate, calcium carbonate, and potassium or sodium bromide) make up over 99.5% of all the conservative elements in seawater. The conservative elements are the ones that do not change in proportion to each other regardless of the total amount of dissolved matter. In other words, the percentage of sodium chloride, for example, in the total salt content is always the same whether the seawater is half strength or full strength. This is very important, for this is why the properties of seawater vary so little all over the world, and why it is such a stable, life-supporting environment in all climates.

The remaining half percent of the inorganic solids is made up of at least 60 elements, found in such tiny amounts that they are called trace elements, and a variable amount (depending on where the water is taken) of pollutants, such as mercury, pesticides, and petroleum, that are released by man's activities. Even though the trace elements are present in extremely tiny amounts, some of them (especially zinc, copper, iodine, strontium, vanadium, cobalt, molybdenum, and arsenic) are essential to many living organisms. Some animals and plants can accumulate these trace elements in their own bodies in concentrations thousands of times greater than the surrounding waters, and some of these elements may even be depleted in areas of the sea due to the activity of marine life.

If this can happen in the open sea, it can certainly occur in a marine aquarium where the ratio of life to water is much greater. These elements are not always released back into the water when the microorganism dies, and if you remove algae from your tank, you are also removing accumulated trace elements. Therefore, it is wise to replenish the trace elements in your tank every month or so, especially if you do not make a water change with natural seawater or a complete salt mix.

The third basic classification of the stuff of seawater is **dissolved organic substances**. These are compounds such as amino acids, proteins, enzymes, vitamins, and pigments. Inshore waters carry a greater load of dissolved organics than clear offshore waters. Natural toxins are sometimes found in seawater, especially during reproductive "blooms" of minute marine algae. These blooms are usually called red tides and can be very destructive to fish life. Some of the dissolved organic substances originate from life in the sea. They are given off by animals, plants, and bacteria during the normal process of living and are also liberated in death. Runoff water from the land adds greatly to the organic content of nearshore waters, and man contributes ever increasingly to this category through discharge of petroleum products, sewage, and agricultural and industrial wastes. These effluents add a number of toxins such as PCB's that can accumulate in the tissues of marine animals, and also, basic nutrients from sewage that enrich inshore waters and cause heavy growths of planktonic algae.

Life is the fourth category of things to be found in that bucket of seawater. No matter how clear the water, there is an astonishing number and variety of living things to be found. Bacteria and microscopic plants and animals occur in each drop of inshore water. Some of these, such as larval fish and crabs, have the potential for great growth; while others, such as one celled algae and copepods, remain as tiny planktonic creatures throughout their brief existence. Life is always gathering and assimilating the elements of the sea, containing them, using them, and liberating them in death and excretion. Thus the sea is a dynamic fluid, filled with life, accepting nutrients from the land and energy from the sun, and balancing the existence of life on earth upon the complex interactions of the life within its waters.

I hope the above discussion makes it easier to understand that a marine aquarium is not a tiny slice of a coral reef or ocean bottom, and that a bucket of seawater and a bucket of marine aquarium water are two entirely different things. How do they differ? Water from a marine aquarium has the same four basic categories of constituents: water, dissolved inorganics, dissolved organics, and life. Water and the conservative constituents (basic salts) are the same in both buckets, but the other, nonconservative constituents differ greatly. Trace element composition changes rapidly because once captive life forms use them, they are not replenished by the vast volume of the sea. Dissolved organics are not as diffused and reused in a marine aquarium as they are in the sea, thus they accumulate from the wastes of animals to a great degree. These wastes are converted to basic nutrients with proper biological filtration, but the concentrations of these nutrients can be much, much greater in the bucket of aquarium water than in the bucket of raw seawater.

Living things are also found in both buckets, but the great variety of tiny plants and animals found in seawater do not exist in aquarium water. Bacteria are the primary life forms in aquarium water. The number of bacteria in one cubic centimeter of seawater varies from less than 10 in offshore waters to several hundred or more in clear inshore waters. In contrast, marine aquarium waters may contain several hundred thousand or more in each cubic centimeter. All bacteria are not bad, however, and their presence in aquarium water does not necessarily make it worse for marine life than raw seawater, just different.

Collection of natural seawater

If seawater were composed of only pure water and dissolved salts and trace elements, collection and use in an aquarium would pose few problems. It is the dissolved organics and planktonic life forms that cause problems for the intrepid aquarist. As soon as the seawater is contained, and is no longer part and parcel of the world's oceans, most of the planktonic plants and animals die, and bacteria proliferate mightily. Eventually all the remains of planktonic creatures are decayed (mineralized) by bacteria, which also utilize some of the dissolved organics.

Most bacteria need a surface of some sort (a substrate) to form a colony and grow, and the sides of the container, precipitated organics (detritus), and dead plankton provide much more surface area than an equal volume of open seawater. These and other factors result in a fantastic proliferation of bacteria in captive seawater, sometimes to levels of several million per cubic centimeter. This is why many authors suggest that newly collected seawater be kept in the dark for two weeks or more before use; for after that period, most of the organic matter has been utilized, oxidized, and precipitated, and all the dead plankton has been consumed by bacteria. Bacteria levels then drop to 10 to 100,000 per cubic centimeter. A brownish flocculent material accumulates at the bottom of the container, and one is instructed to remove the clear seawater without stirring up the sediment on the bottom.

Below, I describe three ways to process collected natural seawater. The first is the classic, sure way and the second is the lazy man's somewhat risky method. The third is an experimental method that I have had good success with, but one that I cannot unconditionally recommend, because I don't really know *exactly* what it does to the water, and I don't know what effect it might have on many species that have not experienced water so treated.

The first thing to do is to decide where the water is to be obtained. Of course the very best water would be clear, offshore water that requires a boat for collection, but your aquarium will operate just as well on carefully collected inshore water. Take your water from an area that has good tidal flushing and no obvious nearby sources of pollution. Avoid sewer outlets, industrial plants, and freshwater creeks and rivers. Don't collect water from areas that show an oil or chemical slick on the surface. Also, look for live fish, crabs, and other life in the area, and if native fish are present and appear healthy, your water should be good. Anyone who lives near the coast should be able to collect good seawater for an aquarium. When you have found the right site, time, and tide, you are ready to collect.

One thing you don't want is a car full of 50 gallons of saltwater. A good, inexpensive way to transport saltwater is with the lowly, but versatile, 20 gallon plastic garbage can. The more plankton and particulate material that can be removed when the water is collected, the better the water will be for your aquarium. I use two buckets, a big plastic funnel, and some fine filtering material. Several folds of clean cloth, a one inch thickness of pure polyurethane foam or, best of all, several layers of filtering floss packed into the funnel do a good job.

[Perhaps the very best one time filtering technique we have used over the years is micron filter bags. These are heavy felt-like bags that will filter water to levels of 10, 5, and even 1 and 2 microns. A lot of water can pass through the bags before they clog and they can also be easily cleaned and reused many times. These filter bags are usually used in the manufacture of beer and other basic liquid foods, and are now also available from some aquatic supply houses.]

Line the plastic garbage can with a polyethylene bag and fill it with filtered water. Leave some room to twist off and secure the bag with a rubber band or wire twist tie, and you have a spill proof container to carry home your water. Be sure not to fill the can so full that you can't lift it into the car.

The best way to treat the water after you get it home is to store it in the dark for two or three weeks prior to using it in the aquarium. Then remove the water carefully so that the sediment on the bottom of the container is not disturbed. The lazy man's way is to use the water immediately and don't bother with storage or treatment. Sometimes you can get away with this approach with no problems at all if the water is well filtered. Sometimes, however, small parasites are introduced this way and can cause hair-pulling breast-beating problems.

The third way of treating your newly collected water is still experimental. However, water treated this way is routinely used to culture marine tropical fish, so the method seems acceptable to most marine organisms. You will need some granular dry chlorine, the type used in swimming pools (65% calcium hypochlorite with no additional algicide), or pure chlorine bleach, an OTO test kit for chlorine (available where swimming pool supplies are sold) and chlorine neutralizer. Sodium thiosulfate is the base for most commercial dechlorinators and is also sold in camera shops as hypo; however, if you use hypo be sure to get pure hypo without film hardeners.

Add a small measure of chlorine to newly collected water until there is at least five parts per million (ppm) chlorine according to your test kit. Let the water sit with light aeration for 12 to 24 hours and test once again for chlorine. If no chlorine is indicated, this means that you have water with a high organic load and you should treat it once again with chlorine. It also means that the dose of chlorine should be doubled if water is collected from the same location again. Chlorine kills all life in the collected water, including bacteria, and oxidizes the organic matter

Figure 9 Granulated chlorine for swimming pools and OTO test kit for free chlorine. Most chlorine test kits also test for pH, however, the pH range in the kits is usually 7.0 to 7.8, a bit below the range of a marine aquarium. The most effective use of the chlorine test is to tell the aquarist when all free chlorine has been eliminated from the water.

dissolved in natural seawater, including natural toxins. After the water has been chlorinated for 12 to 24 hours, it will be very clear and smell a little like a swimming pool.

Now add the sodium thiosulfate in small measure until your test kit indicates that no chlorine remains. It is best to dissolve the sodium thiosulfate in water before adding it to the chlorinated seawater. It won't take much, so just add a little at a time, no more than a teaspoon, until you can estimate how much is required.

Now your water is sterile and may have a slight cloudy appearance. This will clear by itself if the water is left to settle for a day or two under light aeration, or it can be filtered through floss and activated charcoal for a few hours to clear it even faster. In emergencies, I have used water immediately after neutralization with no ill effects, but I don't recommend it as a general practice. To my knowledge, this method of treating natural seawater is quite safe, but I have not used water so treated for many species of invertebrates, which may be more sensitive to loss of trace elements and organic molecules than fish. We have collected water heavily contaminated with oil waste, decaying fish, red tide organisms and toxins, silt and organic matter, treated it with this method, and then used it 24 hours later to rear clownfish and neon gobies. Old aquarium water can also be rejuvenated with this treatment, but repeated treatments will lower the pH of the water, and the effect of this water treatment on invertebrates, especially repeated use, is unknown to me.

[After 10 years, I can't add anything to this section on chlorine treatment of natural seawater. We used this method for many years to prepare water for rearing marine tropical fish—clownfish, gobies, Atlantic angelfish, royal gramma, porkfish, hogfish, and other species—and in maintenance and rearing of spiny lobster and other invertebrates. I never observed any problems that I thought might have originated with the chlorination and subsequent chlorine neutralization of natural seawater. Any prudent aquarists, however, who may wish to use this method of water processing, would be wise to run a few experiments first.]

Synthetic seawater

If you happen to live in Omaha, Nebraska, you may have a tough time deciding whether to go to the Pacific, Atlantic, or Gulf of Mexico to get your saltwater. Even if you live only a few miles from a saltwater source, however, you may not want the hassle of cans, buckets, filters, and hauling water in the back seat of your Mercedes. Fortunately there is a solution for your problem. You can buy a package of synthetic sea salts from your aquarium dealer and carry home the equivalent of 50 or 100 gallons of saltwater in a neat little package on the seat of your car. Synthetic seawater may not be the same thing as natural seawater, but the major brands available today will support marine life in your aquarium almost as well as the real thing, and perhaps even better in some circumstances.

Synthetic seawater differs from nature's own in that the concentrations of the major inorganic salts are not exactly the same, inorganic trace elements are not the same in number or concentration, there are no dissolved organics and, a very important consideration, all impurities present in the makeup water become part of the aquarium's watery environment. This last point is one that could easily be an overlooked problem. One could figure, "Well, I've got this fine grade of expensive sea salt mix manufactured under exacting conditions from carefully tested, time proven formulas. I mix it with the water I drink, so what could possibly be wrong." I hope that at least 99% of the time this is a totally correct attitude, however, remember that the freshwater supply in some areas of the country may be plagued with bacterial contamination (probably not a problem in a marine tank), industrial waste contamination, concentrations of heavy metals (copper, zinc), extreme hardness, nutrients such as phosphate, nitrate, and silicic acid, and detergent contamination.

Freshwater preparation

If there is a suspicion about the purity of your water supply, if you drink and cook with bottled water rather than tap water, then it's a good idea to filter the freshwater through activated carbon before making up the saltwater mix. This will take out most of the impurities and get you closer to the final solution that the manufacturer of the salt mix intended.

[Reef tank aquarists may need to run the tap water through a deionizer to remove excess salts, which makes the RO membrane last a lot longer, and then through a reverse osmosis machine to remove residual nutrients before adding freshwater to replace evaporation in a reef tank.]

Follow the manufacturer's instructions when you mix the salts and add the trace elements, after all, they ought to know the best way to handle their own product. If you are just setting up a new tank, you can mix the first batch right in the tank, but if you are changing water in an established tank, it is best to mix the salts in a plastic garbage can. Never use a metal can or bucket to mix the saltwater. Wait until the solution clears and all the elements are dissolved before adding the newly mixed water to your tank. Some of the elements may not dissolve, even after 24 hours of aeration and will form a white precipitate on the container bottom. Don't worry about this residue unless it is remarkably excessive, just go ahead and use the water, and if some of the sediment gets into the tank it's nothing to be concerned about. It is also good to let the newly mixed saltwater age a day or so to let pH stabilize before adding it to the tank.

Chlorine and Chloramine

The low chlorine content of tap water usually disappears when the salt mix is added and is of no concern since the mix is aerated for at least several hours before use. If there is a question of residual chlorine, a few drops of sodium thiosulfate or of a commercial dechlorinator will set your mind at ease. Unfortunately, in many areas of the country it is no longer possible to dismiss chlorine in tap water with a few drops of a dechlorinator. Due to recent implementation of Environmental Protection Agency regulations on organics in water supplies, municipal water companies are changing the way they treat our tap water. Ammonia is being added to eliminate trihalomethane, a suspected cancer-causing agent. In the past, tap water received only a charge of free chlorine to keep it pure and free of bacteria until it reached our kitchens and bathrooms. Free chlorine is volatile and soon disappears from standing or aerated water and can be quickly eliminated with a little sodium thiosulfate. When ammonia and chlorine are both present in fresh water, however, they form a stable chloramine compound that is toxic to fish just as free chlorine and ammonia are toxic. In fact, it is even a more toxic since chloramine can pass through the gills and into the blood more easily than just chlorine.

Chloramine, unfortunately, does not readily escape from standing water and cannot be removed by a standard application of sodium thiosulfate. When ammonia is already present in the water and the amount of chlorine added is below the "break point reaction" level, then chloramine is formed. If enough chlorine is added to exceed the break point reaction level, the chlorine becomes free chlorine and the ammonia is no longer bonded. Both chlorine and ammonia can then escape as gases over a period of time. As long as chlorine levels are maintained under the break point reaction level, chlorine and ammonia are present as the stable chloramine compound. When sufficient ammonia is present in ground water supplies, chloramine is formed when the treatment plant adds only enough chlorine to stay below the break point reaction. If ammonia levels are not sufficient in the raw water supply, it is added by exposing the water to pellets of ammonium sulphate or adding liquid anhydrous ammonia before it is chlorinated.

Hatcheries, shops, and hobbyists in Texas and Florida have reported considerable loss of livestock due to this development in water treatment technology. If the chloramine levels in your water supply exceed 2 ppm, it may be necessary to remove it from the water before setting up an aquarium. There are ways that the hobbyist can clear freshwater of chloramine *before* making up a synthetic seawater mix. One of the two basic methods described below should work, depending on the particular problems presented by the local water supply. The first and easiest method is to add double the dose of sodium thiosulfate (or a commercial dechlorinator) than would ordinarily be necessary to dechlorinate the water. This should break the chlorine bond and chemically remove the chlorine after a working time of two to three hours.

Aeration of the water will allow the ammonia to escape as a gas over a period of several hours (longer if the concentration of ammonia is high). The freshwater can also be filtered through an ammonia absorbent material, the clay clinoptiolite (zeolite) or a similar commercial product for more positive ammonia removal. It is more important to remove ammonia when preparing water for a partial water change in an established tank than setting up a new tank, since the run in period for a new tank will eliminate any ammonia in the water.

The second method is more involved but may be necessary under some local conditions. First, enough chlorine must be added to break the stable chloramine bond and put all chlorine present into the free state. Addition of 1 cc of laundry bleach (no additives) to one gallon of water (or one teaspoon Clorox, 5.25% sodium hypochlorite, per five gallons) usually accomplishes this after one hour of aeration. Once all the chlorine is in a free state, it can be removed by traditional methods. Addition of sodium thiosulfate until no chlorine registers on an OTO swimming pool test kit is the standard method of chlorine removal. Mix about 4 oz of sodium thiosulfate to one quart of water to make the treatment solution. Start with 5 drops for each 10 gallons of water to be dechlorinated. Retreat if the OTO test shows that chlorine is still present 5 to 10 minutes after the initial treatment. Activated carbon filtration after chlorine removal is also a good idea, for although it won't remove ammonia, it will take out any residual chlorine. A final filtration of the freshwater through an ammonia absorbent material will remove the ammonia if this is desired. Don't just soak a bag of ammonia absorbent or activated carbon in the water as this is most inefficient. Set up a flow through filter to recirculate the water through the filter material.

Synthetic sea salts

Which brand of synthetic sea salt should you use? I've tried several, and they all seem to do a good job. You should rely on your dealer's recommendation or the recommendation of experienced fellow hobbyists in your area. Unless your area has special water problems, any of the major brands of synthetic sea salts mixed with clean, freshwater will provide a good life supporting medium for marine animals and should be the most stable and trouble free element in the whole system. Synthetic sea salts are easy to keep and store. One can keep it in the package in a dry, cool place ready for mixing and use whenever necessary, or if immediate emergency use is anticipated, it can be dissolved and stored in dark containers ready for instant use. Be sure to label the container carefully if you do this, so you will know the date, brand, concentration, and any other pertinent information about the mix that should be known when it is used. Synthetic sea salts have been widely available under numerous brand names for only about the last 15 years. [This is close to 30 years now, and synthetic sea salt mixes are still getting better. The various companies that make these salt mixes are continually experimenting and improving the mixes to keep up with the advancements in the hobby. For example, it is now possible to get sea salts compounded with extra calcium for use in reef tanks.]

The concept and practice of mixing various salts to support marine life in an artificial environment, however, is far older than the marine aquarium hobby. Many formulas have been published during the last 50 years for scientists and advanced aquarists to use in formulating their own experimental synthetic sea salt mixes. In fact, in 1884 H.E. Hoffman published a formula for artificial seawater in Vol. 9 of the Bulletin of the U.S. Fish Commission. It consisted of 13.25 gallons of well water, 46.5 oz of sodium chloride, 3.5 oz of magnesium sulphate, 5.25 oz magnesium chloride, and 2.0 oz of potassium sulphate. Each salt is dissolved separately and then all solutions are mixed and allowed to rest before use. This formula, simple compared with today's claims of 70 or more trace elements, supported marine life but produced, at best, inconsistent results.

If you really want to mix up your own synthetic sea salts, you might try the formula published by Lyman and Fleming in 1940 in an article titled, "The Composition of Sea Water" which appeared in the Journal of Marine Research, No. 3, Vol. 134.

Formula for a simple artificial seawater

Sodium chloride	23.477	grams
Magnesium chloride	4.981	
Sodium sulphate	3.917	
Calcium chloride	1.102	
Potassium chloride	0.664	
Sodium bicarbonate	0.192	
Potassium bromide	0.096	
Boric acid	0.026	
Strontium chloride	0.024	
Sodium fluoride	0.003	

Add water to a total of 1000 grams

The above formula makes up only 1000 grams or one liter (0.9 quarts) of solution. Multiplying each ingredient by 100 will make up close to 25 gallons of solution, and be much easier to weigh out the chemicals. Adding some natural seawater or commercially available trace elements should round out the solution and make an acceptable grade of synthetic seawater. Mixing your own really isn't worth it today because of the availability of commercial brands, but it's good to know that you could do it—if you had to.

Good water quality is very important in rearing marine tropical fish, but it may not be as critical as one would suppose. The larval fish has membranes that protect its internal environment from the great concentrations of bacteria and inorganic and organic molecules that surround it, and this barrier is effective from the moment of hatch. So although water quality must be good, it need not be a sterile laboratory medium or even duplicate the clear offshore waters that are the natural environment of most larval fish. The water quality of a balanced, well maintained marine aquarium is quite adequate for survival of most larval marine fish if all other factors such as food, light, temperature, and freedom from predators are also adequate. Marine fish have been easily reared in several types of synthetic seawater mixes as well as a variety of natural seawater. The rearing tank can be set up with natural seawater processed as usual for a marine aquarium, synthetic seawater aged a few days, or even water taken from a disease free, uncrowded aquarium. In fact, water from a marine aquarium carries an initial load of the "good" bacteria that will aid the chemical balance in the rearing tank. Perhaps most important to water quality in rearing marine tropicals at home is to make sure that chemical pollutants such as insecticides, paint fumes, tobacco, cleaning solutions, other household contaminants, and even air borne agricultural sprays do not get into the water. Such contaminants can create problems that are devastating in effect—yet are extremely difficult to discover and eliminate.

Chapter 3

FILTRATION

Mechanical, Chemical, Biological, and Sterilization

There are a lot of different things that can be done to aquarium water in the name of filtration, but they all fall under one of the four basic categories listed above. Your success as a marine aquarist will depend in great measure on how well you understand and work with the basic principles of biological filtration. The other types of filtration are important and helpful, but BIOLOGICAL FILTRATION is where all the action is. Without it you have a chemical time bomb, an engineer's nightmare, and a pit of fishy despair sitting in your living room. The following discussions provide the basic information on these four basic categories of filtration. More detailed information is available in the *Marine Aquarium Reference* and other books and articles.

There are two basic types of contaminants in aquarium water: suspended, physical particles and dissolved chemical compounds. The physical particles may be as big as a baseball dropped into the tank by the kid next door or as small as a free floating bacterium. The dissolved chemical compounds may originate outside the tank from things such as insect spray or soap and perfume on the hands of an unwary aquarist, but except for these rare instances, dissolved contaminants are produced by the tank's inhabitants. They are created from the metabolic waste materials of fish, invertebrates, and plants, and also develop from the activity of bacteria on the waste organic matter produced in the tank. These dissolved chemical compounds include ammonia, nitrite, nitrate, urea, proteins, amines, fatty acids, phenols, dyes, and many other less abundant compounds. Briefly, this is what each type of filtration accomplishes in your aquarium.

Mechanical filtration

Mechanical filtration removes suspended particulate matter from the aquarium system water. The efficiency of the filter depends on how fast water moves through the straining surfaces, the surface area of the filter, and the size of the trap for the particles. A mechanical filter can use sand, gravel, floss, metal or plastic screens, or diatomaceous earth to strain particles from the water. Obviously, a filter for baseballs and tree trunks is designed differently and operates differently than a filter designed for plankton and bacteria.

A mechanical filter also becomes a biological filter if it is not cleaned or changed frequently. A good mechanical filter that removes very small particles with a rapid water flow is an excellent auxiliary to the basic biological filter because it maintains high water clarity, removes free swimming parasites, and removes accumulated dirt and detritus from the aquarium when it is cleaned. If the media is not cleaned or exchanged frequently, however, the filter clogs and slows water flow, harbors bacteria, and becomes a biological filter. In order to effectively remove organic particles from the aquarium system, the particles must be removed from the filter before they are broken down into dissolved nutrients, thus the filter must be cleaned every few days, no longer than a week, or its efficiency as a mechanical filter is diminished.

A separate mechanical filter, however, is not an absolute necessity for a successful simple marine aquarium, because the undergravel biological filter also acts as a mechanical filter. A good auxiliary mechanical filter does reduce some of the organic load on the undergravel filter and keeps the water free of small particulate matter.

Chemical filtration

Chemical filtration removes dissolved compounds and elements from solution in the aquarium water. There are four basic chemical filtration methods commonly applied to marine aquaria:

1. Activated carbon

2. Ion exchange resins and polymeric adsorbents

3. Protein foam skimming
      (airstripping or foam fractionation)

4. Oxidation through ozonation

Activated carbon

Activated carbon is able to remove dissolved solids from the water because each carbon grain contains uncountable microscopic pores throughout its entire mass. These tiny pores adsorb the molecules of various organic and inorganic substances from the solution and trap them so that they are no longer present in the solution. Of course the complete technical explanation is more complicated, but this gives you some idea of how activated carbon works. When all the pores are filled or coated with organics and bacterial slime, the carbon is deactivated and then functions only as a biological filter, but this takes quite some time depending on the filtering load. The home hobbyist really can't reactivate the carbon by baking it in an ordinary oven, except to drive off some adsorbed gasses, but if the carbon is not exhausted, it can be cleaned of accumulated organic dirt and reused, although its effectiveness will be limited.

The adsorptive properties of activated carbon change as the carbon is used. New carbon has a greater ability to adsorb gasses than old carbon and, in general, will pick up more molecules at a faster rate. Some of the things that activated carbon will remove to some extent from your aquarium water, *depending on the type, amount, and age,* are oxygen and carbon dioxide (but not enough to affect a well aerated aquarium), copper, ozone, chlorine, antibiotics, some dissolved proteins and carbohydrates, iodine, mercury, vanadium, chromium, cobalt, iron, molybdenum, methylene blue, malachite green, sulfa drugs, organic dyes, and many other elements and compounds. Some of these are removed very quickly and efficiently, such as organic dyes, and others are removed slowly. Most compounds are not completely removed by activated carbon, but are reduced in concentration to a variable extent.

Thus, activated carbon is a mixed blessing to us aquarists because it pulls out some good things as well as many of the nasties. It does not effectively remove ammonia, nitrite, or nitrate and cannot substitute for a biological filter. Activated carbon can remain effective in home aquarium application for up to one year in some situations, and it may be that older carbon is better than new carbon, because older carbon may retain the capacity to remove large organic molecules after its affinity for simpler compounds has diminished. **Perhaps the greatest danger in using activated carbon is that it is so efficient in clearing and cleaning the water that it hides the need for occasional partial water changes.**

Properly used activated carbon can be one of the most useful tools of the marine aquarist. My opinions and recommendations on the general use of activated carbon are as follows: Set up the carbon filter as an outside power filter that can be turned off, removed, and cleaned without disturbing the tank. Use it sparingly on invertebrate tanks because invertebrates seem to be more dependent on trace elements in the water than are fish. Carbon can be used constantly or with great frequency on fish tanks, especially older carbon, but give the tank a rest from carbon filtration once in a while, especially immediately after water changes or renewal of trace elements. **Never use carbon filtration on treatment tanks or on a display tank during the, hopefully, rare occasions that you have to medicate the aquarium.** Remember that no one really knows exactly all that activated carbon does or doesn't do to aquarium water, so use it cautiously and let your own experience be your best guide.

[Ten years later, this is still good advice. However, few, if any, marine aquarists are now concerned about any negative effects of activated carbon filtration. In fact, it is a rare marine system that does not have some carbon filtration. Most aquarists renew the carbon every three or four months and keep the system water crystal clear. Fish and most invertebrates don't seem to suffer, but heavy carbon filtration does remove some important trace elements such as iodine. If heavy carbon filtration is used, it is wise to regularly supplement trace elements. Some reef tank aquarists simply drop a bag of activated carbon in the sump tank and replace it every six months or so, but this is not the best way to use carbon filtration. The water flow should be directed through the carbon filter media and not just allowed to flow around it or, as one well known aquarium expert phrased it, "you might as well soak a potato in the tank if you just lay a bag of carbon in the sump". A bag of carbon in the sump tank does do some good, of course, but it is not nearly as effective as flow through carbon filtration.

Most carbon filtration in traditional, undergravel systems is set up in an auxiliary filter that hangs on the back of the tank, and this works very well. Change the carbon every six months or so, or when you begin to notice a bit of yellow color in the water.]

Ion-exchange resins

Ion-exchange resins and polymeric adsorbents are more of an unknown than activated carbon. They are available to marine aquarists as small dull surfaced beads, alone or in a mix with activated carbon, and as fibers in pads and sheets of filter material. Opinions vary from advocation of certain resins as total substitutes for biological filtration to total dismissal of any value of ion-exchange resins to marine aquarists. As in most instances where two great extremes exist, the truth is somewhere in the middle. To a greater degree than activated carbon, ion-exchange resins can be manufactured to attract specific types of molecules. Some resins are used to remove ammonia or nitrate in freshwater sewage treatment and others are effective in removing dissolved organics. Some resins may give off small amounts of toxic chemicals and many are quickly confounded by the large number and type of free ions in saltwater. I prefer to withhold judgement and use of ion-exchange resins in saltwater systems until more information is available on their function and their effects on marine life support systems.

[Use of ion-exchange and polymeric adsorbent resins in marine systems has greatly increased in recent years. They are now manufactured for greater specificity in removal of particular types of molecules and many can be easily regenerated. Some aquarists feel that activated carbon is all the chemical filtration that is needed, and others say that ion-exchange and polymeric resins are very valuable chemical filtration tools, especially for reef tanks. My opinion now is that resins can be beneficial, but that the individual aquarist must determine how useful they are in any particular system, and if the benefits of their use justify the expenditure.]

Protein skimming

Protein skimming, airstripping, and foam fractionation are all terms for the same basic process that is gaining in popularity as a water cleansing method for marine aquariums. The technique is old, but its application to marine aquariums is relatively new. Protein skimming operates on the principle that many of the compounds dissolved in salt-water are attracted (adsorbed) to the interface (surface) between a gas and a liquid. Therefore, if you mix extremely tiny and abundant bubbles of air or other gas into a solution, many of the dissolved organic and some inorganic compounds "stick" to the surface of the molecules and ride them until they burst.

When the organics are heavy, they coat the bubbles and create a surface foam, sort of like soap suds, but not as stable. Now if you can scoop up these suds and discard them, you can remove the compounds that stuck to the bubbles when they formed in the aquarium water. And this is just what the protein skimmer does. It collects the foam created in the foam generation chamber in a small cup where the foam breaks down into a nasty liquid containing all the compounds that stuck to the bubbles. This cup is emptied periodically, or drained continuously, and the aquarium is rid of many things like detergents, proteins, amino acids, some organic dyes, fatty acids, albumin compounds, other complex organic compounds, and some inorganic compounds that tend to hook up with some organic molecules.

There are unknowns, however. Like activated carbon, no one knows exactly what, and how much of it, is removed by an efficient protein skimmer, and it is possible that valuable trace elements and nutrients are removed along with waste compounds. Also, protein skimmers have to be carefully adjusted for peak efficiency in a small marine system, and if the air discharge is not at just the right volume and bubble size, the effectiveness of the unit declines greatly. Wooden air releasers or wooden air "stones", commonly used in protein skimmers because of the tiny bubbles they create, should be changed often for the wood decays and fills with organics, and air release is restricted. [The *Marine Aquarium Reference* has an extensive section on types and operation of protein skimmers, including directions on making a homemade protein skimmer from PVC pipe.]

A protein skimmer can be a very useful tool, especially for heavily loaded fish tanks and coral reef tanks, but you have to make sure that it is operating properly, and remember that it may remove important trace elements and nutrients. The primary value of protein skimming and carbon filtration to the marine aquarist is that when properly employed, they significantly aid water clarity and cleanliness, and decrease, but do not eliminate, the necessity of periodic water changes. Protein skimming is most valuable, because when properly set up and operated, this method of chemical filtration removes dissolved organics **before** they are broken down into basic nutrients.

Ozone

The last method of chemical filtration to discuss is oxidation of dissolved organics through application of ozone. Ozone is the triatomic form (O_3) of oxygen and is a very unstable compound. It is formed just before introduction into the water by air passing through an electric discharge. As the ozone breaks down in the water, it oxidizes or "burns" dissolved organics and kills bacteria and parasites.

Ozone functions as a "chemical filter" in that it changes the structure of many complex dissolved organic compounds if it is abundant enough and in contact with the water for a long enough period of time; and although ozone can oxidize some ammonia and nitrite to nitrate, it cannot substitute for a biological filter. The ozone contact tube should be of a counterflow design for maximum efficiency. This means that the water flow and the flow of ozonated air must go in opposite directions in the reactor or contact chamber (air up and water down) to insure maximum contact time of the ozone with the water.

[The best method of mixing ozone into the water is to use a reactor tube. This is a filter tube or container that trickles water over a large surface area filter media in a pressurized (only 2 to 3 psi above ambient) atmosphere. This is also a good way to oxygenate water, and when used with just air, it is termed an oxygen reactor.]

Ozonation is a delicate and dangerous filtration aid. Too much ozone escaping into the aquarium can burn the gills of fish and the delicate tissues of invertebrates and cause death and distress, and too little ozone mixing with the water will not effectively oxidize the dissolved organics. Ozone escaping into the atmosphere can also cause headaches and stomach distress in humans, but there would have to be a large and constant release before such symptoms appear. If you always smell ozone in the vicinity of the aquarium, then there may be too large a release of this gas into the atmosphere.

Each aquarium carries a different organic load and therefore requires a different amount of ozone, thus it is difficult to maintain maximum efficiency without delicate chemical adjustment. Activated carbon will remove ozone and can be used to prevent a build up of ozone in the aquarium. A carbon filter should be present in the water line that returns water from the ozone reactor to the aquarium or sump tank.

Ozone is frequently used in protein skimmers, and the efficiency of each is enhanced when they work together and both are optimally adjusted. Ozone treatment devices are best left to the advanced aquarist, since they can create problems for the casual or unknowing hobbyist.

Sterilization

Sterilization can be considered a filtering method in that it removes life from the aquarium water. The most common sterilization device for marine aquaria is the ultraviolet light sterilizer in which the aquarium water is passed through a filter tube that contains a short-wave, germicidal ultraviolet bulb. Some chemical filtration is also effected since the device also oxidizes some dissolved organics.

Other sterilizing devices release ozone into a contained tube of aquarium water and an ozone and air mixture. The ozone dissolves in the water and oxidizes the protoplasm of the target organisms. The primary use of sterilization devices is to decrease the abundance of free floating bacteria and control parasitic infections by killing the organisms during the free swimming stages of their life cycles.

Ultraviolet light is a good sterilizing agent when the water is clear, the bulb is new, the UV has to penetrate less than an inch of water, and the exposure time of the water to the UV light is longer than one second. UV works by affecting the function of the living cell through alteration of the structure of the cell's nuclear material, and through some production of ozone in the treated water. The usual structure of a UV unit designed for marine aquarium use consists of a 4 to 8 watt UV germicidal bulb sealed in a watertight jacket that allows the aquarium water to circulate in a thin layer past the bulb. Both UV irradiation and ozonation have the capability to alter the structure of some dissolved chemical compounds. **Therefore, neither ozonation nor ultraviolet sterilization should be used with any drug or chemical medication.**

Sterilization of aquarium water is not necessary for maintenance of a successful marine tank. The most effective application for these devices is reducing the number of free floating bacteria, and such bacteria are usually not a problem in a well maintained, uncrowded tank. However, if you feel that UV treatment helps you to maintain a cleaner, more stable and trouble free tank, then by all means go ahead and use it, but remember that the glass in the UV bulb will gradually change in its ability to transmit UV germicidal radiation, and the bulb should be replaced every 8 to 10 months for the unit to retain its effectiveness.

[There are two very important human safety considerations to be aware of when operating a UV unit:

1. **Never** look directly at the lighted germicidal UV bulb. UV light in a germicidal wavelength can injure the delicate tissues of the human eye.

2. A UV bulb designed to operate within a flow of water should not be operated without the water in the filter. The bulb will heat up when operated in air and may break if it is immersed in water while hot after operation in air, and of course, this can make the tank electrically charged.]

Biological filtration

Biological filtration is the transformation of toxic waste substances, primarily ammonia, into relatively nontoxic nutrients through the activity of living organisms, primarily nitrifying bacteria. Algae also utilize the basic nutrients produced by nitrifying bacteria, thus can function as a type of biological filter under the right conditions. Note that the phrase "removes from the system" is not mentioned in the definition of biological filtration as it is in the definitions of other types of filtration. The only drawback to biological filtration is that the process does not remove waste products from the aquarium, it only transforms the waste to compounds with limited toxicity. These compounds accumulate in the aquarium and eventually have to be removed either through a complicated filtration system, or through the simple process of periodic, partial water changes. Marine aquariums can be maintained for years with only a simple, well aerated, undergravel filter; monthly 10 to 20 percent water changes; and semiannual filter cleanings.

Much has been said in recent literature about the nitrogen cycle, the "new tank syndrome", and nitrification and bacterial decomposition—and rightly so, for they all refer to the basic process that allows life to exist in your aquarium. Just as human communities need septic tanks or sewage plants, aquariums require biological filtration. All animals, including fish, crabs, anemones, butterflies, snakes, and parakeets consume food and oxygen in order to grow new tissues and produce energy for living. Waste products in the form of carbon dioxide, undigested food and intestinal bacteria, and nitrogen wastes from utilization of protein and normal breakdown of body cells are produced by every animal and must be excreted.

In a well aerated tank, the CO_2 content of the water remains relatively stable despite constant production by animals and utilization by algae. Some CO_2 passes slowly back and forth with the atmosphere depending on CO_2 levels in the aquarium. Far more quickly than passive atmospheric exchange, however, CO_2 may be actively produced by large fish and then taken up by algal growth. The carbonic acid—bicarbonate—carbonate—hydrogen ions equilibrium (the buffer system in marine water) shuffles CO_2 between free carbon dioxide gas and carbonic acid, and normally keeps the pH very stable. If the tank is not well aerated, however, CO_2 tends to accumulate in the form of carbonic acid, and the pH drops. In contrast, heavy growths of algae may remove enough CO_2 from the water during the day to cause the pH to rise considerably. The pH of most marine aquarium systems tends to gradually decline due to the accumulation of organic acids that are not part of the buffer system. Regular water change usually corrects this typical decline in pH, and strong aeration and water turnover through the filter helps release excess CO_2.

The solid wastes of fish and invertebrates, uneaten food, an occasional dead fish, and, rarely, an hors d'oeuvre all suffer the same degenerative fate in a marine aquarium. The aerobic (requiring oxygen) bacteria of decay attack this dead matter and produce, among other things, a lot of ammonia from the decomposed protein. This process of decay is termed ammonification or **mineralization**.

The major source of ammonia in a well run aquarium, however, is from the nitrogenous wastes of the aquarium inhabitants. The way an animal rids itself of waste nitrogen depends greatly upon its relationship to water. Ammonia is

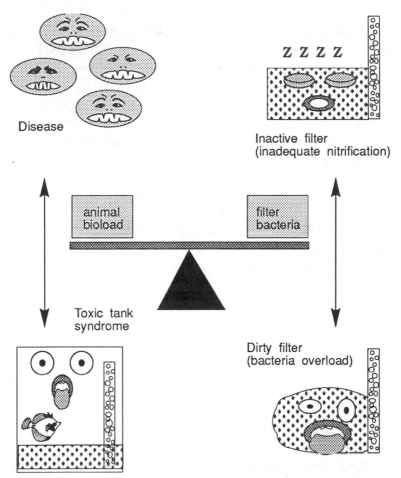

Figure 10 The balance of a marine aquarium. All is well as long as the activity of the filter bacteria transforms and neutralizes all the wastes of the animal load. A tip in either direction creates problems for fish and invertebrates. A filter clogged with detritus and organics fosters disease. A filter with inadequate nitrifying bacteria produces high levels of ammonia and nitrite, the toxic tank syndrome.

rapidly formed in the blood of animals from the breakdown of protein, and it has the characteristics of being very toxic and very soluble. It must be either immediately excreted or rapidly transformed to a less toxic substance. Fish, living as they do in a watery environment, are able to excrete ammonia directly through their gills into the surrounding water.

Land animals cannot afford the water loss that would be the price of direct ammonia excretion and thus, through a clever biochemical mechanism known as the ornithine cycle, they convert ammonia to less toxic urea and excrete it in a concentrated solution whenever the mood strikes them. Some animals that live where there is very little free water, such as desert rats, are so conserving of water that they transform their nitrogenous waste to nontoxic crystals of uric acid that can be stored in the body or excreted in dry form.

So now we have a tank full of highly toxic, soluble ammonia derived from animal excretion and the activity of decay bacteria. Whatever shall we do? Fortunately, Mother Nature comes on like the U.S. Cavalry at this point with her nitrifying bacteria. These bacteria in the genera *Nitrosomonas* and *Nitrobacter* are found throughout the world and have the capacity to oxidize ammonia to nitrite, and nitrite to nitrate, respectively. All we need to provide is a surface for the bacteria to colonize and a source of ammonia. Even if we avoid a biological filter, which is only a device that provides a lot of surface area for colonial bacterial growth, the bacteria colonize every available surface to do their oxidative work. The intermediate product, nitrite (NO_2), is also toxic, but less so than ammonia. Levels of up to 15 parts per million (ppm) can be tolerated by most species of marine fish for a limited period. The end product, nitrate (NO_3), is relatively nontoxic and can be allowed to accumulate in the aquarium without much concern. However, if the tank is allowed to develop pockets of low oxygen or anaerobic conditions, uncontrolled bacterial reduction of nitrate can produce hydrogen sulphide and other toxic compounds.

Ammonia occurs in two states depending on pH, the un-ionized state (NH_3) and the ionized state (NH_{4+}). The un-ionized state is more toxic than the ionized state because it can invade body tissues more readily, but fortunately, almost all free ammonia is in the ionized state at the normal pH of seawater. As pH increases, the nontoxic form of ammonia rapidly decreases and the toxic form rapidly increases. Thus a lethal level of toxic ammonia may be present at a pH of 8.4, while the same total amount of ammonia may be tolerable at 7.8. Fish that are susceptible to ammonia poisoning may suddenly suffer symptoms if the pH increases rapidly when significant levels of ammonia are present. At any rate, levels of ammonia and nitrite should always be very near zero in the aged and balanced marine aquarium.

The *Nitrosomonas* bacteria are the first to populate the filter and rapidly begin oxidizing ammonia to nitrite. *Nirobacter* is inhibited by the presence of ammonia and doesn't begin rapid population growth until after ammonia levels begin to fall. **Obviously these bacteria cannot begin their growth unless the nutrients, ammonia and nitrite, are present in the tank.** These nutrients can be provided naturally by introducing some hardy fish and/or invertebrates that will create ammonia for the bacteria and are able to live though the period of establishment of the biofilter— or artificially by adding a solution of inorganic ammonia. This process is described in Chapter 4 and also discussed in greater detail in the *Marine Aquarium Reference.*

Great populations of bacteria must grow in the relatively sterile, new filter bed, and it takes some time for such numbers to develop, especially if only a few bacteria are present at the start. Bacteria usually reproduce by division, one individual splitting into two; thus the last phase of population growth proceeds much more rapidly than the first phase. This is why ammonia and nitrite levels climb so high so slowly and then drop so rapidly to less than one or two ppm. The nitrite drop usually occurs within a day or two, even though it was building to levels as high as 20 to 40 ppm over a period of several weeks. Obviously, if we start out with a bacteria population of some size, the time required to establish the necessary nitrifying potential will be shortened because the initial period of slow population development is reduced proportionate to the size of the starting bacteria culture. In other words, the populations will

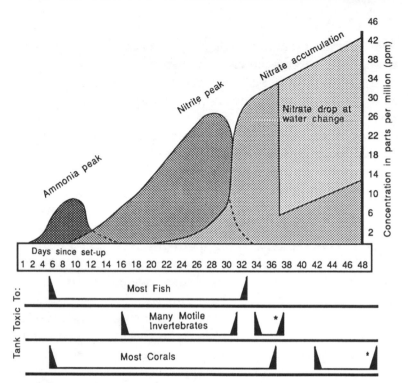

Typical pattern of tank toxicity and relative levels of poisionous, waste nitrogen compounds during the run-in of a new marine aquarium with a traditional undergravel filter.
Note that all aquariums do not cycle exactly the same.

* Tank toxicity after water change is very variable.

Figure 11   Typical run-in pattern of the biological filter in a marine aquarium. Colonies of nitrifying bacteria must become established on the filter media regardless of the type of media or origin of the seed cultures.

develop much faster if we start with two billion bacteria instead of two hundred.

After the populations of *Nitrosomonas* and *Nitrobacter* are well established, oxidization of ammonia and nitrite occurs almost as these compounds are formed, thus they never accumulate in the system and only the end product, nitrate, can build to high levels. Accumulated nitrate can be removed by dilution through partial water changes or, since it is a basic plant nutrient, algal growth can utilize a lot of the nitrate that is produced. Harvest of the excess algae then removes this nutrient, and others, from the system.

[Figure 11 illustrates the typical "run-in" pattern of a biological filter, including the times that a system can be toxic. Ammonia (NH_3), nitrite (NO_2), and nitrate (NO_3) are variably toxic at different concentrations, and Figure 11 provides an indication of when the filter is most toxic to different organisms during the period of typical establishment of bacterial colonies in a biological filter.

Another form of biological filter, a **denitrifying filter,** can be used in marine systems to reduce nitrate. This is a relatively recent development in the marine hobby. Such a filter is mostly used to eliminate nitrate in coral reef tank aquariums, but is also very helpful in breeding and holding systems that produce a lot of excess nitrogen compounds. Severely limiting all the organics and basic nutrients added to reef systems, however, is more effective and less trouble in the long run than maintaining an efficient denitrifying filter, so use of this type of filter seems to be declining. Its most effective use may be on large marine fish systems where denitrification may reduce the required frequency of water changes. Closed system marine fish and invertebrate rearing set ups, however, may make good use of denitrifying filtration. The *Marine Aquarium Reference* has a detailed discussion of denitrification of marine aquarium water.]

Natural systems

The so called "natural system"—a tank established without a filter, only an air stone or two to gently turn over the water, and containing a limited number of fish, invertebrates, and algae—still depends on the same biological process of nitrification that the biological filter is designed to support and enhance. Nitrifying bacteria are still present and working hard, but their populations are restricted to tank sides and most other surface areas present in the aquarium. Even such restricted sites for bacterial activity are sufficient if the tank is well maintained and the biological load is kept well within the range of natural balance. Invertebrates that consume waste matter, and algae that utilize nutrients, greatly aid tank balance in a "natural system" aquarium, and their biological interaction is more important in this system since there is no efficient biological filter to provide a broad base of nitrifying potential. Algae can, and usually do, play an important role in the marine aquarium. They serve as a diet supplement for many fish and invertebrates, enhance the beauty of a natural tank, and can perform as a biological and chemical filter. The type of algae under discussion are the mixtures of single celled and filamentous green, brown, and red algae that form on the sides and rocks of well lit aquariums. Brown algae are usually the first to appear and are really diatoms or golden brown algae. Heavy growths of these diatoms mixed with other algae go by the esoteric name of "lab-lab" and are used in the culture of some marine food fish. Also included are the filamentous green algae in the genus *Entromorpha*. These algae form the thin, hair-like, green filaments that grow on rocks and glass and provide browse for many aquarium fish. Growth of the algae is dependent on intensity and quality of light and amount and type of dissolved nutrients. Diatoms and red algae are most common in marine aquaria because they do not require relatively high intensities of natural spectrum lighting and are tolerant of less than optimum water quality (high nutrient levels and low pH). Good growths of green filamentous algae are indicative of a well balanced, well lit marine tank.

[This was written before the development of nutrient poor, high intensity light, live rock based reef tanks. A reef built of porous live rock in a marine tank can proved ample biological filtration and can eliminate the need for other biological filtration, undergravel or trickle, in a "natural" tank. A moderate growth of filamentous green algae is usually useful and desirable in a traditional type of marine aquarium with moderately intense lighting and a full load of marine fish, but not for a reef tank with a focus on hard and soft corals. Macroalgae in the genus *Caulerpa* is now much more highly desired than green filamentous algae.]

Algae aid bacterial nitrification only in providing some sites for growth of nitrifying bacteria and some detritus for heterotrophic (decay) bacteria. It is as a "chemical filter", however, that algae really have potential. During photosynthesis (the process plants use to make food and energy from sunlight, water, CO_2 and nutrients) algae take up CO_2, which keeps the pH of the aquarium high, and utilize nutrients such as nitrate that are made available by bacteria in the biological filter. Thus algae can clean the water of accumulated nitrates, take up ammonia and nitrite, release oxygen, and remove CO_2, all good things to do for your aquarium.

Abundant algal growth, however, will also remove trace elements, and can be a potential disaster. As algal activity raises the pH, any ammonia present becomes more and more toxic as the amount of un-ionized ammonia increases. Usually ammonia levels are so low and algal activity so limited that no problems develop. Many algae also use ammonia as a nutrient, so ammonia seldom gets a chance to accumulate in systems with heavy algal activity. It is possible, however, for algal activity in closed systems without CO_2 injection, under sunlight or intense artificial light, to raise pH levels to 8 and 9, so it's worthwhile to at least be aware of the possibility.

There are delicate balances in a closed system aquarium between type and quality of algal growth, total animal load, quality and intensity of lighting, frequency and amount of water change, and degree of organic pollution (possibly from overfeeding). It is possible, especially in smaller, overcrowded tanks, to stimulate a luxuriant algal growth for several weeks or months only to have it suddenly die and pollute the tank. If heavy algal growths develop in the tank, the excess algae must be harvested and remaining growth closely watched for changes in type and amount of algae. The best situation is to grow just enough algae to supple-

ment the fish's diet and help maintain a good quality environment, but not to the point where weekly harvesting is
necessary.

Moderate algal growth in the tank is beneficial to the
contained marine environment, but it cannot properly be
termed an algal filter. An external unit with algal growth
controlled by harvesting and special illumination, effectively serves to remove nitrates and CO_2 and performs a real
filtering function. An algal filter is a worthwhile addition to
an external compound filter that is sometimes used with
large, 75 gallons and up, home installations built by skilled,
advanced aquarists for large fish tanks. Nutrient levels required by algal filters are usually too high for coal reef tanks.
The ultimate algal filter is a large, shallow, glass covered
tray that receives natural sunlight during most of the day
and through which the aquarium water is continuously circulated. Care must be taken in such an installation to avoid
extremes of temperature. Also, the effects of algal filtration
are reversed in darkness (oxygen and pH levels drop), so the
aquarist must also be aware of the potential problems.

A tank for **rearing marine tropical fish larvae** can have
no bottom, figuratively speaking. The larvae of almost all
marine fish live in the surface waters of the sea where microscopic food organisms are plentiful and bottom growths
with legions of predators are safely out of reach. Any type of
filtration that collects tank water and directs it through a
device that traps particles is bound to remove tiny food
organisms and perhaps the larval fish themselves. Therefore, the easiest way to rear marine fish larvae is in a bare
tank with no filtration, at least during the first week or two,
except for the nitrifying bacteria that colonize the tank sides
and bottom. Sure, a filter can be developed that will circulate the water through a fine mesh with a large surface area,
but except in the most unusual circumstances, it isn't worthwhile. A 50% water change every few days during the larval
rearing period (three or four weeks) is all that is necessary to
maintain adequate water quality for most species.

Chapter 4

THE BIOLOGICAL FILTER
Function and Construction

Function

A biological filter is a living thing. It consumes oxygen, feeds on the waste products of animals in the system, and excretes wastes of its own. This is very important to remember, because you must treat the biofilter as a living, breathing creature. The nitrifying bacteria in the filter are dependent on the oxygen contained in the water flowing through the filter. If this flow of oxygenated water stops, the good bacteria die, the water fouls, and the entire tank eventually dies. Because of this great demand for oxygen, there must be a rapid flow through the filter at all times. This is one of the major differences between the set up for a freshwater and a saltwater aquarium. The amount of water flowing through a filter designed for a freshwater tank is not adequate for marine tanks, and the proper populations of nitrifying bacteria will not be established. (Note that freshwater contains more dissolved oxygen than saltwater of the same temperature.) The best general rule for an undergravel, biological filter in a marine aquarium is to get the very maximum flow through the filter that your equipment can deliver.

The object behind establishing a biological filter is to bring the nitrifying capacity of the filter into an equilibrium with the waste production of the tank's inhabitants. The more efficient the filter, the more fish the tank can support. Each individual undergravel filter will have a maximum potential carrying capacity, which depends on many things besides the overall size of the filter. First of all, the extent of the surface area of the filter is more important than the depth of the filter bed. This is because the bacteria need oxygen to function, and as the water flows through the filter bed, oxygen is depleted and nitrification decreases. Thus, the top ½ inch of the filter bed does almost all the work.

[In a reverse flow undergravel filter, where the water is pumped down under the filter bed to percolate **up** through the filter bed, both the lower and upper surfaces of the filter bed are exposed to oxygenated water, and biological filtration is a bit more efficient.]

Other factors of importance are the size and shape of the filter gravel, the rate of water flow, whether the filter is new and clean or old and dirty, and how the filter was established. The gravel size should be small enough to provide a large amount of surface area for a high bacteria population and to provide some mechanical filtration, yet large enough to allow a good water flow with some freedom from particulate clogging. Irregular gravel about ¹⁄₁₆ to ³⁄₁₆ inch (1 to 4 mm) in diameter is a good size for a marine undergravel filter. It allows a lot of water to pass through and keeps the filter bed well oxygenated. Large air lift tubes at least ¾ inch internal diameter and a strong air flow broken up into small bubbles are essential to provide the necessary water flow through the filter bed.

A tank with no filter bed, such as a larval rearing tank or a tank set up according to the "natural method" (a few air stones, live rock, many invertebrates, and a few fish), still develops a healthy community of nitrifying bacteria on every exposed surface inside the tank. Sand grains, shells, decorations, tank sides, algal growths, and especially live rock all harbor colonies of nitrifying bacteria. So even a tank with no "biological filter" does, in fact, have a lot of biological filtering going on—it just isn't contained, isn't controlled and, quite often, isn't able to adjust to changes in tank populations, hidden fish deaths, or overfeeding.

In most situations, larval tanks do not need an external biofiltration system. Larval tanks do not carry a large biomass and are in operation for only a few weeks, thus wastes do not quickly build up to toxic levels. Therefore, many fish and invertebrate larvae can be reared in a relatively small tank with a few fairly large water changes during a four week larval period.

A biofilter bed established with an inorganic source of ammonia has a much greater initial carrying capacity than one started with an organic ammonia source such as fish or crabs. The reason for the increased carrying capacity is that all the available sites for bacteria growth are taken by the nitrifying bacteria rather than sharing sites with other types of heterotrophic bacteria that feed on other "foods" such as organic compounds. This allows large populations of the right bacteria to develop, and the filter bed can operate at its maximum capacity. Ammonium chloride (NH_4Cl) is a good compound to use to establish the nitrifying bacteria with an inorganic ammonia source.

Very little is required to develop the proper (1 to 5 ppm) concentration of ammonia in the tank water. You can fly by the seat of your pants and put in a about a quarter teaspoonful (2 to 3 grams) of ammonium chloride for each 20 gallons and let it run until nitrite levels drop to near zero, or you can be scientific about it and add 20 drops of a 6% solution per 10 gallons every three days for nine days. The important thing is to test the nitrite (NO_2) level in the tank at least every three days until the nitrite level has peaked, probably at about 15 ppm at 18 to 20 days after starting. It should then drop to less than 2 ppm, which should occur in 21 to 25 days. Many variables such as temperature, salinity, lighting, actual ammonia concentration, size of the initial bacterial colonies, and type of substrate may extend or shorten this time period. It is **not unusual** for a marine undergravel or trickle filter to take four to six weeks to complete the growth of bacterial colonies. After the nitrite level has dropped to less than 2 or 3 ppm, the tank is ready for fish and invertebrates. If water changes are no problem, a complete or half change is very beneficial at this time, and an inoculation of marine algae, as a unicellular culture or a macroscopic plant, is also a good idea.

[There are a number of products now on the market that claim to provide a seed of nitrifying bacteria in a preserved form. The bacteria are viable when released into a marine aquarium, according to the directions of the manufacturer. Some aquarists claim excellent results from such products and some do not. There are a great many variables when using these products—production variables, storage, effective dosage, water condition, water temperature, lighting, and type of filter substrate, to mention a few. So if you do use a filter run-in aid, always test the water for ammonia and nitrite a few days after adding fish, just to be sure that bacterial colonies have actually formed and that toxic levels of ammonia and nitrite have not developed.]

The table on page 125 (Chapter 6) details the procedure for setting up and maintaining a marine aquarium with the organic and the inorganic methods of biofilter establishment, along with a suggested care schedule for the first year. Remember that not all aquariums will break-in or run exactly by this suggested schedule, but this will give you some idea of the typical maintenance schedule for a marine aquarium with an undergravel filter.

Operation

Way back in the dark ages (the 50's and early 60's), the only biological filters commercially available were designed for freshwater aquariums and had only small diameter, big bubble air lift tubes to provide water flow through the filter bed. Thus, the serious, knowledgeable marine aquarist had to build his own filter plate and air lift tubes to provide the kind of filtration necessary for a good marine tank. Nowadays there are many commercially available biological filters that are designed for marine aquariums and provide the proper construction features.

Selecting an undergravel filter

If you purchase a filter, look for the three basic features a marine, undergravel biological filter must have. We will assume that all commercially available filters are made from non-toxic material. First, the filter plate must fit snugly over the entire bottom of the tank and be designed to allow water to flow evenly through its entire surface. The plate should be positioned well above the bottom of the tank and allow water to flow evenly toward the bottoms of the air lift tubes. The plate should not allow the filter gravel to accumulate underneath and block off portions of the filter or restrict flow through the air lift tubes.

Second, the air lift tubes should have an internal diameter of at least ¾ inch (2 centimeters), however, small tanks, 20 gallons or less, can get by with tubes of only a ½ inch internal diameter, although bigger is better. There should be an elbow on the air lift tubes at surface level to contain and direct the stream of water and air bubbles to various areas of the tank.

Third, the filter material—shell hash, oyster shell, silica sand, dolomite, quartz gravel, limestone gravel, or any combination of these—must be of a particle size that allows free circulation of water yet still removes most suspended particulate matter. A particle size of about ¹⁄₁₆ to ³⁄₁₆ inch diameter (1 to 4 mm) roughly, seems to do the job well. Particles this size do not cake up in various areas and prevent water flow, but do filter out most suspended organic matter. All of the above mentioned materials will work well as a biological filter, but those of carbonate composition—coral gravel, oyster shell, dolomite, or limestone—also serve to chemically buffer the water and prevent the pH from falling too low.

The buffering effect of these materials under average marine aquarium conditions, however, is slight, and will not prevent a drastic drop in pH in a crowded aquarium overloaded with organic matter. In most situations, a calcareous filter material such as oyster shell will prevent the pH from falling below about 7.8, but it may also hasten the fall of the pH from 8.2 to 7.8 through chemical interaction with the buffer system in seawater. A relatively inert filter material, such as silica sand or small plastic or ceramic structures, does not interact with the natural buffer system of seawater, and the pH usually remains higher for a longer period of time without water change. However, when the pH does drop because the natural buffers are exhausted, and there is no extensive amount of calcareous material to provide a pH "floor" in the system, then the pH can quickly drop to really dangerous levels like 7.5 or even lower.

The filter bed

Filter bed material can be obtained at aquarium shops, plant nurseries, and construction supply stores. Whatever the source and whatever the material, be sure to wash it well under running water until all dirt and organic material has been washed out. Be aware that material obtained from sources other than aquarium shops may contain rusty nails, bits of wood, and other contaminants, and must be cleaned and inspected very well. If oyster shell (obtainable from animal feed stores) is used, don't try to wash away all the milky water or the sun will set and rise on your efforts. In fact, even though the filter media is well washed, the tank water will be slightly milky for several hours to a whole day after set up, until the suspended microscopic particles settle. These particles often settle on the glass sides and give the tank a cloudy appearance even though the water is clear. The sides can be easily wiped clean if this occurs, just don't stir up the bottom all over again.

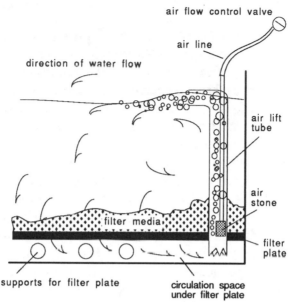

Figure 12 The structure and workings of the undergravel filter.

The filter bed also serves as a mechanical filter by removing suspended particles. Depending on their nature and the condition of the filter bed, these particles are trapped between the grains of filter media or become attached to each other and fill the larger spaces between filter grains. Eventually, the entire filter becomes clogged with organic material, and the biological action of the filter declines. This detritus accumulates most rapidly in an overcrowded, overfed aquarium that receives a lot of light. A little detritus in a filter bed is good because it enhances mechanical filtration and provides some additional sites for nitrifying and heterotrophic bacteria and microscopic life, but too much restricts water flow, cakes the filter bed, and enhances too much "bad" bacterial growth.

Thus the filter bed should be cleaned as required, usually about every 6 to 8 months, depending on the animal load, type and amount of feeding, and size of filter grains. The depth of the filter bed is also important. The deeper the filter bed, the greater the mechanical filtration activity, the greater the build up of detritus, and the greater the risk of developing anaerobic decay in the filter. Anaerobic decay occurs when oxygenated water cannot reach pockets of organic matter, and then the bacteria that do not need oxygen go to work and produce hydrogen sulphide (that rotten egg smell) and other toxins that cause fish great distress.

A filter bed depth of about 2 inches in a 50 gallon or larger tank is about right for most aquarium systems. This depth provides enough media for nitrification and mechanical filtration, and gives the fish enough bottom to stir around without piling up all the gravel in one corner. There are many techniques that can be developed for cleaning filter beds of accumulated detritus, and undoubtedly you will develop the one that works best for you as you gain in experience. Aquariums that receive natural sunlight or intense artificial light and carry a heavy load of animals accumulate detritus more rapidly than lightly stocked, sparingly fed tanks that receive minimum lighting.

Cleaning the filter bed

The basic idea, when cleaning time comes around, is to stir up the gravel to release the trapped detritus particles, and then remove them from the aquarium. Filter cleaning and water changing can go together because the water removed when the bottom is siphoned can be replaced with new water. This is also a good time to give the entire tank a housecleaning, so I'll describe the whole process. It's not necessary to remove the fish from the tank unless you know from experience that they are hyperactive and will continue to bash themselves about the tank during the cleaning. Exposure to some turmoil and dirty water is usually less traumatic to the fish than capture with a net and removal to a holding tank. After all, this sort of situation often occurs in nature during storms.

The first step is to remove any decorations that require cleaning. Some folks like their coral pieces and little castles totally free of green and brown algal growths, and others prefer the natural growths. If these pieces can be cleaned with an old tooth brush and a little water, so much the better. However, if you must be clinical about it, a chlorine solution will quickly remove all organic growths. Be sure to wash off all traces of chlorine before replacing the decoration. Placing any rocks or decorative pieces exposed to chorine in a bucket of water treated with a few drops of dechlorinator is also a good idea. The next step is to clean the sides of the aquarium of any heavy mats of algal growth. Unless a little algae interferes with the aesthetics of your ocean world, it is better for the inhabitants if you leave some algal growth on the sides that aren't used for viewing. The front glass is best cleaned with a plastic abrasive mat or sponge. Just don't carry the grease from last night's frying pan into your tank.

The water will now be a little stirred up, and the fish are looking for a safe place. A flower pot or a rock that they can hide in, or near, gives them some security as their home is being cleaned. This temporary refuge can be moved from one side to the other as necessary. The detritus in the filter bed is much lighter than the gravel and will float up into the water as the gravel is stirred. The gravel can be stirred with a small rake or other implement, but fingers are best because you can feel and break up any caking of the filter material and have greater control over the stirring process. Any hard clumps of filter material that are not broken up are dangerous as water tends to flow around them and not through them.

As your fingers work and stir the gravel, the detritus quickly clouds the water and then begins to settle out on top of the gravel. After the entire filter bed has been worked, the detritus must be removed. Much of it can be taken out by pulling a fine meshed net repeatedly through the water, but probably the best way is to let the dirt settle and then carefully siphon the accumulated detritus from the gravel surface. This removes the major portion of the dirt, and a power filter can quickly pull out the remainder. Any gravel removed by the siphon can be washed and replaced, new salt water can then be added to replace that lost by siphoning, and the tank decorations then replaced. The water will clear in an hour or two, as the suspended particles settle on the bottom. This process will not kill the nitrifying capacity of the filter, but it will knock it back because some of the bacteria have been removed with the detritus and some have been dislodged from their site. Keep a check on nitrite for a week or so after the cleaning to be sure that the tank adjusts properly, and avoid adding new fish until everything is balanced again.

Filter cleaning is, at best, a time consuming, messy chore. It is possible to employ a full time automatic filter cleaner who'll be glad to work for what he can pick up on the tank bottom. A large marine hermit crab, *Pagurus sp.*, can gradually turn a filter bed over completely, and consume uneaten food and algae, and keep the bed loose and free for a long time. Detritus will still have to be removed periodically, but Mr. Hermit Crab makes the job a whole lot easier.

Construction

If you are handy with tools and are looking for a way to cut costs, it is possible to build an inexpensive undergravel filter plate and air lift system that will do a good job in a marine aquarium. Be sure all materials are nontoxic. Don't use metals or flexible vinyl plastic. Rigid American made PVC pipe, available at most hardware stores, is a very good material for air lifts and filter plate supports.

The filter plate The best material that I have found for a homemade filter plate is the plastic "eggcrate" used as a light diffuser for built-in fluorescent lights. This comes in 2 foot by 4 foot sheets and is available at do-it-yourself construction supply houses and electrical supply outlets. It is composed of vertical, half-inch white plastic strips molded in a lattice of half inch squares. It can be cut with long nosed nippers or a hacksaw to conform to the shape of your tank. A piece of plastic window screening (not aluminum!) is cut to the shape of the eggcrate filter plate and is attached with nylon string ties to prevent slipping. The plastic screening prevents the gravel from falling through the eggcrate, and together they make up the basic filter plate. This plate must be kept up off the tank bottom about ½ inch to allow free water circulation. This can be accomplished with small marbles regularly placed about the tank bottom, or short lengths of half inch PVC pipe placed between the tank bottom and the filter plate. (If long lengths of PVC pipe are used to support the filter plate, be sure to cut numerous wide slits in the sides of the pipe to allow a free flow of water through the support pipes.) Whatever you use, be sure the filter plate is evenly supported and will not sag under the weight of the gravel and decorative pieces.

Air lift tubes The air lift tubes can be made from either ¾ or 1 inch diameter PVC pipe cut to a length that will reach from the bottom of the tank to a point about ½ inch below the anticipated water surface. This will allow placement of a PVC elbow on top of the pipe to direct the flow of air and water. Many other air lift designs are available to imaginative aquarists, and decorative air lifts can also be constructed if they function properly.

A good water flow about the tank is most beneficial to fish and invertebrates. Drill a ³⁄₁₆ inch hole in the top of the elbow on the air lift tubes so the air line can extend straight through the elbow down to the bottom of the air lift tube. The air lift tube must project through the filter plate to the tank bottom. The easiest way to do this is to cut a circular hole in the screen and eggcrate that will allow the tube to be forced through the filter plate; it must fit tight to give support and reach the tank bottom. Cut scallops or wedges out of the tube bottom to allow unrestricted flow up the tube.

Another method that requires more precision, but allows greater freedom in air lift placement, is to cut right angled slits in the tube bottom to allow the tube to slip over the cross in a one inch square of the eggcrate. This method also gives the strongest support of the air lift tube. The tube should reach all the way to the bottom of the tank, and additional scalloped cuts should be made to allow good water flow into the uplift tube. Use of a 1 inch internal diameter air lift tube will require careful cutting of a 1 inch diameter hole in the eggcrate or trimming of the tube bottom to fit within the 1 inch square.

The air stone should be positioned near the bottom of the air lift tube, but not so close to the bottom that air escapes from the tube and bubbles up through the filter media. Contrary to the popular expression, water is actually pushed up the tube instead of lifted. When air is mixed with the water contained in the air lift tubes, the mixture is lighter in weight than the water in the surrounding aquarium. This lightweight mix of air and water is then pushed to the surface through the tube by the denser, heavier water entering

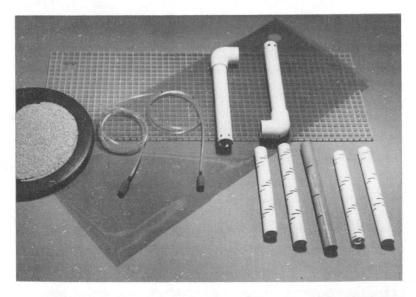

Figure 13 The elements of the homemade biological filter. The slotted 3/4 inch PVC pipe sections support the filter plate above the tank bottom. The fiberglass window screen keeps the filter media above the filter plate and allows water to circulate through the entire filter bed. The air lift tubes bring water from beneath the filter bed to the surface of the aquarium providing water circulation through the filter media. The elbow joints on the top of the air lift tubes restrict spray and direct the water flow around the aquarium.

Figure 14 The construction of the biological filter. All the elements of the filter are in place. It is important for the filter plate to be well supported to prevent sag and possible breakage of the filter plate and screen.

Figure 15 The biological filter in place in the tank with the filter bed partially constructed. Note that there is a 1/2 inch gap between the filter plate and the front glass. The fiberglass window screening folds down in front of the filter plate, allowing the filter bed media to fill this front space and hide the filter. Cut the screening with enough extra width to supprt the front edge if this effect is desired.

the tube bottom. Of course, once in the tube, the new water is also mixed with air, and is in turn pushed to the surface where the air escapes and the water is recirculated. This is a very effective and efficient method of moving water, providing it doesn't have to be pushed very high above the surface of the water.

Now that we know how an air lift works, it's easy to see why very small bubbles of any given volume of air provide more push than large bubbles. The small bubbles rise more slowly, disperse more evenly, and decrease the weight of the air-water column more than the release of large bubbles. Thus, the greater the weight difference, the more push and the more water flow. Wooden air "stones" create very fine bubbles and provide maximum push; however, they also clog and decay relatively quickly and require changing every two or three months. Wooden air stones work well in protein skimmers where tiny, abundant air bubbles are very important. For most air lift purposes, a high quality, fine bubble commercial air stone will give adequate service.

A marine aquarium can be a fantasy world under the sea complete with sunken boats, ceramic divers, little castles, plastic plants, fiberglass coral formations, and fancy colored gravel. Or the aquarist may try to duplicate as natural an undersea setting as possible with algal growths, "living rocks", invertebrates, and coral rubble. We should not belabor one extreme or the other for each represents individual creative efforts and provides delight and satisfaction to the aquarist. However, if the creation of an undersea fantasy kingdom is your desire, be sure all the decor is safe for use in saltwater. Colored gravel should be epoxy coated, or better yet, be composed of inert glass beads or chips, and plastic plants should not have metal weights or ties. Check manufacturer's recommendations and make sure all aquarium decorations are marked as safe for marine use.

[Note: this section was written only for undergravel filters, and it is still a good guide to this basic technology. External wet/dry, trickle, box, compound, and biowheel filters are becoming more and more popular with marine aquarists and each of these has different techniques for establishment and maintenance. See the *Marine Aquarium Reference* for information on other types of biological filters.]

The Compound Filter

Although an undergravel biological filter and a monthly to quarterly partial water change (10 to 20 percent) will maintain an uncrowded marine aquarium very nicely, advanced aquarists may decide to set up a separate water management filter system and circulate the water between the tank and a hidden filter bank.

This is most worthwhile for a large installation, 75 gallons or more, but commercially available external power filters and other filter attachments can be used, if necessary, on smaller tanks as well. The water management system may be set up behind a wall or in a cabinet under the aquarium, and although a lot of work is involved in planning and building a custom-made filter bank, the best possible water quality and largest fish populations can be achieved. An aquarist advanced and skilled enough to construct a separate water management system will undoubtedly do a lot of research and experimentation and will have developed his own ideas on how it should be constructed.

Briefly, the elements that could be included in this type of filter bank, in order of the water flow from the tank through the filter, are a mechanical filter, an algal filter, an activated charcoal filter, and an ultraviolet sterilizer. A protein skimmer is also a very valuable addition and operates most efficiently on water taken directly from the tank before any other type of filtration. These would be in addition to the standard biological filter on the tank bottom. The system can be pressurized except for the protein skimmer, and located below the water level of the aquarium. However, this type of unit is most difficult to service since it must be drained and taken apart to service and clean. A more functional design maintains the filter elements in unpressurized compartments at or below the tank water level. Each compartment should have an overflow, so if flow is restricted in one of the filter elements, the flow can bypass and not pump water out of the system. Also, if you build such a system, make sure the mechanical filter is easy to service, a simple floss replacement or washable foam pad works well. And if an algal filter is part of your system, grow the algae on a surface that can be removed, harvested, and replaced; which is much easier than trying to scrape algae off the sides and partitions of an underwater box. Plan carefully, construct with quality, and you'll have an efficient system.

[The type of external filter briefly discussed above was intended to supplement a standard undergravel marine system with an efficient mechanical filter, use of an algal scrubber to control nutrient accumulation, a protein skimmer to remove organics, and an activated carbon filter to maintain water clarity. All biological filtration was accomplished by the undergravel filter. The intent of this brief section was to introduce the aquarist to the possibility of external filtration on marine aquarium systems. Modern reef type filter systems do all this and also replace the undergravel filter with an external trickle filter, creating a very effective filter system. Back then, an external filter system was a real big deal, nowadays, it's just an ordinary big deal.]

Overcrowding

Don't overcrowd your tank! everybody says that . . . I said that, but what does it mean? Essentially it means that the capacity of the filter bed and the tank water to maintain the existing animal load in good health is nearly exhausted. Of course, if the animal load exceeds the capacity of the system to process their wastes, then the tank balance is destroyed, bacteria populations change drastically, oxygen decreases, toxins appear, and fish die. This can happen suddenly, perhaps due to the introduction of a number of new fish into an already overcrowded tank, or more likely, as a slow breakdown when a well stocked tank is overfed and not maintained for many months. There should be a margin of safety, a buffer zone, between the maximum carrying capacity of the tank and the total animal load occupying the tank at that time. This safety margin allows for a skipped water change, an unobserved dead fish, or a fish sitter's overfeeding, without danger of a tank breakdown.

So how do you know the safe carrying capacity of your tank? Unfortunately, this is one of those situations where the extremes are easily identified—a few fish in huge tank or dozens in a small one—but there is no precise line between too much and too little. There are so many variables that each individual aquarium set up has its own optimum carrying capacity, and this changes with age, maintenance schedule, and fish and algal growth. The filter bed is by far the most important single determinant of a tank's carrying capacity. Many other factors, however, serve to extend or restrict the maximum animal load that can be supported by the system. The following list will give you an idea of the kinds of things that can limit and reduce the carrying capacity of your aquarium:

1. Filter bed too thin or too thick.

2. Filter bed gravel too small or too large.

3. Constricted or channeled flow through a caked up filter bed.

4. Filter bed heavily clogged with detritus.

5. No algal growth.

6. Consistent overfeeding.

7. Infrequent or no water changes.

8. Poor quality lighting.

9. Poor water flow due to small air lift tube, constricted air line or weak air or water pump.

10. Filter bed bacterial action inhibited because of medication.

The wastes and toxins produced by the animal load of a tank are balanced by the efficiency of the filter bed, the capacity of the water to retain altered wastes and still maintain life support quality, and the capacity of algal growth or supplemental filtration to extend the time frame of this balance. Thus, I can't tell you exactly how many fish to put in a certain size aquarium, for a lot depends on how you set up and maintain your tank. However, I can give you a ballpark, maximum figure of 3 to 4 inches of fish for every 5 gallons, assuming that the tank has a mature, full bottom filter bed and is not so high or so narrow that the filter area is unusually restricted, and suggest you watch for signs of overcrowding when this level of occupancy is attained. Some of the indicators of overcrowding:

1. Reduction of green algal growth and more rapid growth of red and blue-green algae.

2. Development of yellow water coloration before the next scheduled water change.

3. Persistent, rapid drop in pH below 7.8.

4. Rapid accumulation of nitrates and persistent traces of ammonia or nitrite. (perhaps the most important indicator of filter breakdown)

5. Distress behavior in fish, fading colors, loss of appetite, hyperactivity, rapid respiration.

Some of these symptoms may have causes other than overcrowding, and if a water change doesn't help, then look for a very dirty filter and/or a disease problem. Remember, the most trouble free marine aquariums are those that are lightly populated with animals and have a moderate, stable growth of algae.

Chapter 5

PHYSICS AND CHEMISTRY
The Essential Information for Marine Aquarists

Physics and Chemistry—two words that strike terror into the hearts of those who would rather stand in awe of the universe than dissect it. But don't worry, this section is designed to tell you in simple language only what you really need to know, so you can put away your calculator.

Light

Light—its intensity, quality, and daily duration—has great influence on all life and all environments, and a marine aquarium is no exception. The major constant through ages of evolution has been sunlight. Temperature, water levels, and even continents changed, but sunlight was always constant, and animals incorporated it into their essence as they evolved. They make vitamins with it, navigate by it, and among other things, control their reproductive periods by its daily duration. Too often we take light and the effects of light for granted, because it is always there at the flick of a switch and does not force our attention as does temperature. (We become very aware of the importance of light in our modern lives, of course, when some idiot gets drunk and runs down the electric pole at the end of the road.) Yet because of its importance, we must take as much care to provide the right lighting as we do to provide the right temperature.

Sunlight in shallow tropic seas is very intense. The warm, clear water allows some sunlight to penetrate hundreds of feet, although 80% of the sun's radiation is absorbed in the first 33 feet. Red, the low energy, long wavelength end of the visible spectrum, is 90% absorbed in the first 15 feet, but blue and ultraviolet, with high energy, short wavelengths, penetrate much deeper. Thus marine tropical fish from shallow coral reefs do best with relatively high light levels that contain at least the normal amount of blue and ultraviolet radiation. These short wavelength radiations are particularly important for the growth of green algae and healthy fish. In fact, long wavelength ultraviolet (black light) is said to have very beneficial effects on marine aquaria. Under normal conditions, only fluorescent lighting should be used, because incandescent bulbs produce too much heat. About 2 to 4 watts per gallon of natural spectrum (daylight) fluorescent light with a good reflector should be ample for a marine aquarium. This is roughly 2 tubes of the proper size for the length of the tank for a 50 gallon tank and 4 tubes for a 100 gallon tank.

It's a good idea to use an inexpensive timer to control the duration of light on the tank. Fish do best when the duration of light each day remains constant or changes very slowly. They should have 8 to 10 hours of darkness every day. Their periods of activity can also be controlled this way. Most aquarists prefer their fish to be active in the evening hours when they are home to enjoy them, so the timer can be set to turn the lights out at 11:00 PM and turn them on again at 7:00 or 8:00 AM. Fish adjust well to such a schedule and are less stressed than under a highly variable lighting schedule. Also, if the room becomes pitch black at night after all the lights are out, a small night light above or near the tank provides enough light to keep the fish comfortable. The natural shallow water environment with moon and stars is never absolutely dark, and a marine aquarium should have some dim night light also. Another good thing to do for your fish is to have an incandescent or blue fluorescent light that comes on about 15 to 30 minutes before the main tank lights come on and stays on about 15 to 30 minutes after the main tank lights go out. These crepuscular (dawn and dusk) lights don't have to remain on all day, but they make for a natural transition between light and dark and reduce stress on the fish. (You know, when you take your fish to the movies in the middle of day, how they bash around in the bowl when you come out of the theater into the bright light. Well this eliminates that kind of stress.)

[Even though there has been a great revolution in lighting for marine aquarium systems over the last few years, the above discussion of lighting is still relevant and topical for the traditional, undergravel fish tank, which is still the basic home marine aquarium system. Note that it is a mistake to put high intensity lighting over a tank with an undergravel filter that holds a lot of fish and accumulates a lot of nutrients. Good lighting is important, a couple of 40 watt, full spectrum fluorescent bulbs are fine as they help the fish do well and grow some good macroalgae, but high intensity lighting will create an algae monster in the undergravel filter and greatly increase the need for water changes and maintenance. The kind of lighting I am talking about here is not the little fixture that comes with some commercial freshwater tanks and has one or two 20 watt red/orange fluorescent tubes. These may be fine for freshwater tanks, but they are inadequate for marine fish. There are some good commercially made light hoods available that carry 40 to 80 watts of full spectrum or high blue light fluorescent lights, and these are fine for marine fish tanks and low-tech reef type systems. One must be aware of the lighting requirements for the kind of marine system that is planned and be sure that the light hood that is selected will deliver the necessary light.

High intensity lighting—10 to 15 thousand lux at the surface—should be put above reef type systems with external trickle filters and live rock reefs that are intended for heavy macroalgae culture or coral culture. A tank for only, or mostly, marine fish can do quite well on lesser lighting, although most marine fish also do very well, if not better, in reef type tanks with high intensity lighting.

A marine aquarist now has a great selection of various types of lights designed and developed for marine aquarium systems. There are many types of the standard 40 watt fluorescent bulbs that display various spectral qualities and intensities, some even have internal reflectors, and there are High Output (HO) and Very High Output (VHO) fluorescent bulbs **that require special ballasts** and produce double and triple the lumens of standard bulbs. Expensive metal halide lamps designed and built expressly for marine aquariums are now also available, and these fixtures allow marine aquarists to almost capture the sun and place it above their own little coral reef. *The Marine Aquarium Reference* has an extensive section on light and lighting and should be consulted if one wishes to build a custom light fixture or needs more information on aquarium lighting.]

Temperature

All animals, with the exception of humans who can engineer their environment, have a range of temperatures that define the limits of their existence. Internal chemical reactions and external physical characteristics have adapted to particular environments through ages of evolution, thus polar bears aren't found in Florida, and queen angelfish don't frequent New York Harbor. Fish, as all other poikilothermic (cold blooded) animals, are totally dependent on the proper environmental temperature range because they cannot regulate their internal temperature. Lizards and snakes can bask in the sun to raise their body temperature or hide under a log to lower it, but fish can only be the same temperature as the water around them, so we must meet their temperature demands rather precisely. The broad temperature range for most marine tropical fish and invertebrates is 65°F to 90°F. A few species can exist above and below these limits, and a few have somewhat narrower tolerances. Please note that this does not mean that fish can be moved from 65°F to 90°F with one quick kerplunk. Fish can withstand some rapid changes of a few degrees. I've seen such quick changes occur on the reefs due to varying current patterns, but slow changes are much easier on the fish. The extremes of the temperature range allow life to only survive.

Optimum temperature for a marine aquarium ranges from 75°F to 82°F (24°C to 28°C). In these days of air conditioning, one seldom has to worry about tank temperatures rising above 85°F, since heat loss from evaporation usually keeps the water a couple of degrees below room temperature. Tank temperatures can easily drop too low, however, and a good aquarium heater should be used to keep the tank at a comfortable, for the fish, 78 to 80°F.

A heater can be very dangerous in a saltwater tank because it produces heat through the electrical resistance of a wire coil, and if saltwater gets into the heater, it can be a very shocking experience. Glass immersion heaters with an internal thermostat are the most commonly used and are quite adequate providing they are designed for saltwater use and have safeguards against intrusion of saltwater and salt spray. An important safety measure is to unplug the heater while working about the tank. This prevents destruction of the heater through inadvertent lowering of the water level or removal of the heater while it is still active, since the glass tube quickly overheats and shatters if it is exposed to the air when the coil is heating. Be sure the heater is of the proper wattage for the gallonage of the tank. Too small a heater may not do the job when the room is cold, and too large a heater can quickly "cook" a tank if the thermostat malfunctions. Figure the heater at about 2 to 4 watts per gallon or follow the manufacturer's instructions. If the heater malfunctions, tank temperatures can easily creep up or drop without your notice, so be sure to have a water temperature thermometer always in or near the tank for ready reference.

[Cooling water is a bigger deal than heating water. The water must be passed through coils that are being cooled by a thermostatically controlled chiller, and this is usually an expensive addition to a marine aquarium system. The only time that a chiller is necessary is usually on a large reef tank system that holds delicate hard and soft corals when the tank environment will not keep the tank below 80 °F. The best temperature for a coral reef tank system is about 76 °F.]

Salinity

Salinity is a measure of the quantity of inorganic solids (salts) that are dissolved in the water. It is usually measured in parts per thousand (ppt or ‰), and most tropical seas are 34 to 35 ppt (35 grams of salt in one kilogram of water). Coastal waters are often diluted by freshwater runoff and vary between 5 and 30 ppt. "That's easy to understand," you might be thinking, "But what's all this 1.025 S.G. stuff? " Well, this requires a little bit of an explanation. When three pounds of salt are dissolved in 10 gallons of water, it disappears. The salt is no longer visible, but it hasn't gone away. The atoms of chlorine, sodium, and the other elements that made up the white salts dissociate into their ionic states and slip in between the water molecules—and if the water didn't taste salty, you would never know they were there.

There are other changes though, one of the most important is that a given volume of saltwater is heavier (more dense) than an equal volume of pure freshwater. A floating object is pushed upward by a force equal to the weight of the water it displaces. This means that an object light enough to float is more buoyant in saltwater than in freshwater (it floats higher), and the more salt in the water, the greater the object's buoyancy and the higher it floats. Specific gravity (S.G.) is a ratio or comparison of the weight (density) of saltwater, or any other substance, to the weight of an equal volume of pure distilled water. Thus, since 1.0 represents the value for distilled water, a heavier substance (such as lead or saltwater) sinks and has a S.G. greater than 1.0; and a substance lighter than pure freshwater (such as oil or wood) floats and has a S.G. less than 1.0.

Now our problem is to find out just how much salt is in the water, and there are four commonly used methods to do this. In the traditional oceanographic research method, the quantity of chlorine ions (chlorinity) is measured by chemical analysis, and the total salt content is calculated from this figure. Two other methods now commonly used are to measure the electrical conductivity of the water, which increases as the salt content increases, or to measure the refractive index (how light is bent by a thin film of water), which also changes with salt content.

These methods are too complicated and expensive for most marine aquarists, so the method of choice is to determine the specific gravity, a measure of density. Since water gets denser as salt is added, we can determine its specific gravity by observing the relative buoyancy of a small glass float, and then determine how much salt is in the water by consulting a graph or table that converts S.G. to salinity. There is one variable, however, and that is temperature. Molecules of warm water are further apart than molecules of cold water, because they have more energy and move faster. This means that warm water is less dense than cold water; thus a floating object sinks a little deeper in warm water. Therefore to get an accurate S.G. reading from a hydrometer, water temperature has to be considered.

A hydrometer is a weighted glass or plastic bulb with a calibrated stem that protrudes above the water surface. The hydrometer floats higher as the salt content of the water increases, thus S.G. can be read directly from the point where the calibrated stem is intersected by the water surface. The *meniscus* is the little upward curve the surface film makes as it tries to climb up the side of the glass stem. For greatest accuracy, take your reading at eye level from the flat surface of the water, not from the top of the *meniscus*. Most hydrometers are calibrated to give an accurate S.G. reading at 59 °F (15 °C), although there are a few now that are made specifically for the marine aquarist and are calibrated at higher temperatures. [One new design has an arm that floats in a plastic case with an indicator line that points at a specific gravity reading printed on the outside of the case. This is a quick and easy method for a marine aquarist to get an approximate specific gravity reading, but one must be sure that all air bubbles that might be stuck on the indicator arm are knocked off, since these air bubbles make the arm lighter and will cause a false reading.]

Because of the temperature effect, a hydrometer calibrated at 59 °F and read at 80 °F will give a reading of about 1.022 at 34 to 35 ppt instead of the true S.G. value of 1.026. Translated into salinity, a true reading of 35 ppt will read 30.8 ppt at 80 °F on a hydrometer calibrated at the standard 59 °F, so you can see that the temperature effect is very significant.

Table 1 on page 111 allows you to convert observed S.G. to true salinity quickly and easily. First record the temperature and the S.G. reading from the water sample. If the water temperature corresponds with the calibration temperature of the hydrometer, go directly to Box A and determine the salinity (in ppt) directly from the S.G. of observed hydrometer reading, since no temperature correction is required.

However, if the hydrometer is calibrated at 59 °F (15 °C) then go to Box B. Select the vertical temperature column that most nearly corresponds with the tank temperature, find the S.G. reading that is nearest your actual reading, and then move over horizontally on that line into Box A to determine the true S.G. and the correct salinity in ppt. If your observed S.G. value falls between two listed values, you can achieve greater accuracy by interpolation.

ppt ‰	True S.G.	68°F / 20°C	69.8 / 21	71.6 / 22	73.4 / 23	75.2 / 24	77.0 / 25	78.8 / 26	80.6 / 27	82.0 / 28	84.2 / 29	86°F / 30°C
	BOX A	BOX B			Observed S.G. (hydrometer calibrated at 59°F/15°C)							
20	1.0145	1.0134	1.0132	1.0130	1.0127	1.0124	1.0121	1.0118	1.0115	1.0112	1.0109	1.0106
21	1.0153	1.0142	1.0140	1.0137	1.0135	1.0132	1.0129	1.0126	1.0123	1.0120	1.0116	1.0113
22	1.0160	1.0150	1.0147	1.0144	1.0142	1.0139	1.0137	1.0134	1.0130	1.0127	1.0124	1.0120
23	1.0168	1.0157	1.0155	1.0152	1.0150	1.0147	1.0144	1.0141	1.0138	1.0135	1.0132	1.0128
24	1.0175	1.0164	1.0162	1.0160	1.0156	1.0154	1.0151	1.0148	1.0145	1.0142	1.0139	1.0135
25	1.0183	1.0172	1.0170	1.0167	1.0165	1.0162	1.0159	1.0156	1.0153	1.0150	1.0146	1.0143
26	1.0191	1.0180	1.0176	1.0174	1.0172	1.0169	1.0166	1.0163	1.0160	1.0157	1.0154	1.0150
27	1.0198	1.0187	1.0185	1.0182	1.0180	1.0176	1.0174	1.0171	1.0168	1.0165	1.0162	1.0158
28	1.0206	1.0195	1.0192	1.0189	1.0186	1.0184	1.0182	1.0179	1.0175	1.0172	1.0168	1.0165
29	1.0214	1.0202	1.0200	1.0197	1.0195	1.0192	1.0189	1.0186	1.0183	1.0180	1.0175	1.0172
30	1.0222	1.0210	1.0208	1.0205	1.0202	1.0199	1.0196	1.0193	1.0190	1.0187	1.0184	1.0180
31	1.0229	1.0217	1.0215	1.0212	1.0209	1.0207	1.0204	1.0201	1.0198	1.0195	1.0192	1.0188
32	1.0237	1.0225	1.0222	1.0219	1.0217	1.0214	1.0211	1.0208	1.0205	1.0202	1.0198	1.0195
33	1.0245	1.0232	1.0230	1.0227	1.0225	1.0221	1.0218	1.0215	1.0212	1.0209	1.0205	1.0202
34	1.0252	1.0240	1.0238	1.0235	1.0232	1.0229	1.0226	1.0223	1.0220	1.0217	1.0214	1.0210
35	1.0260	1.0248	1.0245	1.0242	1.0240	1.0237	1.0234	1.0231	1.0228	1.0225	1.0221	1.0218
36	1.0268	1.0255	1.0253	1.0250	1.0247	1.0245	1.0242	1.0238	1.0235	1.0232	1.0228	1.0225
37	1.0275	1.0263	1.0260	1.0258	1.0255	1.0252	1.0249	1.0245	1.0242	1.0239	1.0236	1.0232
38	1.0283	1.0271	1.0268	1.0265	1.0262	1.0259	1.0256	1.0253	1.0250	1.0247	1.0244	1.0240
39	1.0291	1.0278	1.0275	1.0273	1.0270	1.0267	1.0264	1.0261	1.0258	1.0255	1.0251	1.0248
40	1.0299	1.0286	1.0284	1.0281	1.0278	1.0274	1.0271	1.0268	1.0265	1.0262	1.0258	1.0255

Table 1   Conversion of Specific Gravity (SG) to Salinity(‰)

In actual practice, you needn't get all in a dither about salinity. I don't think that the salinity of a marine aquarium **must be** any one particular value within a range of 28 to 35 ppt, (1.020 to 1.026). With the possible exception of certain invertebrates, marine animals and biological filters do better at salinities a bit lower than oceanic seawater. Lower salinities keep more oxygen in the water, allow the nitrifying bacteria to work more efficiently, and reduce the metabolic work load of the fish. It is entirely possible to maintain a beautiful tropical marine aquarium at salinities of 20 to 25 ppt instead of 30 to 35 ppt. The only difficulty is the gradual acclimation of new fish to the lower salinities. Some fish are euryhaline and can easily move between salt and freshwater, adjusting their osmoregulatory system to abrupt salinity changes. Most coral reef fish are stenohaline, and must remain in seawater although they can adjust to lower salinities than those found on coral reefs.

All fish, freshwater or marine, carry salt levels in their blood and tissue of about 12 ppt, roughly equal to those of land animals. Freshwater fish do metabolic work to prevent loss of salt to the surrounding freshwater, and marine fish work even harder to prevent loss of freshwater from their bodies. Marine fish even drink seawater to increase their water content and excrete excess salt through special cells in their gills. Theoretically, lower salinities ease this metabolic work load and allow the fish to put this energy elsewhere. However, unless you want to do a lot of salinity response experimentation on fish and invertebrates, it is best to maintain your aquarium at salinities between 30 and 32 ppt (a specific gravity range of 1.022 to 1.024). This slightly lower salinity does not seem to increase acclimation stress on the fish, and allows a comfortable evaporation margin.

Loss of ½ or 1 inch of water to evaporation from the tank will not push salinity up past the normal range. Be sure to put a mark outside the tank at the water surface right after filling it to the proper level. This allows you to add **freshwater** to replace evaporation loss without concern for salinity.

You know, of course, that only the water molecules evaporate off into the atmosphere. The salt molecules stay behind, and the solution becomes more concentrated. If you must add a great deal of freshwater to make up for evaporation loss, do so gradually and avoid adding tap water heavy with chlorine or with a large temperature differential. Some salt may be lost through spray encrustation on the outer surface of the tank, but this is seldom enough to even detect through salinity measurements.

It is possible, however, to inadvertently increase the salt concentration in marine systems by adding saltwater when freshwater should be added. One may notice that a lot of water has been lost to evaporation and then think, "Oh, this is a good time for a water change." A 10 or 20% water change made at this point replaces the freshwater lost to evaporation with saltwater and tends to increase salinity. Salinity may also be increased if specimens and the saltwater in their bag are added to the tank when replacement of evaporated water is needed, as this replaces some freshwater loss with saltwater. Over time, if one is not aware of the potential to increase salinity in these ways, salinity can increase to levels higher than necessary.

Oxygen

The two things most essential for life in a marine aquarium are water and dissolved oxygen gas (O_2). Fish can live a short while without the other things, but without water and oxygen they die immediately. Dissolved oxygen is used by all the animals and the biological filter, and is replenished almost entirely by oxygen entering through the air/water interface at the surface of the tank. Algae produce oxygen during lighted hours, sometimes a considerable amount if growth is heavy, but these same algae use oxygen during dark hours, so the gain is not completely positive, and oxygen levels quickly drop to normal saturation or below when algal photosynthesis stops. Some additional oxygen enters the water from air bubbles in air lifts, but this amount is quite small compared to oxygen entering through the surface. The tank water must be well circulated to maintain proper oxygen levels, and this is one of the most important functions of the air lift system. Oxygen cannot diffuse through water rapidly enough to replace that used by animals and filter bacteria, thus without good circulation, oxygen is quickly lost in lower levels of the tank. Colonies of nitrifying bacteria in an undergravel filter can die after only a few hours without oxygenated water circulating through the filter.

Water does not hold a great deal of dissolved oxygen, and the amount it can hold decreases as temperature and salt content increase. Warm saltwater holds only about 4 to 6 ppm dissolved oxygen at saturation levels. Algal activity can supersaturate the water with oxygen and push it up to 8 to 12 ppm, but this is under unusual conditions. Most fish suffer severe stress when dissolved oxygen drops below 3.5 ppm and die when the level sinks below 2.5 ppm. Thus, in a tropical marine aquarium, there is only a difference of 2 or 3 ppm oxygen between a living tank and a mass of anaerobic decay.

It is not necessary for the typical aquarist to measure oxygen levels, a rather complex procedure. [New test kits are now out that allow advanced marine aquarists to test for oxygen.] **But it is important to know that oxygen enters water very quickly and that normal oxygen levels are dependent on active water circulation throughout the tank.** The biological filter also has a great need for oxygen, and if circulation stops, the filter will quickly use up most of the oxygen in the lower levels of the tank. Watch for black discolorations in the filter and/or a "rotten egg" smell from anywhere in the tank. These are both sure signs that circulation is restricted and oxygen is being depleted in certain areas of the tank or filters. Another sure sign of oxygen depletion is if all the fish gasp at the surface and even try to jump from the tank. The latter is an extreme situation and would only occur under very crowded or dirty conditions when water circulation has completely ceased.

[There is a type of "filter" that will slightly supersaturate aquarium system water with oxygen and keep oxygen levels at saturation or above in almost all situations. This is an oxygen reactor, which is a sealed, pressurized tube filled with an open filter media. Water trickles over the high surface area filter media and is exposed to air at slightly higher than normal air pressure by about 2 to 4 psi. Oxygen enters the water at levels above saturation at normal atmospheric pressure and returns to the tank with this higher than normal dissolved oxygen level. See *The Marine Aquarium Reference* for more information on oxygen reactors.]

Nitrogen

Nitrogen and oxygen occur in the tank water bound up in numerous molecular compounds, nitrite (NO_2) for example, or as dissolved gases. Nitrogen in the form of dissolved gas is not a consideration to the average marine aquarist. In some instances, water supersaturated with nitrogen and then compressed can cause "gas bubble" disease in small fish, but this seldom, if ever, occurs in home aquaria.

[Supersaturation with nitrogen gas is now a greater possibility than it was 10 years ago. This is because more aquarists are now using electric pumps to move water around marine systems. An air leak on the intake side of a pump can pull air into the water, and the impeller of the pump may create enough pressure to force considerable air (nitrogen) into the water while it is in the pump. Then when the water gets into the unpressurized aquarium, it comes out of the water in very, very tiny bubbles. These tiny bubbles make the water actually look milky, and an aquarist may think that the tank has a bacterial or algal bloom. One can easily check to see if it is tiny bubbles by filling a glass with the milky water and setting it on a table. If so, after about 10 to 30 minutes, tiny bubbles leave the water and the glass of water will be clear. Another source of air into the water line just before the pump in reef systems is a sump tank with a low water level. If water lost to evaporation is not replaced, the sump level may fall so low that air is sucked into the pump intake line, and this can cause super-saturation of air in the tank water. This often makes an audible sound such as "sllllluuuuuurrrrppppppp". This is known in some reef system circles as the scary, surreptitious, slurper syndrome, but most aquarists need not be concerned about it.]

pH

One can be a successful marine aquarist without ever taking a pH reading, because if you go by the rules of good aquarium management, the pH of the tank water will take care of itself. However, the pH of your water is a good indicator of water quality, and how slowly or rapidly water quality changes occur, and it is well worth knowing. pH is a measure of acidity and alkalinity expressed on a scale of 1 through 14 with 1 being the most acid, 7 neutral, and 14 the most alkaline. The symbol pH stands for the "power of hydrogen" or "weight of hydrogen". The H is capitalized because it represents the chemical symbol of the element hydrogen. An acid condition is caused by an excess of the positively charged hydrogen ions (H^+), and the alkaline condition is caused by an excess of the negatively charged hydroxyl ions (OH^-). When there is an equal number of each, the solution is neutral, with no acidity or alkalinity. pH is expressed on a logarithmic scale, each point being 10 times more concentrated than the one before. Expressed mathematically, each point is a power of 10 (10^0 to 10^{14}). Table 2 on page 117 illustrates the pH scale.

Measuring pH is not at all difficult. It can be done with an electronic pH meter, with pH test paper, or with a liquid pH indicator. The latter two depend on color changes to indicate the pH of the solution. Liquid pH indicators are

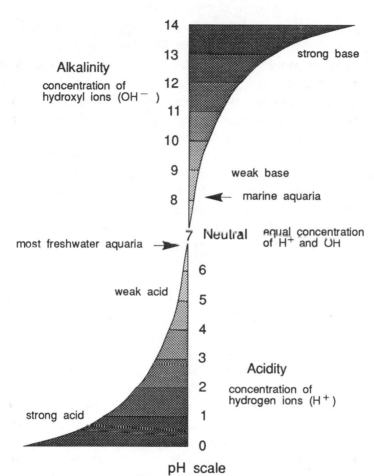

pH scale

Table 2 The pH scale (hydrogen ion concentration).

inexpensive and suit the needs of the typical aquarist very well. There are a number of pH tests on the market for freshwater and saltwater aquariums.

The acceptable pH range for a marine aquarium is 7.8 to 8.3, with 8.2 as the ideal point, if such a thing exists. Most well kept home aquaria fall between 7.9 and 8.2. There are a number of problems that can cause a drop in pH and if the water is filtered with activated carbon, these conditions may remain masked by the clarity of the water until the pH has fallen below 7.6. It is very important to test pH if you do not change a percentage of water regularly, and use activated carbon to maintain water clarity. A pH drop to less than 7.6 under these conditions indicates that it is way past time for a water change.

Seawater has a considerable natural buffering capacity, that is the ability to "absorb" excess H^+ ions without lowering the pH. The biological activity of the filter and the animals, however, eventually overcomes this built in buffer, and the pH begins to drop. The decline is hastened by overcrowding, heavy detritus accumulation, lack of calcareous material with exposed surfaces, and accumulation of dissolved organics. Regular partial water changes dilute accumulations of dissolved organics and restore natural seawater buffers. Sodium bicarbonate (baking soda) is frequently used to push pH up the alkalinity scale when water changes are not possible, but pH will drop again soon, and water changes must be made eventually. If it becomes necessary to artificially buffer the tank to bring the pH up, it can be done as follows.

In a cup of water from the tank, dissolve one teaspoon of sodium bicarbonate for each 20 gallons and slowly add the solution to the tank. Wait for thorough mixing to occur and then test pH. Do this repeatedly to bring the pH up to 8.0, and then test pH frequently until a water change can be accomplished.

The consistent trend in a marine aquarium is always toward a lower pH. Once in a while, however, pH can rise above 8.3, even to 9.0 in some cases. This is a result of CO_2 uptake by vigorous algal photosynthesis and is not in itself harmful. If such a high rise in pH is noted, it is probably more than evident that the algal crop should be harvested.

Dissolved organics

Organic matter is added to the marine aquarium in the form of new animals or plants, as food for fish and invertebrates, and, sometimes, in the water used for water changes.

This organic matter is cycled and recycled by the living organisms in the tank, and eventually accumulates as either detritus or dissolved organics. Many organic compounds including proteins, amino acids, peptides, fatty acids, urea, ammonia, organic dyes, amines, and phenols fall under the category of dissolved organics. Unless physically removed from tank through filter cleaning, algae harvesting, filtration, and water changes, organics continue to accumulate and cause changes in the tank environment detrimental to its inhabitants. Excess organics accumulate slowly in uncrowded, sparsely fed tanks and rather quickly in heavily stocked, well fed tanks, but in either case, they must be controlled by good aquarium management.

There are three sure signs of excess dissolved organics: a heavy persistent foam on the water surface, a yellowish color in the water, and a drop in the pH. These become most evident if the maintenance routine has been skipped for two or three months, and indicate a need for a filter cleaning and water change. Although partial water changes are the best way of controlling dissolved organics, they can be reduced to some extent by carbon filtration, good protein skimming, and UV irradiation. New filtration products that claim removal of dissolved organics are appearing on the market, and if effective, should ease the life of a marine aquarist by extending the intervals between partial water changes. As with all new innovations, time will prove or disprove their utility.

[The best way to remove dissolved organics is with a well designed, efficient protein foam skimmer. A little skimmer that sits inside a big tank and foams away once in a while is helpful, but only marginally so. A tank over 50 gallons really needs a tall (18 inch or so) external skimmer that can really process a lot of water, or, better yet, a good venturi powered skimmer. This is the only process I know that will **remove** a large amount of dissolved organics from a marine aquarium system. A mechanical filter that is frequently changed (every two or three days) will also capture and remove some microscopic particles and dissolved organics, but it is not as efficient as a good skimmer. The comments above on products that might remove dissolved organics referred to some resins, carbons, and powdered filter media that might remove dissolved organics and basic nutrients. There are now some filter media available (polymeric styrene and acrylic polymers) that remove some organics from saltwater solutions and some aquarists use them extensively, but, again, they do not take the place of good protein skimming.]

Caulerpa racemosa

Chapter 6

SETUP, MAINTENANCE, AND TROUBLE-SHOOTING
The First Day, The First Year

The big day! You're ready to put together a marine aquarium. This chapter should answer most of your questions and can serve as a basic maintenance guide during the first year of operation. First of all, watch your bottom. Most commercially manufactured tanks have a bottom supported with a plastic frame, but if this is not the case or if it is a large home made tank, be sure to set it up on a ½ to 1 inch thick sheet of styrofoam. This will even the stress on the bottom glass and prevent cracking. Placing a glass bottomed tank on an uneven surface is a sure way to warp, stress, and crack the bottom piece.

Position the filter plate and air lift tubes in the aquarium. Hook up the air stones in the tubes and make sure that they are about an inch off the bottom so all the air goes up the tube. Next, spread the washed filter media to a depth of two to three inches over the filter plate. It can be a little deeper in some places and a little thinner in others if you are trying to produce a special effect. Any decorations such as rocks, corals, and ceramics can now be put in place. These things are much easier to do before the water is in the tank and won't be disturbed when the water is added, if it is done carefully.

If you do things the right way, the water is all made up, settled out, and ready to go into the aquarium. However, if you are the casual type, you may just pour the salt package into the aquarium and fill it with tap water. Although the latter method will work, it doesn't give you precise control over salinity, because a tank holds less than its listed gallon volume when rocks and filter media take up space. Usually, at least 15% of the volume of a typical aquarium is taken up with rocks, coral, and other structures. Mixing is also a big problem if you have an undergravel filter already in place, and it will be more difficult to remove chlorine and/or chloramine from the freshwater (see Chapter 2).

Place a china dinner plate on the gravel bottom and pour the water into the tank on top of the plate. This will prevent the filter media from washing out of place. The plate is removed when the tank is full. Hook up the air pump and run the undergravel filter right away, as this will help the tank to clear. Don't run any auxiliary power filters until the tank clears, for this just puts unnecessary sediment in the filters. In fact, auxiliary power filters are not really helpful until after the tank has been conditioned (run-in) and has established its first balance between the filter bed bacteria and the animal load. Be sure the tank has a close fitting, non-metallic cover. The cover should fit inside the edges of the tank to contain drips and condensation and prevent salt encrustation on the tank and table or stand. A good cover also limits evaporation from the tank.

The air in heated and air conditioned rooms is dry and will take up substantial quantities of water from an aquarium. The salt, of course, stays behind, and salinity increases as the tank level drops. Make a mark on the tank side at the original water level, and when the level drops ¼ to ½ inch, refill the tank with freshwater to the original level. **Never** replace evaporation losses with saltwater, for this just increases the total salt content of the tank water. Besides containing water and salt spray, a good cover prevents fish from jumping out of, and odds and ends from falling into, the tank.

The conditioning process can be enhanced by addition of "seed" bacteria from an already established tank. The advantages of seeding a tank with active filter media are first to introduce the proper kinds of bacteria, and second, to reduce the time required to build the proper bacteria populations. The disadvantages of this method is the possible introduction of disease organisms, both protozoans and bacteria. However, gravel from a good, trouble free tank is usually a safe bet. Seeding the new aquarium shortens the conditioning time by a week to 10 days depending on the amount of seed media used. Seeding is not worth the risk of disease introduction unless you are sure that the source aquarium is healthy and disease free. Note that the time frames described below for tank conditioning are estimates, and individual tanks can vary considerably depending on circumstances. See Figure 11, Chapter 3, for a chart of the typical tank run-in pattern. Warm water and low salinity are two factors that will reduce the conditioning period.

It is now possible to purchase nitrifying bacteria in freeze dried form that can be added to the aquarium when it is first set up, to provide a large dose of the right kind of bacteria. This does not give the tank an "instant balance", but if the product is good, it can significantly decrease run-in time. An initial "food" (a source of ammonia and/or nitrite) is usually provided in the product, but it is still wise to start off with a few hardy fish until the nitrifying capacity of the tank is well established. One can also now buy bottled unicellular green algae cultures to add to new and established tanks to aid the growth of green algae. Some nitrifying bacteria are also introduced into a new tank with these cultures. Neither of these is a substitute for careful run-in and good aquarium maintenance, but they will aid the "balance" of the aquarium within the limits set by the conditions of the individual aquarium.

Chemical testing for ammonia and nitrite are important during the run-in period because it keeps you informed of the changing condition of the tank, and most important, it lets you know when the process is complete and the nitrifying bacteria are established. The ammonia test can be skipped if necessary, because when nitrite (NO_2) levels rise, you know that ammonia (NH_3) is being converted and that ammonia levels in the tank have dropped. Nitrite levels appear in the tank about day 10, and rise gradually to a peak of 20 to 30 ppm about day 20 to 25. The most toxic period for a new tank is the period from day 15 to day 25 when nitrite levels are at their peak (see Figure 11). At some point, usually between day 24 and day 30, nitrite levels drop within a day or two to only 1 or 2 ppm. Thus testing for nitrite during the conditioning period tells you when the tank is most toxic and when the conditioning period is complete. It is possible to run-in a marine system even if you can't test for nitrite, but be sure to allow at least 40 days for run-in before adding delicate and/or expensive species.

An important point to remember is that a tank will not run in by itself. It **must** have an organic or inorganic source of ammonia to feed the developing bacteria populations. Keep a small notebook near your aquarium, and make it a habit to record test results, water changes, algal growth, new acquisitions, spawnings, and other events. This will take a lot of the guess work out of maintenance ("Lets see now, did I change water before or after Aunt Gert's visit?") and provide an interesting history of your aquarium.

Ulva lactuca

Table 3 Conditioning and Maintenance Chart for the Marine Aquarium

Time	Organic conditioning method	Inorganic conditioning method
Day 1	Set up tank and filter. Run undergravel filter and allow tank to settle and clear. Add a cup or two of disease free, active seed media if available.	Set up tank. Run undergravel filter and allow tank to clear. Add ammonium chloride (NH_4Cl) to about 3 to 5 ppm. (A quarter teaspoon for each 20 gallons, or better yet, 20 drops per 10 gallons of a 6% solution.) Add a cup of disease free, active seed media if available.
Day 2	Wipe off any sediment that has settled on the sides. Add a source of organic waste matter. A couple of crabs or a few hardy and expendable fish will do fine. Feed sparingly.	Wipe off any sediment that has settled on the sides. Let it run and test ammonia if test kit is available.
Day 3	Feed sparingly twice a day, satisfy the animals, but do not let uneaten food accumulate. Continue feeding throughout conditioning period. Note if appetite declines and then decrease the amount fed.	Add another dose of ammonium chloride.
Day 5	Continue animal maintenance. Test ammonia if kit is available.	Test ammonia if kit is available. Add another dose of ammonium chloride if ammonia levels are below 2 ppm. Skip dose if test is not made.
Day 7	Check ammonia and nitrite levels. Observe fish for signs of stress.	Add another dose of ammonium chloride if ammonia levels are below 2 ppm. Add a dose anyway if an ammonia test is not made. Begin to test for nitrite levels.
Day 10	Test nitrite level, it should begin to show up at levels of 3 to 10 ppm. Keep an eye on the fish for signs of stress.	Nitrite should show up now at levels of 5 to 10 ppm. Add a half dose of ammonium chloride and let it run. Check nitrite every other day until it peaks and drops to less than 3 ppm.
Day 15	Nitrite should be rising well above 10 ppm. Watch the fish and remove any dead or very distressed fish. Do not replace dead fish if nitrite levels are higher than 15 ppm.	Nitrite still rising. Should be above 10 ppm. Add a half dose of ammonium chloride.

Day 20	Same procedure as day 15. Nitrite levels should be near peak.	Nitrite should be near peak. Test levels every day if possible. This shows you when they begin to drop.
Day 25	If your fish aren't stressed yet, you know you have a hardy species. Nitrite levels should peak and fall off within the next 5 days, although it's quite possible for high nitrite to run on for another 10 days.	Nitrite levels should fall off within the next 5 days, but may remain high for a longer period in some situations.
Day 30	Most likely nitrite levels have peaked and fallen off to less than 2 or 3 ppm by this time for both methods of conditioning. If not, don't worry unless you want to, for nitrite levels will surely drop within the next 10 days. If temperatures are cold, below 75˚F, it may help to warm the tank up to 80˚F	
Day 30 to 40	Begin the next phase as soon after the nitrite drop as possible, certainly within 5 days. Make a partial water change, 25% is about right at this time although you can go up to a total change if clean saltwater is no problem. Now is the time to begin adding the fish and invertebrates you desire. Don't put in a great load all at once, and begin with the specimens recommended as most tolerant of aquarium conditions. Add 1 or 2 animals to a 20 gallon tank and up to 5 or more in 50 gallons and up. Allow 7 to 10 days between each introduction of animals to let the tank adjust to each increase in the animal load.	
Day 60 Month 2	Time for a water change. Clean the front glass if necessary and remove any heavy build up of algae. Siphon out any accumulations of dirt that may be present on the bottom. Change 10 to 20 percent of the water with new saltwater, either synthetic or treated natural saltwater.	
Day 90 Month 3	Repeat the maintenance performed at month 2. Change 20 to 25 percent of the water if you feel you have a heavy load of animals in the system. A 10 percent change is adequate if the tank is lightly populated. Make this procedure a monthly routine and you should have a trouble free tank.	
Month 6, 7 or 8	Time for a filter cleaning (see chapter 4). It could come as early as month 6 or may drift to month 10 to 12 depending on lighting, animal load, feeding rates and invertebrate populations. A partial replacement (10%) of the filter bed media may be helpful.	
Year 1	Six to 8 months after the first filter cleaning your tank should be ready for another housecleaning. By now you probably have 2 or 3 marine aquariums and enough experience to write your own book, so good luck and give a helping hand to a fellow marine aquarist whenever you can. Another partial replacement of filter bed media (10 to 20%) may be helpful.	

[A marine aquarist (novice or old hand) may run into a problem now and then that is perplexing and worrisome. Sometimes the problem may be just unsightly, or in the worst case, involve the death of valued specimens. The novice, of course, is more prone to such problems, but even experienced marine aquarists are surprised once in a while. I have had the opportunity to talk with many marine aquarists over the years, and to run many a marine tank myself, since the first edition of this book; thus I have been exposed to many of the problems and difficulties that can be experienced. So as an aid to marine aquarists, I have listed the most common problems, and a few rather uncommon difficulties that might occur, along with the possible cause and solution that (hopefully) will solve the problem.

The following chart does not include all the problems that can plague a marine aquarist, (I don't know all of them yet), but if you have a problem, there's a good chance you may find an answer, or a least a clue, in the following chart. **Note that many of the symptoms listed in this chart can have different or multiple causes.** I have tried to mention the most likely causes for each symptom, but please be aware that a chart like this is inherently oversimplified. Captive marine ecosystems are complex, and it is easy to misdiagnose a problem, especially if one does not have broad experience with marine systems. Therefore, if you have a problem, don't just assume that the first thing you come across that sounds like it might apply is truly the cause of the problem. Check out all the potential problems and discard them one by one until you have only a few real possibilities left. General environmental problems within the system are listed first, and more specific, fish related problems are listed later. Note, however, that disease and distress is often caused by an interaction of events in both the environment and in the organism. **A good environment (light, water quality, habitat, and diet) is the best prevention and basic treatment for disease and distress!**

The chart doesn't give complete information on each possible cause. It is intended only as guide to steer you in the right direction toward a solution to the problem. One should refer to the section of this book where that subject is discussed (see the index), or to the *Marine Aquarium Reference*, or to other books, videos, or computer programs that also deal with these subjects in great detail (see the reference list at the end of the book).]

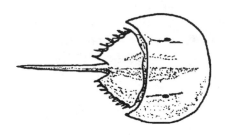

Horseshoe crab, *Limulus*

The Marine Aquarium Handbook: Beginner to Breeder Trouble-shooting Chart for Marine Aquarium Systems

© Moe

Symptom	Possible Cause(s)	Possible Solutions
Yellowish water	Lack of water change, exhausted activated carbon, and/or heavy algal growth	water change and change or addition of activated carbon filtration
Red slime algae on the bottom and sides of the tank	improper lighting, high nutrient load, especially in a reef tank	remove nitrate and especially phosphate from system water, remove all detritus from system, consider treatment with erythomycin (this may destroy filter bacteria)
Brown dust-like algae on bottom and sides of tank	diatom bloom, improper lighting, high levels of silicic acid (silica) in system water	remove excess nutrients, use deionized and/or RO water for all freshwater additions
Persistent foam and/or shiny film on surface	high level of dissolved organic compounds, the tank may be overcrowded or overfed	water change, add use of protein skimmer, add surface skimmer
Reduced water flow from uplift tubes	caked filter bed and/or clogged air stones	clean filter bed, replace some filter media, replace air stones
Cloudy water, green or white	A bloom in the tank water of microscopic algae (green) and/or bacteria (white)	reduce lighting (algae bloom), increase/ add fine mechanical filtration, reduce nutrients
Cloudy white water, tiny bubbles in eyes and fins of fish	teensy weensy, itty-bitty, teeny tiny air bubbles in the water	relieve supersaturation of air in the water, look for an air leak in the intake side of the pump
Fish trying to jump from the tank	external toxin such as pesticides	water change and/or add heavy, new activated carbon filtration,
Fish gasping at the surface and/or showing rapid respiration	low oxygen levels, possible toxins, possible *Amyloodinium* infestation	increase aeration, water change, treat for *Amyloodinium*
Fish shimmying, rapid gilling (respiration), hanging in one place, apparent weight loss in small fish, fish death, the "wipe out" or "toxic tank" syndrome	bacterial toxins, usually *Vibrio* (vibriosis)	move fish to different system or treat in treatment tank with antibiotics (Neomycin at 250 mg/gal and Streptomycin at 40 mg/gal)

Symptom	Possible Cause(s)	Possible Solutions
Fish display rapid respiration, rapid, irritable movement, little feeding activity	new tank syndrome, ammonia and/or nitrite poisoning	check ammonia and nitrite levels, change water, move fish
Fish holding mouth open, abnormal swimming patterns, excess mucus production, slow respiration, listlessness	*Amyloodinium* infestation, Ichthyophonus, high CO_2 levels, piscine TB, fungus disease, copper poisoning	look for *Amyloodinium*, increase aeration, look for other disease in fish, check copper level
Fish mildly irritable, invertebrates stressed, something not quite right, fish may be inactive or too active	possible electric charge in system water, possible temperature problem—too high or too low, possible low pH, possible high nitrite level	check, clean, and replace electrical equipment; ground tank water; check, adjust temperature; adjust pH; do a water change
A pool of water slowly enlarging on the floor around the tank.	If the water level in the tank is dropping at about the same rate as the pool is expanding, there is probably a crack in the bottom or side of the tank. If the tank level is not dropping, then there may be a leak in the filter sump, or perhaps the bathtub in the next room is overflowing.	Fix the leak. (Note: If you have this problem, and you had to run though this chart to figure it out, you may want to switch your hobby to collecting stamps, or chewing gum.)
Tiny, whitish specks, dust-like, on the sides and fins of the fish, fish respiring rapidly and brushing against rocks	*Amyloodinium* infestation	freshwater dip, copper treatment of fish and tank
Small white pimples on the sides of the fish	*Cryptocaryon* ciliate infection	freshwater and formalin dip (1 minute), 30 minute to 1 hour saltwater formalin bath, copper treatment, repeat as necessary
rough white areas on the sides of the fish with excess mucus and skin loss	*Brookynella* or other ciliate infection	freshwater and formalin dip (1 minute), 30 minute to 1 hour saltwater formalin bath, repeat as necessary
tiny black spots on the side, mostly on tangs	tubellarian worm infestation (Black Ich)	formalin bath, frequent cleaning of filter and tank bottom
Extended eyeball, (popeye or exothalmus)	fish TB, internal fungus infection, bacterial infection	bacterial treatment, TB treatment, feed antibiotic foods

Symptom	Possible Cause(s)	Possible Solutions
Rapid respiration, open mouth, raised scales, fins clamped	fish TB	TB treatment, streptomycin (40 mg/gal)
Soft, distended abdomen (dropsy)	fish TB, internal bacterial infection, parasites, tumor	TB treatment, feed anitbiotic treated food
Frayed and red edged fins, open sores on sides, fins may be clamped to the body of the fish	bacterial infections (*Pseudomonas, Vibrio*), possibly secondary to parasitic infection, high level of dissolved organics in system	antibiotic treatment: neomycin, tetracycline, erythromycin, streptomycin; water change; reduction in tank population; improve lighting
Apparent blindness, fish may be unusually dark or pale in color	Fish TB, internal fungus, bacterial infection (*Vibrio*)	TB treatment, feed antibiotic foods
Fish swimming in circles and/or upside down, disoriented, also shrunken stomach, ragged fins, poor color, cloudy eyes	internal fungus infection (*Ichthyophonus*)	no proven cure, good diet and good environment best control and preventative
Cotton-like, wispy external growths	external tufts of fungus and/or bacterial growths (*Saprolegnia*, columnaris)	treatment with malachite green, acriflavine, furanace, copper
Cauliflower-like, small white clumps on fins and/or mouth parts	a virus disease, Lymphocystis	no cure, good diet and good environment speed recovery
Sunken abdomen	starvation, possible cyanide poisoning	supply proper diet
Slow decline, feeding without thriving, loss of appetite, loss of vigor	possible cyanide poisoning including liver, kidney and intestinal damage	no cure, good diet and good environment aid recovery If recovery is possible, support efforts to eliminate cyanide
Stress intolerance, deep shock at netting and/or environmental disturbance	liver damage, great fatty infiltration of liver tissue as a result of poor diet	remove fat from diet, particularly animal fats designed for freshwater fish, reduce feeding
Hard, swollen abdomen, good health otherwise	eggbound, eggs in female developed fully but not spawned, possible encysted parasite	treat normally, eggs will gradually be absorbed or will remain encysted
Frayed fins, marks on the body, not feeding, hiding	harassment by other fish	remove or isolate one or the other of the interacting fish

Symptoms	Possible Cause(s)	Possible solutions
Erosion of the skin around the eyes and in and around the pores of the lateral line	lateral line or "hole in the head" disease, probably caused by inadequate diet or light	add vitamin C and B and perhaps E to the diet, find a food with "stabilized" vitamin C, feed green algae
Anemones turn white, shrink and die	inadequate intensity and/or spectrum of light, high nutrient level	improve lighting, water change, add protein skimmer
Hard corals do not grow and may even recede	lack of calcium and strontium	add calcium and strontium
Green hair algae invades hard corals	high nutrient levels, (nitrate and phosphate)	water change, remove nutrients in tank and in makeup water
Hard corals fading, soft corals stretching upwards "trumpeting"	inadequate lighting	increase light intensity, increase blue peak in spectrum, move specimen toward light source
Algae (*Caulerpa*) turn white and die back	loss of essential nutrients in the system, algal reproduction	add iron supplement to system, harvest excessive algal growth
A chocolate chip cookie floating in the tank.	This can be a baffling problem, but the best guess is an unauthorized fish feeder, probably below the minimum age recommended by the International Association of Professional and Amateur Fish Feeders - Marine Division. (IAPAFFMD)	A net, a heavy cover, and a serious talk about what little fishies eat.

The Marine Aquarium Handbook: Beginner to Breeder

© Moe

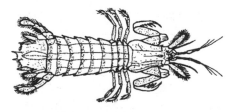

Squilla, mantis shrimp

Chapter 7

FISH SELECTION

What to Look for:
Condition and Compatibility

That healthy, alert, beautifully colored specimen in the tropical fish shop or a friend's tank probably had many a rough time before it became adjusted to aquarium living. Unfortunately, collection, holding, shipping, and distribution techniques are designed more for the convenience of humans than fish; and many fish arrive at their final destinations poisoned, stressed, diseased, and starved. Many, perhaps most, of the marine fish that enter the trade do not survive more than a few weeks if they are captured on the reefs. This problem will diminish as more tank reared fish become available, but for now, we must live and work with the existing situation.

[Now, ten years later, things are a bit better. We—meaning hobbyists, retailers, wholesalers, and collectors in the US and all countries that produce live tropical marine life—are becoming more and more aware that harvesting methods that destroy the environment and the resource, also destroy the future of humanity. Destructive collecting practices still exist, and the job of education for all concerned is never ending. The very least that marine aquarists should do is to never purchase a specimen that cannot be properly cared for, to avoid purchase of specimens that were collected with destructive harvesting methods such as cyanide or dynamite, and to work to advance responsible collection and the cultivation of marine aquarium species. Organizations such as The International Marinelife Alliance and national and international marine aquarium societies (The International Marine Aquarist Association and The Marine Aquarium Society of North America) are working hard to educate people in the use and conservation of natural resources and need the support of marine aquarists. The addresses of these organizations are listed in the back of the book.]

Condition

Acquiring new fish, either for an old aquarium or a new one, is fraught with anxiety and weighty considerations. Is this fish in good shape? Will he eat for me? Is that spot a scar or a parasite? Was he collected with cyanide? Will he get along with the other fish in my tank? Will his coloration clash with my wallpaper? Most of these questions, and others like them, you have to answer for yourself. Your dealer may know some of the answers, but chances are he puts his faith in a wholesaler that has given him good fish in the past, and doesn't know the history of each fish in his stock. One of the most important considerations, and one that I may be able to give you a little help with, is whether or not the fish is in good health. There are two basic areas for your evaluation: appearance and behavior.

When you judge the appearance of a prospective acquisition for your marine aquarium look closely at the eyes, mouth, skin and scales, abdomen, and fins. The eyes should be bright and clear and normally set in the head. Internal bacterial infections are often first seen in the eyes as a cloudy grey mist, or in more advanced cases as an outward protrusion of the eyeball. Sometimes only one eye is affected, and of course the fish keeps his good eye looking out at you; so be sure you observe both eyes when you evaluate the fish.

Cloudy eyes and/or popeye can be treated; neomycin is usually effective, but you, and the retailer, should know about it should you decide to buy him. A fish with sunken eyes (eyes that seem too small for their sockets) is bad news, especially when the fish displays shallow respiration and little movement. This condition may be a result of exposure to a poison, and his days are probably numbered.

The mouth should open and close normally in respiration and feeding. Most species seldom open their mouths more than just slightly during normal respiration. A fish that keeps its mouth rather wide open all the time has problems that are hard to cure and is usually on a downhill ride. Respiration rates vary with species, age, and size; but extremely rapid gilling, except when the fish is upset by being chased with a net or fighting with other fish, is also a sign of trouble. Disease or parasitic infection (*Amyloodinium*) is the usual cause of rapid respiration, and the fish merits very careful evaluation when this condition is observed. The tissues of the mouth should be firm and uninjured. Mouth parts are often torn in fights with other fish, and these torn tissues are potential sites for fungus and bacterial infections.

The skin and scales should be smooth and well colored. Indistinct, discolored blotches on the upper sides are usually a sign of an internal disease, especially when linked with rapid respiration. Uplifted or raised scales are also a bad symptom (piscine TB). Scales should be indistinct unless their edges are accentuated by the natural coloration of the fish. Missing scales are indications of fighting and are potential sites for infections. Fish are generally very hardy creatures, and given a good environment and good nutrition, they can usually repair minor damage quite rapidly if they are not deeply stressed, poisoned, or diseased.

A fish usually stops eating when it is taken from its oceanic home, and is subjected to crowded holding situations and unnatural foods. The period of starvation lasts until the fish encounters a wholesaler, retailer, or hobbyist that takes the pains to set him up in at least a semi-natural situation and offer food regularly until he begins to feed. During the period of starvation, the fish subsists on energy stored in its fats and liver, and no great harm is done unless the fish goes without food past the point where the liver can recover. The abdomen or stomach area should be well rounded and slightly convex in profile in a healthy fish. As the fish loses condition, the abdominal profile becomes straight, and then concave. In extreme cases, the stomach is pulled up almost to the spine and the dorsal muscles are wasted and shallow. Needless to say, such a fish seldom recovers. The condition of the abdomen offers clues to the recent history of the fish and some indication of how easy it will be to get him to eat. Beware the sunken stomach.

The fins should be clear with smooth edges, and the fish should extend them to their full spread with some frequency. Tightly clamped dorsal, anal, and pelvic fins are a sign of problems. Frayed fins indicate fighting or bacterial infections. Fins with frayed and bleeding edges and red spots have bacterial infections. If not checked, these will turn into open sores and invade the body, usually where the pelvic or pectoral fins touch the sides, and ulcers on the body will result.

Amyloodinium is often first seen on the fins. The cysts on the body of a light colored fish might be overlooked, but the white pinpoints are noticeable on thin fins. A few *Amyloodinium* cysts on a fish can be readily treated with a freshwater bath and a copper medication, but this parasite can quickly get out of hand and overrun a stressed fish in a few days. If one fish in a tank has *Amyloodinium*, it's a sure bet that the others either have or will have the infection soon. If you spot *Amyloodinium* in the tanks of a dealer, be sure to point it out to him, for it can cause a dealer heavy losses of money and good will if allowed to progress unchecked.

Behavior is an important clue to the general health of the fish. It helps to know something of the normal behavior of your prospective fish, for then you can properly evaluate his (or her) actions. If the fish is normally nocturnal or secretive, then there's nothing wrong with hiding under a rock or in a corner. A fish of this persuasion, however, swimming slowly in the middle of the tank with fins clamped tight to its sides, is in trouble. Conversely, a fish that normally swims about in the open waters above the reef should not hide continuously. Feeding is a very important sign of well being. If a fish feeds well on standard aquarium fare, the chances are that he is either in good condition or strong enough to shrug off any minor ailments. An active interest in his surroundings is also a good sign. The fish should respond quickly and actively to movements just outside and inside the tank. Although the term "bright eyed and bushy tailed" may not apply to fish, the basic concept does; so when you pick out your fish look for the ones that are bright eyed and full finned. A large part of the skill of a good marine aquarist lies in the selection of compatible fish that have the promise of surviving well in home aquariums.

Compatibility

There are perfectly good reasons why some fish are compatible in community aquariums and others are not, why some fish communities are peaceful and others are like a frontier bar on Saturday night. Unfortunately, there is no sure way of always knowing what behavioral interactions are going to occur between specific fishes in a particular aquarium situation. The relationships between species that make up natural communities—not just fish but inverte-brates, plants, and bacteria as well—have developed over millions and millions of years of living together and surviv-ing to reproduce in a harsh and changing environment. Predator and prey, parasite and host, must coexist on the species level for each to survive. Each species must maintain its numbers within an optimum range—too many and the food supplies dwindle, too few and the reproductive effort is not adequate.

When we build a marine aquarium, the inhabitants we select bring along all their accumulated instinctive behavioral baggage—one of the things that makes a marine aquarium so fascinating and unpredictable. After all, a marine aquarium is like a multimillion piece jigsaw puzzle. All but a few pieces are missing, however, and the few that we have may not fit together just right, or in exactly the same way they did in nature. In the vastness of the reef and nearby environs, there are species that seldom encounter each other, species whose separate instinctive methods of fulfilling their drives for food, protection, and reproduction never bring them directly into competition with one another. Packed into an aquarium environment, however, they must now interact with each other as they compete for available food and space.

The more active, mobile, and aggressive species usually get the lionfish's share of attention, food, and occasionally, a tankmate. Some fish almost always cannot coexist with other fish in a small aquarium for one of two reasons. They either feed so aggressively and actively on other fish that tankmates can find little shelter from them, or they are so docile and restrictive in food habits that most other fish easily out compete them for food and space. Fish in these categories should be kept in tanks to themselves or with tankmates chosen by trial and error, and in these cases, experience is the best teacher. Most of us do not choose to carry a study of species compatibility into the intricate web of coral reef ecology. We are content with knowing how certain species of fish and invertebrates commonly behave in marine aquariums, and how to expect, and thus avoid, loss and damage of valuable fish. To this end, it is helpful to have an understanding of why some fish are aggressive toward others.

The most important considerations in assessing compatibility are species, individual size, state of sexual maturity and activity, feeding habits, size of the aquarium, numbers of fish in each species group, and type and amount of habitat built into the aquarium. All these factors help determine the nature and intensity of aggressive behavior between aquarium inhabitants.

Table 4 summarizes the kinds of aggressive interactions that can take place in marine aquariums. The most obvious type of aggression is the predator/prey interaction. There is little question as to why a large grouper is aggressive toward a small damselfish. The interaction is quickly settled by the disappearance of the damselfish, either into the grouper or into the protective network of the reef. The aquarist uses this aggressive behavior to good advantage when feeding guppies or mollies to a prize grouper or lionfish. Few aquarists are so naive as to expect the lion to lie down with the damsel in their aquarium. Most of the fish we keep in aquariums feed on smaller fish or invertebrates in the wild.

Table 4 Types of Aggressive Behavior in the Marine Aquarium

Type of Aggressive Interaction	Recipient of Aggressive Behavior	Example
Predator/Prey	Perceived food organism	Moray eel consuming a small clownfish
Territory Protection	Others of the same or similar species	Juvenile angelfish and jewelfish attacking others
Mate and Status Protection	Other fish of the same species	Paired clownfish attacking others
Spawn Protection	All other fish near the nest area	Triggerfish
Instinctive Feeding Patterns	Corals	Butterfly fish feeding on coral polyps

Predator/Prey relationships

Fish eating fish, except for sharks and barracuda, usually take their prey in one gulp, so food organisms are seldom larger than a mouthful. Therefore, size differences are important considerations. A moray eel can coexist with a large angelfish, but a small clownfish may only be a tasty tidbit. The three factors that work to the aquarist's advantage when keeping predatory and prey species in the same aquarium are size, familiarity, and habitat. A small fish may coexist with a large predator on a peaceful, if tenuous, basis for a long time simply because they both have a recognized habitat in the aquarium. The small fish avoids the predator and the **well-fed** predator is not stimulated to attack the familiar tankmate. Another small fish added to the aquarium is seldom so lucky. The predator's attention is drawn to the unfamiliar fish, the fright and anxiety behavior patterns displayed by the new fish arouse the feeding instincts of the predator, and a strike is made.

Under these conditions, the old time tankmate may also become a target. The old timer, however, has a better chance of survival since it is familiar with the protective cover and behavior patterns in the aquarium. Protective habitat, such as honeycombed rocks and coral growths that provide numerous safe havens, are necessary in tanks that hold groupers, lionfish, moray eels, and other predators as well as small reef fish. Even with the protection of extensive habitat and a good feeding program, however, small fish will occasionally disappear in such a situation.

If one wishes to maintain fish with a predator/prey relationship in a large tank, it is often helpful to separate the species with a partition of glass or transparent plastic for a week or so to allow the prey species to become acclimated to the tank and established in the mind of the predator. The reasons for other types of piscine aggression are not so obvious. Proper habitat is the key to survival in nature. Although numbers of some species, such as high hats and cardinalfish, can peacefully share a small habitat, others, such as angelfish and some damselfish, require some individual space. In nature, each species requires a particular type of habitat to survive. Jewelfish require fire coral; clownfish require anemones; neon gobies must have large coral heads; high-hats need dark, intricate reef formations; small angelfish need sponges and crevices; and so it is with all fish species—some with broad and some with restricted habitat requirements. The fish that occupies, and holds onto, the right crevice, the right section of the reef where the proper food organisms occur, is the fish that will survive.

Territory defense

What would you do if you returned home one day and found a stranger fixing dinner in your kitchen with his suitcase in the bedroom. "Nice place you got here, buddy, I'm sure you won't mind if I move in for a while." With a little help from the police, I'm sure said stranger would soon find himself in different surroundings. In other words, you would aggressively remove the intruder from your private space. Individuals of many fish species protect their own living space (food, shelter, and potential spawning sites) from others of their species in basically the same manner.

A little queen angelfish may comfortably occupy the same crevice with a high hat, a blenny, a pair of gobies, a few cardinalfish and a puffer, but will not tolerate another queen angel within three feet. Other species do not compete for exactly the same resources as the queen and therefore are not a threat to its existence. These other species occupy different apartments in the same building, but another queen would be moving into the same apartment—not an acceptable living arrangement. The original owner has the power of occupancy—a power great enough to enable him to drive off even a slightly larger angelfish. When such an encounter takes place, a little nipping and posturing usually sends the intruder off to find an unoccupied apartment a few coral heads away. The angelfish may occupy this space for a few weeks or months until he outgrows the area and moves on to a new habitat more suitable to his size. Another small angelfish soon finds the deserted habitat and moves in, much to the delight of the tropical fish collector who has "staked out" that particular hole and collects a queen angel at the same spot every month or two.

In the aquarium, the same instincts prevail even though there is no shortage of food or shelter. A territory is a territory, and no other small angel is allowed within a certain distance. If this distance happens to be four feet and the aquarium is only three feet, then somebody has a problem, and it's usually the smaller of the two angels. In nature, the loser has a vast expanse of ocean bottom to escape into, but in an aquarium he is imprisoned with the owner of the territory. He can't fight back because he already lost the fight, and the winner can't stop fighting because the loser won't go away. The result is either a dead fish or one that is so intimidated that he seldom ventures from a secluded hiding place.

Size is important to the intensity of intraspecific aggression. Often a large angelfish will tolerate a small fish of the same or closely related species because the size difference puts them in slightly different ecological niches and territorial aggression is muted. Another way of diffusing territorial aggression in an artificial situation is to contain many fish of the same size and species together, perhaps 20 to 200 or more in a relatively small tank. Aggression is then so diffuse, because there are so many fish, that no one fish can become dominant, and no one fish can become the sole target for the aggression of all the others. All the fish give and take a little aggression and all survive. There is some indication that fish reared in such a situation are not as aggressive toward others of their own species as wild fish, however, this tendency probably disappears after the fish is kept alone for a while.

Young angelfish were used as an example of territorial aggression, since it is often pronounced in these species, and aquarists often try to keep them together, which is usually a mistake. Two small angelfish of the same species can seldom be kept together unless there is a significant size difference, and even in this situation, the smaller fish is barely tolerated and shows little or no growth.

Sexual territory (mate protection)

As a general rule, the more distantly related the species, the more tolerant they are of each other. In certain families of marine fish, notably some species of angelfish and wrasses, a harem type of relationship exists between the sexes. One physically large male, often distinguished by color and form as well as size, maintains a territory with several females and aggressively protects his females from intrusion by other males. Some groupers may also exhibit this pattern in natural populations, but this is difficult to observe. It is interesting to note that protogynous hermaphroditism (functional females changing to males) is found in each of these, as well as in other families of coral reef fishes.

The loss of the male in these harem groups apparently stimulates a large female to begin to change into a male, which can take place within a matter of weeks. Behavior patterns change along with form, color, and sexual organs. An opposite pattern, protanderous hermaphroditism, occurs in anemonefish. In this case, one large, dominant female, a smaller male, and a variable population of subadult fish inhabit a large anemone or area of anemones. The subadults are tolerated by the pair, but are kept in their place and they do not develop into adults. Upon loss of one of the pair, the largest subadult becomes an active male. If the female is lost, the active male changes to a female and pairs with the now maturing subadult male.

We are just beginning to investigate these fascinating physiological and behavioral changes that are apparently so common in coral reef fish. We have much yet to learn, much that will advance our understanding of how to care for these fish in aquariums. Development of aggressive behavior in a tank that has long been peaceful may be due to onset of sexual maturity or even sexual change. Individuals of some species protect their status within a sexual hierarchy as well as, or perhaps without regard for, a specific territory. For example, one male pygmy angel, *Centropyge*, may tolerate, interact, and even spawn with several females in a single aquarium; yet introduction of another male may cause intolerable aggression and loss of the new male. If the aquarium is large enough, however, a new female may fit into the harem and not cause undue problems. It is also possible for a small juvenile clownfish to occupy an anemone with a pair of the same species and suffer no more than an occasional nip; and if the relationship is well established, the juvenile will grow only very slowly. A mature intruder into a tank with an established clownfish pair stands little chance of survival, unless it is so big and powerful that it can displace one of the pair. A female will be violently attacked by the resident female and a new male will be harried and picked upon by both male and female.

It is possible to have two or perhaps three pairs each establish a territory in a large tank, but this usually happens only if the fish have grown up in the tank together. Once sexual maturity and subsequent pairing takes place in anemonefish, each mature fish protects its status by attacking all who might threaten this status.

Reproductive territory (spawn protection)

Spawn protection is more intense and focused than status protection. This aggression is directed at all species of fish that venture near the nest. It only exists when a spawn is present or imminent. Damselfish and clownfish are most commonly observed protecting spawns since their nests are usually somewhat exposed. Royal grammas and neon gobies, on the other hand, are secretive spawners, their nests well hidden under a rock or in a crevice. Even though the nests are well hidden, an observant aquarist will notice the increased aggressive activity exhibited by the male near the entrance to his carefully guarded treasure. Many species we keep in aquariums become adults at relatively small size and form strong pair bonds between a male and female. Most commonly encountered in this category are some species of butterflyfish, gobies, clownfish, a few angelfish and, to a certain extent, royal grammas. These fish are often easier to keep as mated pairs than as singles, but when paired they seldom tolerate other fish of their own or similar species in the same aquarium.

Random aggression

Territorial protection is present in many species to a greater or lesser degree and usually results in loss or intimidation of one or more tankmates. There are some fish, however, that are so aggressive that few if any fish can be kept with them, and triggerfish are the prime example. They nip and bite the fins and body of all other fish kept in the same tank. This is not territory protection in the true sense, it is merely an aggressive, non-specific feeding behavior on a victim that cannot avoid the slow swimming triggerfish because of the confines of the aquarium. (Once the trigger fish gets near its prey, however, it is quick on the trigger.) Invertebrates are also subject to this never ending torment. This is just an extension of their behavior on the reef. They investigate anything that might be remotely edible with nips from their sharp teeth and small, but powerful, jaws. In fact, I once thought I had lost half an ear to a curious grey triggerfish one day as I was collecting angelfish. (Incidently, grey triggerfish fillets are good eating.)

Triggerfish are among the most colorful and responsive of marine fish and are easy to keep, by themselves, in an aquarium. They are well worth a separate tank just to observe their behavior and beauty. Some triggerfish are said to recognize their owners and can even be taught to perform particular behavior patterns when food is offered. Behavior patterns, developed over millions of years, that adapt a species to life in a particular ecological niche, do not fundamentally change when the fish is placed in the confines of an aquarium. The fish adapts to the aquarium only to the extent allowed by these innate behavioral patterns. Some spe-

cies have behavioral characteristics that allow them to adapt
to aquarium conditions quite well. The clownfish, for example, has a restricted range in nature, is active during the day,
feeds on a wide variety of food organisms, and is of small
adult size—all characteristics that allow it to survive with
vigor in a typical marine aquarium.

Shy, delicate, and dietarily restricted fish

Incompatibility is not always a result of unconstrained
aggression caused by predatory behavior and territorial or
reproductive defense. Some fish, such as jackknife fish and
other reef drums, are physiologically delicate, do not withstand capture and handling very well, and have a wide
natural range in nature. Fish that remain associated with
reef structures usually acclimate better to captivity in small
tanks than fish that range widely over reef, grass bed, and
open ocean. It is difficult to keep these fish in good condition during capture and shipping, and they seldom withstand these stresses well enough to survive in an aquarists's
tank. Small specimens usually do much better than large
fish.

Other species, such as mandarin fish and sea horses,
may be physiologically hardy enough to survive capture
and transport very well, but are so restrictive in diet and/or
so shy in feeding behavior that they often starve before
taking typical aquarium foods. Such fish are best kept in a
tank devoted to that specific species, and the aquarist must
be sure to meet the dietary needs of the species with the
proper foods and feeding regime. Mandarin fish, incidently,
and some other difficult to keep small fish that require tiny
invertebrate prey species, do quite well in reef tanks and
other systems with much live rock and natural invertebrate
fauna. So despite the docile nature and spectacular form and
color of some fish such as jackknife, mandarin, some puffer
fish, and shrimpfish, they do not adapt well to life in a
community tank, although a careful and attentive aquarist

can create a good captive environment for a these difficult species. Reef tanks now supply the kind of captive environment that many of these delicate species require.

Survival

There are many pathways to survival on the reef. Some species have found that there is safety in numbers, and interspecific competition for food and shelter has been reduced to the point that they can exist in groups or schools to the benefit of all the individuals. Surgeonfish, some damsels, grunts, jawfish (providing there is enough bottom area), cardinalfish, some wrasses and reef drums (high hats) are examples of fish that form compatible living groups. Fish that live in groups or schools in nature usually get along well with themselves, and most other species, in the aquarium environment. Survival in the aquarium, however, is much different than survival on the reef.

The greatest compatibility problems in the aquarium usually occur when the aquarist brings home a valuable new prize acquisition to an old, established tank with fish that are well adapted to the tank and each other. Occasionally the new fish will be met with indifference, especially if it is a large fish that does not establish a particular territory, or if the aquarium is relatively uncrowded. But more often, the old timers harass the newcomer unmercifully. There are several things the aquarist can do to ease the introduction process. New habitat, a rock or piece of coral added along with the new fish, may provide the new arrival with some cover unfamiliar to the established fish. Changing the position of all the tank habitat is a bit more drastic, but it causes confusion in the established territories and allows the new fish to find a spot in the subsequent reestablishment of space claims. However, if the new fish is a large specimen of a species that is known to be aggressive, it is probably better to add it without any establishment aid, since the old fish will be better able to maintain an already established position against a larger intruder.

One of the best methods of bringing a new and delicate fish into an active community tank is to separate the new fish and a bit of habitat from the rest of the tank with a transparent piece of glass or plastic for about 10 days. This allows the old timers to see and accept the new fish before they can attack. It also allows the new fish to develop the behavior patterns of an established fish and defend its status when it does move into the tank's social structure.

[The development of coral reef tank systems has created many new problems in the area of compatibility of marine organisms. Now the fish to fish interactions that we used to worry about are relatively simple when the whole mix of fish, plants, hard and soft corals, and other invertebrates are packed together in one little tank. Advanced marine aquarists are still—and will be for quite some time—working out the compatibility problems that show up in these environmentally complex small marine systems.

In general, it is important to know the feeding habitats of any fish placed into coral reef tanks, especially whether or not corals are included in the diet of the fish. Some butterflyfish, for example, feed on coral polyps and can quickly destroy valued hard coral specimens. John Tullock, in his *Reef Tank Owner's Manual*, has a good chapter on fish for reef tanks, and Helmut Debelius' *Fishes for the Invertebrate Aquarium* is also a good reference on fish for reef tanks.

Various species of corals are also incompatible with each other. If placed too close together, they expand and touch each other and the polyps wage "war" with their stinging cells. One coral will usually prevail and may even kill the other if one of them is not moved. Anemones can move about the tank and may find a location where they damage other invertebrates. A good reef aquarist is aware of these interactions and keeps the reef tank under close observation to avoid any coral "wars".]

Chapter 8

INTRODUCTION
AND QUARANTINE
Purposes and Methods

Way back in 1864, Louis Pasteur proved that there is no such thing as spontaneous generation. Therefore, everything that shows up in your marine tank, except for air borne bacteria and algal spores, has got to be there because someone, somehow, put it there. This goes for disease organisms, copepods, parasites, and algae as well as fish, invertebrates, and coral rock decor. Consequently, it is wise to stop and consider how things that you don't want, such as disease organisms and chemical toxins, could possibly get into your tank and what can be done to prevent their introduction. Remember that introduction of a nasty life form is not limited to the time of initial setup, indeed, this is the period when you are most concerned and aware, and work hardest to avoid contamination. Slip-ups usually occur after a year of trouble free operation, when you've developed the "Oh, I can throw anything in there and it does fine" attitude.

Introductions

We are most concerned with preventing the introduction of marine protozoan parasites *Amyloodinium*,

Cryptocaryon, and *Brooklynella*, and bacteria *Pseudomonas*, *Vibrio*, and *Mycobacteria*, since these organisms cause most of the disease problems in marine tanks. Although it is true that a healthy fish in a good environment can fight off a few bacteria, protozoan parasites are another story—they can quickly destroy a tank of fish if introduced and allowed to reproduce unchecked.

The second concern (only because it is relatively uncommon) is the introduction of "unnatural" toxins such as nicotine, pesticides, rat poison, heavy metals, perfume, paint fumes, and industrial chemicals. Anything that enters the tank has to be considered a possible source of contamination, especially if persistent problems are occurring, and the history of each routine introduction should be traced to make sure it is above suspicion. Keep in mind, however, that a marine tank is not an operating room, and you need not try to keep it "clean and sterile." Indeed, that attitude could almost give one an ulcer since algae and detritus are part and parcel of most marine aquariums. We are only interested in avoiding introductions from already contaminated marine sources or accidental introduction of external poisons.

Perhaps the most common disease problem (and probably the most dangerous to captive fish populations in a marine aquarium) is caused by the introduction of the *Amyloodinium* parasite. This parasite exists as a free swimming dynospore, a cyst on the external surfaces of a fish, and as a cyst on the bottom of the tank. Thus it can enter a tank (1) with water from a contaminated source, (2) with gravel, a live rock, or a decoration from a contaminated tank, or (3) the most likely mode, attached to a new fish.

Be sure to see the section on *Amyloodinium* in Chapter 9 for more information on diagnosis and treatment. It is important to be aware of the various ways a parasite can gain entry to an aquarium system. Table 5 lists the most common modes of contamination of *Amyloodinium* and other parasites and toxins and offers suggestions on prevention.

Table 5 Sources of Disease in a Marine Aquarium

Mode of Contamination	Methods of Prevention
Introduction of new saltwater either as initial fill or as water changes.	Natural saltwater should be treated (dark storage for two weeks) to prevent introduction of protozoan parasites. Synthetic seawater is safer, but be sure containers and hoses are rinsed with freshwater if they have recently held saltwater from another source.
Introduction of active filter media when seeding a new tank.	The only precaution here is to know and trust your source.
Introduction of new fish and invertebrates	Quarantine is the answer. See the following section.
Introduction of "living rock".	"Living rock" covered with attached invertebrates and algae can add much natural beauty and interest to a marine tank, but, depending on the source, they can introduce protozoan parasites. Quarantine for a week or so in a fish free tank is good insurance.
Fish and invertebrate food.	Every day food goes into your tank, and if you do a good job as an aquarist, the food is varied and from both plant and animal sources. Generally, any food that has been processed (freezing, cooking, drying, freeze drying, canned, etc.) is free of parasite problems. The greatest danger comes from live foods (brine shrimp, plankton, live minnows, worms, etc.) and dead unprocessed foods (shrimp, fish flesh, and algae) are next in line. The answer is to be careful, but not paranoid. Know and trust your sources as well as possible. Don't introduce water that live foods are packed with, and rinse natural foods well.
Introduction and transfer of coral, rocks, or other decorations.	Make sure all coral or rock not intended to be alive is properly processed. Rinse and scrub well any transfers from possibly contaminated sources.
Introductions through nets, siphon hoses, and cleaning implements.	It's easy to pick up a net, remove a dead fish from one tank, put down the net, then pick it up a few minutes later and use it in another tank. Get in the habit of rinsing all nets and cleaning materials in freshwater after each use and storing them in a dry place. Not only will they last longer, but possible parasite transfer will be prevented.

Introduction from air borne spray or splash over.	Aquariums set up close to one another, or over and under each other, have the potential for spreading problems through drip and spray. Isolate the tanks as well as possible by space and covers, and in the unfortunate instance that a tank develops a parasite problem, prevent any spray, splash, or drip.
Introduction through casual or accidental means.	"Oh look Barbie, one of Uncle Mike's fishies is on the floor. Lets put him in that tank over there. I wonder why he isn't swimming?". Good covers on tanks are important for obvious reasons. They keep fish in and little fingers out. The better your control over the tank environment, the less problem you'll have with accidents.

The best preventative for protozoan parasite introduction, besides careful selection and a good dealer, is a one to two minute freshwater bath before introducing the fish to the tank. As long as the freshwater is the same temperature and close to the same pH as the tank water, the fish is only momentarily inconvenienced; but any external parasites not deeply imbedded in flesh or mucus quickly take up water until they burst from the increased internal osmotic pressure. If you also avoid introducing any of the water the fish were packed in, there is very little chance of contamination.

[This is not completely true! A freshwater bath will remove most parasites from the external surfaces of the fish, and it will also kill many invertebrate parasites, but in the case of *Amyloodinium*, the parasite cyst only falls off the fish and remains alive on the bottom of the bath bucket. Do not ever, never, add the freshwater from any freshwater bath to the marine aquarium!]

Introducing a new fish

A good method of introduction, assuming the fish is not severely stressed, is in relatively good condition, and the bag was packed with oxygen, is to float the packing bag unopened in the tank for about 15 minutes to allow temperatures to equalize. The bag is then opened and water from the tank equal to about one fourth the original volume is added to the bag. This allows the fish to gradually get used to the tank water and allows you to observe the fish's behavior as the tank water is introduced. If the fish becomes stressed when the tank water is added, something is wrong and the introduction process must be watched very carefully. Add the same volume of water about every 15 minutes three more times. Remove water from the bag and discard it before each addition of tank water to prevent the bag from filling. Now take a good look at the fish. If he is respiring very rapidly, listing to one side, and in general looks very stressed, it's probably best to skip the freshwater bath and put him directly into the quarantine tank, unless there are obvious evidences of parasite infection.

If the fish is in good shape, however, a one minute freshwater bath is good insurance. Make sure the freshwater is the same temperature and close to the same pH (7.8 to 8.1 should be about right) as the tank water. Lift the fish with a clean net or hands and place him in the container of freshwater. Cover the container with something transparent if possible to keep the fish in and still let you observe. Time the bath and watch for signs of shock. If severe shock does occur, remove him from the freshwater bath and place him in the tank immediately. After one minute, put the fish in the tank and give him a day or two to settle down before worrying about whether or not he is eating. Other cleansing methods include use of copper compounds, medicinal dyes, and antibiotics for periods of days or weeks before introduction to display tanks. Such treatments add to the stresses on the fish and are best avoided unless a disease becomes evident during the quarantine period or fish from a particular source consistently display disease.

Quarantine

The term quarantine can mean different things to different aquarists. To some it's a sterile-looking, medicated, bare tank that houses new fish for a day or two to see if any disease develops, and to others it's a second fully set up smaller tank that maintains new fish and invertebrates for several weeks to be sure all is well before introduction to the main tank. Both methods have their advantages and disadvantages. The bare tank allows effective use of medication, good observation of the fish, and opportunity to keep the tank bottom clean. However, the fish cannot survive long or well in such a set up, and the water should be discarded after each use. In my opinion, the bare tank finds its best application as a treatment tank, for use when a disease has been detected and a course of medication determined.

A small tank, 10 to 15 gallons, set up with an undergravel, biological filter and a natural tank decor, is more functional for quarantine than a bare tank. It allows a new fish to be maintained under good aquarium conditions for two to four weeks to get used to the water, the tank routine, and available foods away from the competition of the main tank. If a fish does bring a problem home with it, this should be evident within two or three weeks and, depending on the disease, treatment can be effected in the quarantine tank or in a bare treatment tank. A small quarantine tank is a lot easier to keep free of disease than a large display tank, and can be used to brighten up another corner of the room. Also, if neccessary, a 0.2 ppm copper treatment level can be better maintained in a small tank that does not contain calcareous gravel or rock.

Following the simple procedures of selecting top quality fish, giving a one minute freshwater bath before introduction to a tank, providing a two or three week stay in natural type quarantine tank, feeding a varied diet, and adhering to a good maintenance schedule, will give you a marine tank relatively free of death and disease.

Chapter 9

DISEASE AND DISTRESS
Identification and Treatment

[This chapter has been greatly enlarged and changed for the new edition. There were so many new comments that they could not all be marked off with bold brackets( ]), but wherever possible I did identify the new information. Descriptions and treatments of a few relatively rare diseases have been added since the great increase in marine aquarium keeping has made encounters with a greater variety of marine disease organisms more frequent. Some illustrations have also been added to make it easier to identify specific ailments. Although they are simple in technique and execution, they should serve the purpose and may have even saved a thousand words. The emphasis on treatments has continued to be on those that are basic, yet effective, and within the scope of most marine aquarists to obtain and use with modest cost and relatively little danger.]

Problems

Suppose, despite your best efforts to avoid contamination, disease does strike. This is not an uncommon occurrence in marine aquaria, and sooner or later every marine aquarist has to deal with a disease problem. This section is designed to help you identify the problem and suggest a method of treatment. Disease diagnosis is an involved and complex subject, however, and although this chapter will help you cope with the most common problems a marine aquarist encounters, please be encouraged to seek other references and learn all you can about marine fish diseases and treatments. The trouble shooting chart in Chapter 6 will also be helpful in identifying many problems and diseases, and determining a course of action.

Most fish and invertebrate health problems fall under one of three major categories:

1. Problems caused by poor environmental conditions.

2. Problems caused by poor nutrition.

3. Problems caused by an organism that causes disease.

Usually, poor environmental conditions and/or poor nutrition cause debilitation, create stress, and reduce the natural resistance of an animal to disease organisms. A disease can strike quickly, from within a few hours to a few days or a week, but problems due to poor environment and/or poor nutrition develop slowly, over weeks and months. Generally, if the problem develops quickly, suspect a disease organism; if the problem develops slowly, try to improve conditions and nutrition. There are exceptions, of course; piscine TB and some parasites may be chronic and plague the fish for a few months or more, while a drop in oxygen levels in the tank may affect the fish very quickly, but with application of a little common sense, the rapidity of onset is a good clue to the source of the problem.

Note that the very best disease control in an aquarium consists of prevention, and the very best disease prevention technique consists of providing good nutrition and a good environment, and using a quarantine procedure. Good environmental conditions, good nutrition, and quarantine will not eliminate the possibility of disease, but will certainly reduce the incidence of disease and greatly increase the ability of the fish to withstand the stress of the disease and the treatment. When disease and distress happens, and it will, a good marine aquarist must know what to do.

First of all, it is important for a marine aquarist to understand something about the relationship between fish and disease. Fish have a natural resistance to disease, and, in nature, disease causing organisms seldom destroy their host; for if they do, they also usually die. A "natural balance" exists between host and parasite that has developed over eons of evolution, and both species have adapted to survive within the natural web of life in tropical seas. The aquarium, however, is an unnatural environment, and whatever the "natural balance" may be on a coral reef, it no longer exists in the captive environment. Parasites, bacteria, and host are contained in a restricted environment where nutrients that feed bacteria and algae accumulate to very high levels, natural nutrition is seldom available, and natural controls on bacteria and parasites are seldom present. It is the responsibility of the aquarist to provide for what is lost from the natural environment. Does this mean that you have to keep a shark to eat any fish that might get sick? No, there are limits to your responsibility, but you should do all you can to keep the life that was borrowed from the sea as healthy as possible. When disease strikes, it is important to act quickly—intelligently, but quickly.

Problem (disease) identification

There are three steps to solving a disease problem:

1. Determining that a problem exists.

2. Identifying the cause of the disease or source of the distress.

3. Successfully curing the fish and eliminating the disease or cause of distress.

The first step—determining that a problem exists—may seem very simple: "Gee, when I got up and looked at my tank this morning, half the fish were dead and the rest were covered with little white spots." The real key to disease control, however, is to catch the problem as soon as possible. The aquarist quoted above is actually saying that the first time in well over a week that he really looked at his fish, he discovered a problem that had been around for some time. Make it a point to observe the fish carefully at least every two or three days. Make sure they are all present, their behavior is normal, and there are no white spots, fuzzy skin, cloudy eyes, red fins, or open sores.

Behavior is often the best first indicator of disease, so watch for lack of feeding, listlessness, rubbing against rocks, color changes, and other unusual appearance and behavior patterns. These are the things that tell you to look more closely and keep the tank under careful daily observation. The quicker a disease is identified, the better the chances for treatment and recovery. Once you have determined that a problem exists—that things are not right with one, several, or all of your fish—the first thing to do is to stay calm and analyze the problem.

Don't act until you are reasonably sure of the cause of the distress and have a carefully thought out plan of treatment. Treating a tank with a panicky dose of copper, for example, does nothing to cure a bacterial disease and may even make it much worse. Remember that the treatment can sometimes be worse than the disease, so never rush blindly into treatment. Frequently, and especially in a neglected or overlooked situation, treatment will be complicated by the presence of two or more problems. An unchecked *Amyloodinium* infestation, for example, often leads to secondary bacterial infection through damaged skin and mucus layers and general stress. A fish weakened by harassment from other fish or poor environmental conditions is also a ready victim for bacterial disease. Keep in mind that certain basic problems such as bad environment and poor diet can be the underlying cause of continuing disease problems. There are several important things to note and consider as you observe the fish. Consider the following questions and keep the answers generally in mind as you try to identify the cause of the problem:

1. How long has the tank been in operation?

2. Has biological filtration been fully established?

3. What are current ammonia and nitrite levels?

4. When was the last water change and filter cleaning?

5. How many fish and what species are affected?

6. What is the tank water temperature?

7. What is the pH of the tank water?

8. How long ago was the newest fish introduced?

9. When was the tank last treated with copper, if at all, and is there any free copper left in the tank water?

10. How long has the distressed fish been in the aquarium?

11. What and how often do the fish eat?

12. Any past disease problems? If so, how long ago and due to what cause?

13. Any recent unusual introductions such as ornaments or chemicals?

Keeping a brief log book on your aquarium, as mentioned before, will easily provide answers to these questions and will increase your skill as a marine aquarist manyfold.

After you are sure that a problem is present (and hopefully you catch it so early that you can't be sure without careful observation), it must be identified and a course of treatment determined. It is difficult to prepare a check list or key to follow to arrive at a specific cause of distress, because many problems cause similar symptoms. The trouble shooting chart (Chapter 6) may be helpful in focusing on the possible causes of various problems.

Careful evaluation of the problem and attention to the following chart of ailments (Table 6) and the discussions of symptoms and treatments should enable you to cope with the majority of disease problems that may develop. There are a great many diseases of marine fish that may appear in an aquarium, far too many to discuss them all in a basic sort of book. Only a few of them, however, cause most of the problems. These few, the most frequently encountered ailments, are listed in Table 6 in the order of the frequency that they are likely to occur. This is a subjective arrangement based solely on my experience. The only reason for listing them in this order is to suggest to you which ailments seem to be most common. Actually, only the first few on the list are the ones that most marine aquarists commonly encounter, and these are also the ones that respond best to treatments.

Another guide in the list is the check that indicates whether the ailment is usually common to all fish in the tank, fish of one closely related species group, or just one or two individuals in an otherwise healthy tank. Two checks indicate the most common circumstance even though it may also occur more broadly. [There are now more than a dozen entries, but I still like the original name of the table.]

Yellow tang, *Zebrasoma flavescens*

Descriptive names	Scientific name	all fish affected	one species affected	several fish affected
Amyloodinium, Oodinium, Coral fish disease, velvet disease, oodiniasis, saltwater ich	*Amyloodinium ocellatum*	√√	√	
Cryptocaryon, white spot disease, cryptocaryoniasis, saltwater ich	*Cryptocaryon irritans*	√	√√	√
Brooklynella, clownfish disease, angelfish disease, skin spot disease	*Brookynella hostilis*		√√	√
Poor diet	Nutritional deficiency	√	√√	√
Poor environment	grubbyosis tankii	√√	√	
Toxins present				
Generated within the tank		√	√√	
Introduced into the tank		√√	√	
Harassment	lack of *lebensraum*			√
Fungus disease				
Internal fungus, Ichthyophonus	*Ichthyosporidium hoferi*	√	√	√√
External fungus	*Saprolengia*		√√	√
Piscine TB, Fish tuberculosis	*Mycobacteria marinum*		√	√√
Black Ich, tang tubellarian disease	Tubellarian worms		√√	√
Bacterial diseases				
Vibrio disease, saltwater furunculosis, "the wipe out"	*Vibrio anquillarium*	√	√	√√
Fin rot, red spot disease, ulcers *Pseudomonas*	*Pseudomonas sp.*	√	√	√√
Viral disease, cauliflower disease, Lymphocystis	Lymphocystis virus		√	√√
Fish flukes	*Benedenia (melleni?)*	√√		√
Fish lice	*Argulus sp.*	√√		√
Old age	acquisition of time			√

Table 6 The Dirty Dozen Ailment Chart

Diseases, Symptoms, and Treatments

This part of the disease and distress section provides basic information about the most common ailments, a description of the most obvious symptoms, and details of one or two treatments that, in my experience, usually effect a cure or solve the problem. The recommended treatment chemicals and antibiotics have been developed from a number of sources, including my own experience, and many, if not most, are available in the pharmaceutical section of your favorite aquarium store in a commercial preparation. Be sure to read the labels of commercially sold aquarium pharmaceuticals to know what the active ingredients are, and, of course, how to use them. First, two very important points:

- **Always read the ingredients and directions on aquarium pharmaceuticals and use as directed.**

- **Always keep aquarium pharmaceuticals out of the reach of small children.**

Some medications can also be obtained from drug stores, animal supply (feed) stores, and scientific and chemical supply houses. There are usually a variety of effective treatments for each malady, and I have tried to include the ones that are most effective and most available.

[There have been a number of books and articles written that discuss marine fish diseases and disease control since the *Handbook* was published in 1982. There have been few new treatment techniques or medications, however, and this chapter is still substantially current. Even so, changes and additions have been made to include more information, and most of these are so noted. Additional information on disease and treatment is also available in the references listed at the end of the book. If you're into computers, you may want to get the computer program that is now available that helps identify disease and suggests commercially available treatments. This is also listed in the reference section.]

Amyloodinium

[Note: The scientific name of the organism that causes this disease is *Amyloodinium ocellatum*. When the *Handbook* was first written, the generally accepted genus for this species was *Oodinium*. It is now generally accepted that this species belongs in the genus *Amyloodinium*. This change in scientific nomenclature is the reason that the generic name of this disease causing organism is *Oodinium* in the first edition and *Amyloodinium* in this new edition of the *Handbook*.]

Amyloodinium ocellatum is also known as coral fish disease, white spot disease, velvet disease, and frequently as saltwater ich. [The name ich, incidently, comes from the freshwater parasitic ciliate, *Ichthyophthirius multifiliis*, which is very similar to the saltwater parasitic ciliate, *Cryptocaryon irritans*. "Ich" is an abbreviation for *Ichthyophthirius*, which was used by freshwater aquarists and then transferred to the marine parasite.]

The secondary names for *Amyloodinium* are, in common usage, sometimes also applied to the protozoan disease *Cryptocaryon*. There is a tendency for the novice aquarist to use the term "ich" for any condition that results in a white spot on a fish. **Beware of this confusion, because mistreatment can be the result.** *Amyloodinium ocellatum* is a marine one celled alga, a dinoflagelate, a member of the same group of organisms that cause red tides in marine waters. *Amyloodinium* does not cause red tides, but it is parasitic on fish during one stage of its life cycle; and in a closed or open system marine aquarium, this can be as devastating as a red tide. The reason *Amyloodinium* can be such a scourge is that, unlike some other marine pests, it can readily complete its life cycle in the aquarium, and can quickly reach numbers that overwhelm the captive fishes. In nature, their numbers are kept in check by planktonic predators, dilution by ocean currents, movement of fish, and the cleaning activity of parasite pickers. It is very rare to encounter a fish in nature with a severe case of *Amyloodinium* parasitism, but on the other hand, fish with a few *Amyloodinium* cysts (trophonts) tucked away here and there are not rare at all.

The life cycle of this parasite begins with the release from a mature cyst (tomont) of up to 250 very tiny, free swimming algal cells called dinospores. The tomont cyst is either trapped in the mucus of the host fish or has fallen off to the bottom of the tank. Division of the daughter cells within the tomont occurs within three to six days depending on temperature. The higher the temperature, the more rapid the maturation and release of the dinospores. The free swimming dinospores must find a host fish to obtain the nutrients needed for further development. The dinospores cannot live long without finding a host. Some strains may not survive 48 hours, but others may last up to a month. High temperatures also reduce the time that the dinospore can survive in the free swimming state.

The dinospore attaches to a host fish when it comes in contact with the external tissues of the host. Since fish are constantly pumping water through their gills, these soft respiratory tissues are the most frequent sites of infection. After attachment, the dinospore becomes a cyst (more properly termed a trophont) and sends filaments (rhizoids) into the tissues of the host to draw nutrients for its further development. After several days, the filaments are withdrawn and the parasite becomes a tomont (another type of cyst). Cell division occurs and mature dinospores eventually develop and are released, and the life cycle begins all over again.

The number of dinospores produced depends on the nutrition obtained in the trophont stage, temperature, and the genetic characteristics of the strain. The tomont cyst usually falls off the host fish at maturity (if it isn't caught in mucus and cell debris in the gills), and development is completed on the tank bottom or some other resting place. Depending on temperature, the life cycle of *Amyloodinium* is completed in 6 to 12 days. Often, an aquarist not familiar

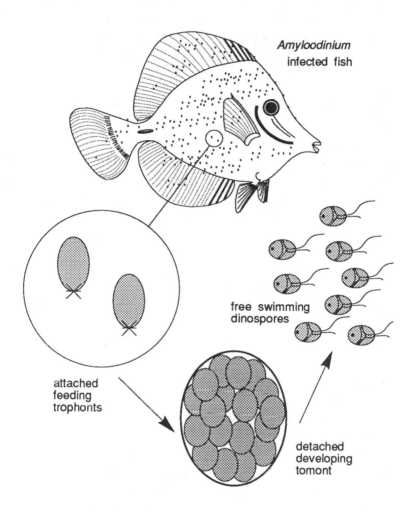

Amyloodinium infected fish

free swimming dinospores

attached feeding trophonts

detached developing tomont

with the life cycle of *Amyloodinium* will notice that the cysts on the fish are gone and assume that the parasitic infection is miraculously cured and all is well. Then, 6 to 9 days later, the cysts reappear on the fish like traffic on the freeway at 8 AM on Monday morning, and the aquarist is scrambling to save the fish with freshwater baths and copper cures.

One or two, or a half dozen of these parasites would have little effect on a fish in the open ocean; however, it is easy to see that in a closed system aquarium this parasite can reach population levels that totally overwhelm any fish that may be present.

Symptoms

Amyloodinium infestations typically begin in the gills. Damage to the delicate gill tissue stimulates fish to produce excessive mucus in the gills, and this condition restricts the exchange of respiratory gasses. The result is an increased respiratory pace (rapid gilling), which may be the first outward sign of *Amyloodinium* infection. As the infestation progresses, the cysts become visible on the fin membranes and body surfaces. These cysts are about the same size and color as a grain of table salt and, especially on light colored fish, are difficult to see. They can usually be first observed on the clear fin membranes, and show up best on the body when the fish is viewed lengthwise along its side and light reflects off the numerous tiny cysts.

Infected fish often scratch their sides on the bottom or on rocks, and sometimes shake or shudder while swimming. As the infestation progresses, colors fade, a powdery or dusty appearance becomes very noticeable as the cysts proliferate, and secondary bacterial infections often develop. Respiration is now very rapid, and the fish begins to lie on its side on the bottom of the tank. It is usually too late at this point to save that particular fish, but some of its less infected tank mates may pull through if treatment is quickly provided. The time period between first observation of rapid respiration and terminal infestation may be as short as three to four days or may be two weeks or more depending on temperature, tank population, type and efficiency of filtration, and the resistance of individual fish to this parasite.

Treatment

A successful treatment for *Amyloodinium* consists of treating *both the infected fish and the infected tank*. If the parasite is not eradicated from the tank, reinfection will occur no matter how effectively the fish have been treated. *Amyloodinium* can be treated successfully with formalin, copper, hydrogen peroxide, quinacrine, malachite green, and a number of other compounds. The most common treatment used in large and small marine systems is copper in the form of cupric sulphate complexed with citric acid or chelated with EDTA. A solution of just copper sulphate quickly precipitates out of saltwater; copper sulphate complexed with citric acid stays in solution much longer (at least a few days); and copper sulphate chelated with EDTA remains in a saltwater solution for considerably longer, but is less toxic to the parasite, and most chelated copper medications require treatment at higher apparent copper levels.

The most effective, no nonsense treatment for *Amyloodinium* is as follows.

The freshwater bath: Prepare a freshwater bath of one to three gallons depending on the number of fish to be treated. Dechlorinate the tap water if necessary by aerating it for several hours or add one small crystal of sodium thiosulfate or one drop per gallon of a weak solution of sodium thiosulfate. (Note: If the freshwater contains chloramine and not just chlorine, it may not be very easy to remove the chloramine. Chapter 2 has more information on removing chloramine from freshwater.) The pH of the freshwater should not be more than 0.5 points off that of the tank water. Add baking soda or a commercial buffer if the pH is too low. Remove **all** the fish from the infected tank and give them a one to two minute bath in the bucket of freshwater. The fish can easily withstand the abrupt change in external osmotic pressure, but the parasites have no protection (unless they are deeply embedded in mucus) and quickly swell and burst. Thus the freshwater bath efficiently eliminates

nearly all cysts on the fish as well as their potential off-
spring.

[This is not completely true. I always thought that the
cysts on the fish burst after the fish was placed in a freshwater bath, because I had read that this was so in various
reference books; and when affected fish were removed from
a freshwater bath, it was obvious that the cysts were gone
and the tissues around the cyst area were ragged giving the
appearance that the cyst had burst.

Then one time we had some half inch clownfish that
were badly infected with *Amyloodinium* cysts. Since they
were such small fish, I gave them a freshwater bath in a
small fingerbowl and watched the process under the dis-
secting microscope. Sure enough, the cysts disappeared,
and there were little ragged spots on the tiny clowns where
the cysts used to be. Then I noticed a lot of little white specks
scattered over the bottom of the fingerbowl. I removed the
clownfish and kept the specks in the fingerbowl under observation for several hours. No change was noted. Then I
sucked up some of the specks in an eyedropper and placed
them in a fingerbowl of saltwater. I left the fingerbowl of
saltwater on the table and observed it once in a while over
the next few days. After a day or two, most of the little white
specks were gone and there were numerous tiny dinospores
swimming about in the saltwater in the fingerbowl. Thus a
freshwater bath does not burst all the cysts, but only makes
them fall off the fish. They are then able to complete development if they get back into saltwater, and continue the life
cycle if they can find a host. **So never put the freshwater
from the bath into a marine tank!**]

After the freshwater bath, the fish are placed in a treatment tank with only an airstone for aeration and water
circulation, and some rocks or ceramics for fish shelters. A
five to ten gallon tank is a good size unless a large number
of fish need treatment. Avoid placing coral, limestone, and
other calcareous materials in the treatment tank since they
tend to remove copper from the treatment water. Treatment

for fish infected with *Amyloodinium* consists of a three week exposure to a copper level of 0.2 to 0.3 ppm (parts per million) to destroy all dinospores that may be liberated before they can encyst on a fish, and, if the fish are held in a separate treatment tank, exposure to an antibiotic (neomycin, erythromycin, tetracycline, or furnace) to control secondary bacterial infections. Refer to the bacterial disease treatment section for dosage or follow the instructions on a commercial antibiotic treatment for marine fish. If a level of 0.15 to 0.2 ppm copper can be maintained for three weeks, this is adequate to destroy *Amyloodinium* dinospores. (Some scientific studies show that dinospores are destroyed by copper and tomonts are not, and other studies demonstrate the opposite result.) However, 0.15 ppm is the minimum effective dose, and it may not be adequate under normal aquarium conditions where proper levels of copper are difficult to maintain. Most fish are not harmed by levels up to 0.3 ppm, thus concentrations slightly higher than 0.15 (0.2 to 0.25 ppm) provide a more sure cure since even if a slight drop in concentration occurs, copper levels are still effective.

Treatment of the fish is only half the cure. The *Amyloodinium* cysts resting on the bottom of the tank or in the filters must also be eliminated. There are two ways to do this, both effective, and the best way for you depends on your own attitudes and methods. Time and temperature can be used together very effectively. Like all organisms with no internal temperature control, the *Amyloodinium* life cycle progresses faster at high temperatures because the chemical reactions of life take place more quickly. *Amyloodinium* also requires a host fish to survive. Generally, the free living dinospore stage survives for only a few days if it cannot find a fish host. (Some strains, however, can survive 15 to perhaps 30 days before finding a host.) Therefore, the life cycle of the parasite can be broken if the fish hosts are removed from the system, and are not returned until after all the dinospores have hatched and have died for lack of a host. The process can be speeded up by increasing the temperature to 85 °F, perhaps even to 90 °F. All *Amyloodinium* cysts and dinospores can be eliminated from an aquarium in two weeks (three is almost a sure thing) if the fish hosts are removed and temperature is elevated—and if the fish do not carry the parasite back with them when they are returned to the tank. The undergravel filter should be thoroughly cleaned and all detritus removed at the start of the treatment to remove all possible *Amyloodinium* cysts that may be in the bottom debris. The bare bottom of tanks with external filters should be siphoned clean.

[**Reef Systems:** *Amyloodinium* is usually not as big a problem in reef tanks as it is in fish tanks. This is not to say that this parasite does not occur in reef tanks. To the contrary, it can be major problem in some coral/fish reef tanks when fish sensitive to the parasite are in the tank and can't be removed without pulling out every piece of rock and coral, which is seldom a worthwhile endeavor. The special characteristics of a reef tank—super filtration, strong water movement, and the presence of lots of filter feeders—tend to keep parasite populations in check and even occasionally seem to eliminate them. Most often, however, the parasite remains in the system at a low level of infection, and may someday become a serious problem if other fish are added to the tank. The only way to clear a reef tank of *Amyloodinium*, aside from removing all corals and other invertebrates and treating with copper, is to keep the tank **completely** fish free for at least a month, preferably two. The fish must be captured and removed or the parasite will probably find a host and survive at low levels. Even a resistant fish may harbor a few cysts and keep the parasite viable. If the fish cannot be captured and removed, the aquarist must either wait for the fish to succumb to the parasite, or keep only fish that are resistant, and live with an occasional outbreak of *Amyloodinium*.]

Copper treatment: The second way is to treat the tank with copper. The most effective method is to remove any invertebrates and all calcareous objects. Sometimes it is not possible to remove all calcareous material, especially when the undergravel filter is composed of a calcareous media. If possible, however, the undergravel filter should be cleaned very well before treatment, to remove detritus and some, hopefully most, of the free *Amyloodinium* cysts (tomonts) also. The tank can be treated with or without removing the fish to a treatment tank. If no other tank is available, give the fish a freshwater bath to remove the cysts (trophonts) that are currently on the fish, and replace the fish in the tank. Treat the tank with a 0.3 ppm dose. (If all fish and invertebrates have been removed from the tank the initial treatment can be as high as 0.6.) Test the copper level the next day (if the tank has never been treated with copper and if calcareous material is present, the copper level may have dropped to almost zero) and elevate the dose back to 0.25. Wait two days, test the copper level again and bring it up to 0.20 if necessary.

Thereafter, test copper levels every other day and maintain the dose at about 0.2 for two to three weeks. The fish may be replaced in the tank after two to three days if necessary since the copper levels that are maintained in the tank water will prevent reinfection. Be sure to test the copper level before replacing the fish in the tank, especially if an elevated copper dose was added to the fish-free tank. Adjust the copper level to 0.2, or close to this, when the fish are replaced in the tank. If copper levels are too high, lower the level with water change or activated carbon filtration.

The copper concentrations must not be allowed to fall below 0.15 during the treatment period. After treatment, free copper in the tank water can be removed with activated carbon filtration, and the invertebrates replaced after copper levels fall to zero.

Once a tank is treated with copper there will always be some precipitated copper in the tank, and the water should always be tested before retreatment with copper, especially if species sensitive to copper are kept. Symptoms of copper

poisoning in marine fish are slow respiration and listlessness.

For the more casual aquarist, there are shortcuts to this
treatment method that can be effective, although less precise
and far more dangerous to the fish. The simplest method is
to just dose the tank with a double dose of copper treatment
at the first sign of *Amyloodinium* (hopefully winding up with
a 0.3 ppm level). Add a second single dose two days later,
another single dose three days later and keep your fingers
crossed that this will take care of the problem. It may, and
then again it may not. The tank can be retreated whenever
Amyloodinium is observed, for the presence of *Amyloodinium*
is a good sign that copper levels are below 0.05 ppm. A
freshwater bath for those fish most heavily infested will also
be helpful. They can be returned to the tank immediately if
the tank has been treated with copper. Such a shortcut is not
good treatment technique, but it's better than none as long
as copper levels do not rise above 0.4 ppm, and this may be
too high for some sensitive fish species.

Now a word or two about copper: Copper is not a cure
all, in fact the primary, almost only, use of copper in the
marine aquarium is to medicate for *Amyloodinium* infestations. This parasite is so common that without judicious use
of copper treatments, collecting, shipping, stocking, and
keeping marine fish would be extremely difficult. There are,
however, several problems inherent with the use of copper.
First of all, it is a poison to fish as well as to *Amyloodinium*.
The only reason we can use it is because it is slightly less
toxic to fish than to dinoflagellates, and by carefully regulat-
ing the dose, we can wipe out the *Amyloodinium* and not
injure the fish. The second problem is that it is difficult to
maintain the proper level of free copper in an established
marine aquarium. Many organisms, including bacteria and
algae, and also detritus and calcareous material, remove
copper from the water and can rapidly reduce its concentration below the effective level. However, repeated applica-

tions may quickly push the concentration into the toxic zone (0.5 ppm and up) for fish.

The third difficulty is that low levels of copper are quite toxic to many invertebrates such as anemones and corals and should **never** be used when these animals are in the tank. There is also evidence that copper treatment inhibits biological filtration to some extent. Thus the biological filter is at risk if high copper treatment levels are used. Note too, that the presence of heavy metals, especially copper, contributes to the growth and development of *Vibrio* bacteria. Thus, treatment with copper may cause or contribute to vibriosis, a virulent bacterial infection! So try to avoid the use of copper in the main tank with an effective quarantine system (Chapter 8), and before you use copper, be sure that you have an *Amyloodinium* or ciliate problem and not a bacterial infection.

Copper treatment preparation: Proper copper levels are relatively easy to maintain in a bare treatment tank if the copper solution is correctly prepared. There are many copper preparations available on the market today and most are compounded to deliver a 0.15 ppm concentration at a dose of one drop per gallon, but some deliver 0.25 ppm at the same dosage. It's important to know what concentration of copper is programmed to end up in the tank with a commercial preparation. The best way to find this out is to put a drop into a gallon of saltwater or 10 drops into 10 gallons and test the resulting concentration with a copper test kit. The copper in most commercial preparations is complexed, usually with an acid, to keep the copper in solution as long as possible. Other medications such as formalin are frequently added.

Unfortunately, treating a marine aquarium with copper is not a simple, straightforward operation. Even if you know precisely what concentration of copper the medication is designed to deliver, the tank may not be at all cooperative. Each aquarium set up has a certain capacity to pull out free copper from the water. Old tanks with a lot of detritus and calcareous material and infrequent past copper treatments can pull out much more copper than clean tanks with silica sand filters. It's possible to treat a tank with a full dose of copper only to have copper levels fall to almost zero in the space of a few hours. This is why it's important to test copper levels in the tank to make sure that the proper treatment level is maintained.

If you've a mind to, you can make up your own copper treatment solution. I'll give two formulas below, one for those with access to a laboratory type gram scale and metric volume measurements and one for those with only kitchen equipment and no other alternatives.

Dissolve 2.23 grams of copper sulphate (pentahydrate) and 1.5 grams of citric acid in one liter of freshwater to prepare the stock solution. Treatment with this stock solution at one milliliter per gallon of tank water results in a maximum concentration of 0.15 ppm. If the amount of copper sulphate and citric acid is doubled, the resulting solution will produce a concentration of 0.3 ppm at a dose of one ml per gallon.

If you are really stuck and can't get a commercial preparation and can't find someone to weigh out the chemicals for you on a gram scale, and don't understand all this metric stuff anyway, you can prepare a stock solution as follows. Copper sulphate and citric acid can usually be purchased at a drug store or a plant nursery. The copper sulphate should be in the form of small blue crystals (it's sometimes called bluestone) about 1/16 to 1/8 inch long (1 to 3 mm). Dissolve one level teaspoon of copper sulphate and one rounded half teaspoon of citric acid in three liters of freshwater. If you can't measure out three liters (100 ounces) use three quarts plus four ounces. A one gallon jug makes a good mixing and storage container for this stock solution. One milliliter (ml) of this stock solution per gallon of tank water should deliver about 0.3 ppm copper. There are about five ml per teaspoon (20 to 25 drops per ml), so one teaspoon of this solution for every ten gallons of tank water will produce about a 0.15

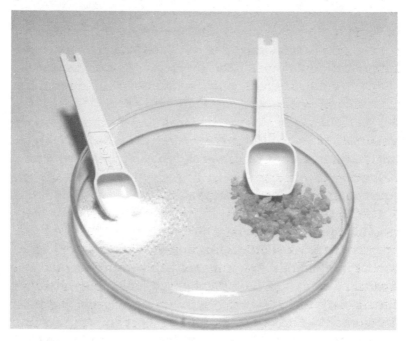

Figure 16 Copper sulphate and citric acid in the proper pro-
portions to make three liters of copper treatment stock solution.

ppm concentration. **Note that this method of preparation is
quite inaccurate, and there is a substantial risk of over or
under treatment, especially if you do not test the aquarium water for copper concentration.**

When adding any medication to your tank that calls for
a certain dose per gallon, remember that there is more than
just water in your tank. The undergravel filter and decorations, as well as fish, take up space that reduces the total
volume of water. To determine how many gallons of water
in the tank, multiply the length times the width times the
height of water, all in inches, and divide the product by 231.
This will give you the number of gallons that space will
hold. Then deduct 10% or more, depending on the individual tank, to allow for the volume of the filter and the decorations.

Cryptocaryon

Cryptocaryosis is most commonly known as white spot disease and is also known as saltwater ich. Inexperienced aquarists frequently confuse *Cryptocaryon* and *Amyloodinium*. It is quite different from *Amyloodinium* although there are similarities. The ciliate, *Ichthyophthirius multifiliis*, causes the fearsome "ich" that is the freshwater counterpart of *Cryptocaryon irritans*. Thus cryptocaryosis is best known by the common name, saltwater ich. Like *Amyloodinium*, *Cryptocaryon* can complete its life cycle in a closed system aquarium and also has the capacity of overwhelming and destroying captive fish.

The tomite is the motile, infective stage of the life cycle. They are small ciliated protozoans about 50 microns long, and their function is to find a host fish within a day or two, or die in the attempt. Once they attach to the gill or body of a host, they develop into the second stage, the parasitic trophont. This stage burrows into the host and feeds on the host's tissues, often causing extensive damage. The well fed trophont eventually stops feeding and encysts, becoming the outwardly inactive tomont stage. This final stage may stay trapped in the mucus of the fish or may fall off and drift to the bottom. Within 6 to 10 days, about two hundred new tomites may emerge from the tomont and seek another host fish to begin the cycle again.

Despite similarities in the life cycles, it has been my experience that *Cryptocaryon* does not overwhelm aquariums as rapidly as *Amyloodinium*. Perhaps fish have a greater natural resistance to *Cryptocaryon*, although the individual trophonts of *Cryptocaryon* seem to inflict greater damage than single *Amyloodinium* dinospores.

Symptoms

Although *Cryptocaryon* frequently infects the gills and causes respiratory distress, the first sign of the disease is usually several to a dozen white spots on the body and fins

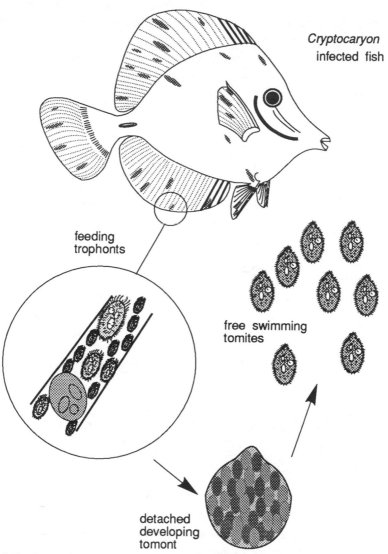

Cryptocaryon
infected fish

feeding
trophonts

free swimming
tomites

detached
developing
tomont

of the host fish. These spots are about the size of a pinhead
and look very much like a small single pimple. The fish do
not have the "dusted" or "salted" appearance that charac-
terizes a severe case of *Amyloodinium*, unless of course, both
parasites are present. These discrete white pustules become
more numerous as the disease progresses. The gills become
clogged with tomonts, mucus, and tissue debris. Bacterial

infections invade the lesions caused by the trophonts, and the fish declines rapidly. Scratching on the bottom or on rocks is a common symptom. Loss of color also occurs in patches or blotches as the erosion of the trophonts destroys pigment cells.

Treatment

As with *Amyloodinium*, the fish and the tank must be successfully treated to eliminate *Cryptocaryon* infestation. There are several methods of treatment that generally give good results. Unfortunately, copper is not as effective against *Cryptocaryon* and other ciliates as it is for *Amyloodinium*, although it does attack the free swimming tomite stage and is therefore useful, but other medications are necessary. The first step in treatment is a freshwater bath since this will explode all trophonts and tomonts on the surface of the fish. This is not as effective as with *Amyloodinium* because *Cryptocaryon* burrows deeply and is protected by mucus and tissue.

The traditional treatment for *Cryptocaryon* consists of a one hour formalin bath (½ hour for sensitive species) every other day for a total of three baths, and a copper treatment for the aquarium (as described in the *Amyloodinium* section). In this case, the fish can be returned to the aquarium after each bath, as it is also under treatment. If you do not wish to treat the tank with copper and plan to maintain the fish in a separate treatment tank with a light (0.15 to 0.2 ppm) copper treatment, the tank can be cleansed of *Cryptocaryon* with a time-temperature treatment of 10 days at 85°F. This period allows four to six days for all tomonts to release their tomites, and at least three days for all tomites to die for want of a fish host.

The formalin bath: Prepare the formalin bath by adding one ml of formalin for each gallon of saltwater in the bath (one teaspoon to five gallons). Aerate this preparation very actively because formalin tends to reduce oxygen saturation, and carefully time the hour of treatment. If signs of shock appear, terminate the bath immediately. Formalin is a commercial preparation of a 37% solution of formaldehyde gas. It is commonly available at drug stores and janitorial supply houses. Full strength formalin is potent stuff, so don't inhale it or get it in your eyes or on your skin. Formalin works as a preservative (and poison) by denaturing protein. Proteins, as you know, are the basic building blocks of life, and formalin, figuratively speaking, rushes in and changes the arrangements of the blocks and binds them permanently together so that the chemical reactions of life cannot take place. At very low exposure levels, formalin destroys the parasites without bothering the fish. It also does the same thing to most bacteria, thus a good dose can wreak havoc with a biological filter. Formalin breaks down over a period of weeks in solution, so it stays in the aquarium for some time. It is a useful treatment tool for *Cryptocaryon, Amyloodinium*, external fungus, external bacteria, fish flukes, and fish lice, but keep effective doses in a separate treatment tank or you may pickle organisms you don't want pickled.

Quinacrine treatment: A treatment developed by Dr. Edward Kingsford works well on *Cryptocaryon*. This treatment uses the antimalarial drug, quinacrine hydrochloride, at a dosage of 4 to 6 milligrams per gallon applied directly to the infected tank. Quinacrine can be obtained through chemical supply houses and occasionally at drug stores. The drug does not affect the biological filter, but is active against protozoans. It may also be detrimental to anemones and corals, so these animals should be removed from the tank before treatment. Carbon filtration removes quinacrine, so these filters should be taken off and flushed with fresh water to remove any stray cysts before reuse.

The treatment requires two doses of 4 to 6 milligrams of quinacrine hydrochloride, spaced 24 hours apart, applied to the infected tank. Light levels should be reduced during treatment, so the tank lights should not be turned on. After 10 days, residual quinacrine can be removed by activated carbon filtration. A water change after treatment is also a good idea. This medication leaves a yellow stain in tissues of fish and invertebrates that gradually disappears.

Malachite green treatment: Another effective treatment for *Cryptocaryon* and other ciliates is a five day exposure to the dye malachite green. One or two drops per gallon of a 1% solution makes up the treatment bath. After four to five days in a treatment tank, the white spot disease should be gone.

I think the best treatment for cryptocaryosis, in terms of effectiveness and ease of use for most marine aquarists, consists of first removing the fish to a treatment tank. The main tank can then be treated with copper or left without fish for 10 to 15 days. If the fish are set up in a treatment tank, then the treatment tank should carry a 0.15 to 0.2 copper level. The fish should be given a one minute fresh-water bath with one ml of formalin per gallon added to the bath water. Transfer the fish to a standard 30 minute to one hour saltwater formalin bath and then return them to the treatment tank. The bath process can be repeated after three days, especially if any recurrence of *Cryptocaryon* is noticed on the fish. After two weeks under copper treatment, the *Cryptocaryon* infestation should be cured. Although the quinacrine treatment is usually effective, I feel that the for-malin/copper treatment is generally better.

Brooklynella

Cryptocaryon irritans is not the only ciliate parasite that plagues marine fish. It is the most common and the best known, but there are others, a little smaller, but just as nasty. *Brooklynella hostilis* is known for its occurrence on clownfish and is often called clownfish disease. Other species of ciliates parasitic on marine fish are *Uronema marinum*, *Miamiensis avidus*, *Caliperia* sp. The diseases caused by these and possibly other species of ciliates differ in expression and virulence depending on the species under attack, condition

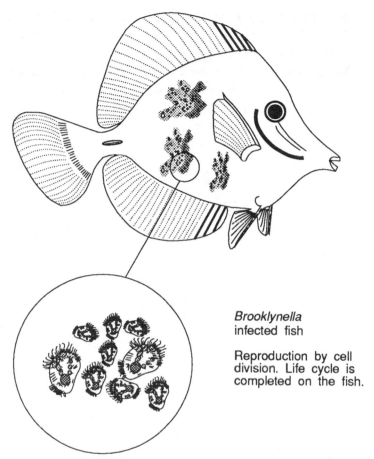

Brooklynella
infected fish

Reproduction by cell
division. Life cycle is
completed on the fish.

of the host, and environmental conditions. Small French and black angelfish from Florida are often infected during the warm summer months, and other species such as Cuban hogfish may also develop ciliate infections. The stress of capture, handling, and closed systems may reduce the resistance of the fish to the ciliate attack and cause a small occurrence that might well be shrugged off in the wild to bloom and kill the fish in captivity.

Symptoms
The fish at first has small whitish spots with indistinct borders on the sides and sometimes on the fins. These small

whitish areas begin to enlarge and soon mucus and skin begin to slough off and the affected areas become red and raw with loose scales. In some host species, the ciliates may also invade the internal organs and blood system of the host. The disease advances rapidly and the fish usually dies within a few days. Small fish are most affected.

Treatment

As with *Cryptocaryon*, copper treatment is ineffective without co-treatment with formalin, quinacrine, or malachite green. The formalin treatment recommended above for *Cryptocaryon* is probably the best that a marine hobbyist can do to cure other ciliate infections as well.

Poor Diet (including starvation)

A diet that provides all the essential nutrients is necessary to keep marine fish in good health over a long period of time. Fish suffering from malnutrition become susceptible to many other maladies, and although death may be caused by a specific disease, the underlying problem is a fish weakened by malnutrition. Except for total starvation, nutritional deficiencies do not occur quickly. They are the result of habitual poor feeding practices and, unfortunately, many fish keepers do not expend the little bit of extra effort that would keep their fish well fed. Underfeeding is a common problem. Most fish need to be fed at least once a day, twice is better. The exception is a reef tank where food is usually constantly available to small fish.

In nature, many fish, particularly plankton pickers and sponge and algae browsers, feed almost constantly during their active hours. In an aquarium, they can do very well on two or three feedings per day, if the food provides their basic nutritional needs. Underfeeding becomes a problem when no one feeds the fish for days at a time and then, after a big argument about who's supposed to feed the fish, someone sprinkles a little dry flake food in the tank and then

Nutritional deficiency (starvation)

lets it go for another few days. Fish don't have to eat a lot to be healthy, but they do need the right foods on a consistent schedule.

Overfeeding is bad for the fish and bad for the tank, especially consistently overfeeding dry flake foods. There are some aquarists that cannot pass a fish tank without feeding the fish a little sprinkle of food. This may make the fish feeder feel good, but it quickly overloads the fish and the tank. Small fish that consume too much flake food too often, have a tendency to bloat after feeding and become so buoyant that they have difficulty staying near the bottom. Feeding the same food week after week without change promotes underfeeding for those fish that don't or can't eat well on the offered fare, and nutritional deficiencies for fish that require a wide range of nutrients. Many species require vegetable matter, preferably algae, in the diet to provide roughage and the proper balance of nutrients. One condition that often plagues marine fish is the fatty degeneration of the liver. Feeding most marine fish a diet high in animal fats gradually causes fat to infiltrate the liver, and that organ then declines and eventually ceases working.

As this happens, the fish is very susceptible to stress, often going into complete shock when disturbed or netted from the aquarium. Sometimes a fish in deep shock will not recover and will die from the shock, but often it gradually recovers consciousness. Fatty liver degeneration may be reversible, but I have not successfully restored a fish that suffered from the obvious symptoms of this condition. See the section on foods and feeding for a positive approach to marine fish feeding practices.

Symptoms

The symptoms of malnutrition are very much like, and often are, the symptoms of a variety of diseases. However, some of the things to watch for that may be attributable to dietary deficiencies are a tendency to bloat after feeding, a sunken stomach, overall thinness (especially behind the head under the dorsal fin), fading colors, loss of color in blotchy areas, erosion of the skin behind the head (especially angelfish), and general listlessness. A large fish can live a long time without feeding. If the proper food is not available, or if another condition prevents the fish from feeding, the fish will slowly starve. When this happens, the abdomen of the fish is slowly shrunken upward toward the spine giving the lower profile of the fish a decided concave appearance. The musculature on the sides behind the head also wastes away and the fish becomes quite thin. A fish in this condition is not feeding, or is feeding very little, and most likely will not survive.

Treatment

Provide a good, varied diet. Provide something for all the various types of fish. One would not feed a cow and a tiger the same diet and expect both to survive, so don't feed a tang and a grouper the same food either. Refer to the foods and feeding section. Several brands and formulas of frozen, complete diets for marine fish are now available, and some even include stabilized vitamin C in the preparations.

Hole in the Head Disease (lateral line erosion)

This is a condition that often plagues fish, particularly tangs and angelfish, in marine systems. It also occurs on butterflyfish, groupers, damsels, and other species. The fish appear to be in good health in terms of body shape, feeding behavior, and general tank deportment; but color is often faded or washed out, and the tiny pores that make up the

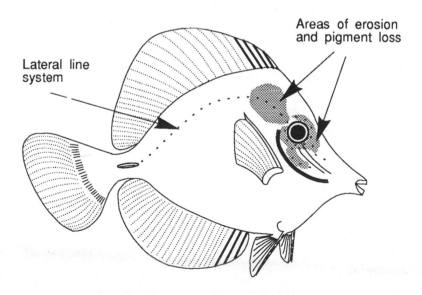

Hole in the head (lateral line erosion) disease

lateral line sensory system and extend along the side of the body and then wind around the face and eyes of the fish are enlarged and external layers of the skin in the vicinity of these pores seems to erode away. Large areas of the face and head, particularly about the eyes, are often affected and lose pigment. Eventually, if the condition is not reversed, the fish waste away and become susceptible to various diseases.

One simple, single specific cause has never been demonstrated for this condition; however, the strongest evidence implicates poor diet—a deficiency of vitamin C (ascorbic acid). Anecdotaly, a number of aquarists report that feeding foods rich in stabilized vitamin C seems to cure or at least improve the condition of affected fish. George Blasiola found that addition of vitamin C in the diet improved this condition in a study done with one species of surgeonfish, the palette tang. Access to natural algae is also reported to be beneficial. Improvement in lighting or exposure to natural sunlight is also reported to improve this condition, and even elimination of stray electrical charges in the system by grounding the saltwater with a stainless steel probe attached to a good ground is said to have a beneficial effect. At this time (1992) the best treatment seems to be to feed a diet that contains stabilized vitamin C.

Poor Environment

The aquarium environment has been well discussed in other areas of the book, and obviously, a bad environment can have detrimental effects on the fish. Some of the most common problems are a lack of the proper kind and intensity of light, inadequate circulation through the biological filter, high organic load (yellow water) and subsequent drop in pH, and high or low temperatures. Some of these maladjustments of the aquarium environment can cause ammonia and/or nitrite toxicity (discussed under toxins), but more often they lead to general debility and reduce the life span of the fish.

Symptoms

Fish subjected to a poor environment show a fading of color, often due to a whitish film over the body (which may be a touch of external fungus or excess mucus production or both); are very susceptible to bacterial infections; lack a strong interest in feeding; and may stay in one small area of the aquarium with little ranging movement.

Treatment

Check water chemistry, the filtration system, and physical factors (light, temperature, water flow, etc.) to make sure that all is well. If you still can't identify the cause of the problem, and if no disease is evident, make a 50% water change, clean all or part of the filter, and watch the fish carefully for either improvement or the appearance of a disease problem.

Toxins

Fish toxins get into aquariums in one of two ways. They develop within a tank through natural biological processes or they are introduced from an external source. Since these are very different in cause and effect, they will be discussed separately.

Internally Generated Toxins

A poor environment can cause toxins such as ammonia, nitrite, phenol, cresol, hydrogen sulfide, indole, and skatol to develop in the tank. The latter three are the result of anaerobic (oxygen lacking) bacterial processes and are very odorous. They develop only when a dirty outside filter has been turned off for several days and then turned on without cleaning or flushing, or when an undergravel biological filter is so clogged that aerated water does not circulate through all or part of it. Both conditions show severe neglect by the aquarist. A good aquarist usually discovers the problem when toxin levels are still very low and contribute only to a generalized poor aquarium environment as discussed previously. However, sometimes things degrade quickly and toxins reach a level where they cause severe distress, and even death, before the aquarist is aware of their presence.

The average marine aquarist may encounter two problems caused by internally generated toxins. These are ammonia and/or nitrite poisoning (the "new tank syndrome") and a sudden unexplainable loss of almost all fish in a healthy looking tank within 12 to 24 hours ("the wipe out"). The "wipe out" or "toxic tank syndrome" is not a particularly uncommon occurrence, but it is very misunderstood, and the effects are usually attributed to a disease. The syndrome most often occurs in tanks heavily populated with young fish of a single species, although it can occur in any type of marine closed system. The water is often very clear and uncolored, with no trace of ammonia or nitrite, and it usually has an acceptable pH when the syndrome occurs. My experimentation has shown that a virulent toxin is released from the biological filter and is often species specific, or may be more toxic to certain species than to others, especially when numerous young fish of one species are present. Possibly a substance released from the fish stimulates the filter bacteria (not necessarily nitrifying bacteria) to produce a toxic substance; or perhaps a new type of toxin producing bacteria is stimulated into a population bloom. Fish showing early symptoms of the toxic tank syndrome that are removed and placed in a totally different system almost invariably recover, and those left in the affected system almost inevitably die. Laboratory investigations showed that no ammonia/nitrite levels or *Amyloodinium* are present. Total water changes slow, but do not stop, the syndrome.

Although I knew that tanks of fish were mysteriously "wiped out" from time to time, it was always easy to put the blame on many possibilities such as tobacco, insecticide, *Amyloodinium*, bacterial disease, or anything else that could cause such mortality. The specific nature and apparent source of the "toxic tank syndrome" was not apparent to me until I began to work with large numbers of young, tank reared fish in closed systems. Extensive work with very large numbers of small fish in small, closed systems enabled us to identify the symptoms of this syndrome, and subsequently trace the cause to a toxin released from the biological filter. It is possible that this toxin can be removed by chemical filtration, however, very little is known about it, and much additional research needs to be done.

[Ten years later, I still don't know *exactly* what causes the "toxic tank syndrome", but I have some strong suspicions. Bacteria in the genus *Vibrio*, possibly the species *V. anguillarum*, has many characteristics that make it a prime candidate as the cause of this syndrome. It proliferates rapidly, displaces other species of bacteria, attacks fish externally and internally, and produces a toxin that is quickly lethal to fish whether or not the live bacteria are actually present. My best guess is that the "toxic tank syndrome" is caused by a toxin released by large populations (a bloom) of *Vibrio* bacteria residing in the biological filter, and quite possibly on the external surfaces of the fish themselves. Reducing the amount of toxin currently present and in production by moving the fish to a new system, changing water, cleaning the bio filter, and treating the fish with an antibiotic, reduces the toxic effect on the fish and relieves the symptoms. Leaving a large population of *Vibrio* bacteria in the system, however, probably just prolongs the bloom and postpones the development of lethal levels of toxin. The best treatment, especially in the case of large numbers of small fish of the same species, remains a transfer to new, unaffected systems. Modern, well maintained systems filtered with protein skimmers, ozone reactors, trickle filters, and activated carbon and resins, limit accumulation of detritus and dissolved organics, and apparently control bacterial blooms much better. Thus, a marine fish breeder with a modern closed system may not have as great a problem as we did with the toxic tank syndrome.]

Symptoms

Ammonia/nitrite poisoning leads rapidly into bacterial disease because of the impaired functioning of the kidneys and liver. Excessive mucus is also produced in the gills and rapid respiration is one of the first signs of ammonia/nitrite toxicity. (If a water test shows no ammonia or nitrite, suspect *Amyloodinium*.) The fish may also keep their mouths open and move restlessly about the tank. In extreme cases, movement is rapid and the fish may try to jump from the tank, eventually colors fade, eyes get dull, and the fish goes into shock and dies.

The **"toxic tank syndrome"** progresses very rapidly. As little as six hours may pass between onset and death, but usually 24 to 30 hours pass before it's all over. Only the most virulent of bacterial diseases or severe poisoning destroys fish this rapidly. Only a few fish out of several hundred survive this syndrome.

The early symptoms are very rapid, shallow respiration and shimmy-like swimming movements that keep the fish active, but do not move them about the tank. There also seems to be tremendous weight loss, especially in small fish, that gives them an emaciated appearance overnight. Possibly the biological mechanisms that maintain osmotic barriers break down and the fish lose body fluids to the surrounding saltwater. Young fish also tend to group in schools facing the water flow and shimmy and shake almost in formation. Unless removed from the system, the fish soon lie on the bottom and die.

Treatment

Note that a high pH, 8.3 to 8.5, increases the toxicity of ammonia. If your fish show signs of ammonia poisoning and the pH is high for some reason, lowering the pH will bring the fish some relief. This would be a rather unusual occurrence, however, for pH in a marine aquarium rarely rises above 8.0 to 8.2 unless there is a great deal of algal growth, and if there is, the algae keep ammonia levels low.

Ammonia/nitrite poisoning usually occurs during the early life of the aquarium before the nitrifying bacteria are established or when the activity of the bacteria are repressed by medication, especially antibiotics, or after filter removal or cleaning. The best treatment is removal of the fish to a balanced, ammonia/nitrite free environment. If this is not possible, remove the most severely affected fish (or the most valuable) to an aerated bucket or unfiltered tank for several days until the ammonia/nitrite levels drop in the display tank. Add one ml per gallon of a 1% by weight methylene blue solution to the holding water to aid respiration and provide a mild medicant against fungus problems. A furanace preparation is also very effective in this situation. Leaving ammonia/nitrite sensitive fish in an unbalanced tank, even with a water change, is usually a death sentence. The only real cure is to allow the tank to build the nitrifying bacteria population levels necessary to balance the animal load in the tank.

Persistent toxicity problems with newly made synthetic seawater may be the result of a new water treatment process for municipal water supplies. This process binds ammonia and chlorine in a stable compound that remains in the water despite typical treatments to remove chlorine from tap water. See Chapter 2 for a description of the problem and its remedy.

Fish suffering from the initial symptoms of the **"toxic tank syndrome"** present a little different situation. Usually the only way to save the fish is immediate transfer to another totally separate system. Water changes slow the progress of the syndrome, but do not prevent its reoccurrence 24 to 48 hours later, especially if only biological filtration is in use. There are two methods of treating the tank for this syndrome. The first is a good filter cleaning and water change and 5 to 10 days "rest" from fish occupation. The tank should be watched carefully for the next several weeks to catch any re-occurrence. It is wise to change the species composition of the tank after a bout with a wipe out, for the tank may become "sensitized" to a particular species group.

The second method is sterilization of the entire system—tank, filter, and decorations—and reestablishment of the biological filter. Entirely new bacterial populations develop and any "sensitivity" to any species group that may have developed in the tank is destroyed. Tank sterilization is probably the best thing to do if two or three "wipe outs" occur within a six to nine month period. See the end of the disease and distress chapter for details on tank sterilization.

Externally Introduced Toxins

Outside poisons seldom find their way into a tank, but when they do, they create many difficult problems. There are three ways such poisons can get into a tank:

1. On or in something the aquarist introduces into the tank.

2. An accidental introduction?

3. Sabotage!

A poison strong enough to cause death and distress was probably introduced within a few days, or more likely, within a few hours of the onset of the symptoms. If you suspect a poison from an external source, review everything done to the tank within the last three days. Suspect new ornaments, new food, new water, and any unusual introductions. Remove these if possible and investigate carefully. Medications perhaps? A double, double dose of copper? More than one person treating the tank?

Under number 2, review who had access to the tank (did your three year old nephew put moth balls from the closet into the tank?) Were there any recent paint or chemical fumes, any cigar butts, perfume spills, or martinis after a party? How about the most obvious, a zealous insecticide sprayer working behind and under the tank in the vicinity of the air pump intake? Number 3, sabotage, is another problem altogether, and if you worry about it, you're either paranoid or you've got problems way beyond the scope of this book.

Symptoms

Severe poisoning is very evident from the behavior of the fish. In most instances, there is violent swimming about the tank mixed with moments of rapid, heavy respiration. Fish will frequently jump from the tank, shudder and shake, and finally convulse and die. When this happens to all the fish in the tank, you know something is bad wrong. Perhaps worse than this though, is the mild case of poisoning that gradually kills the fish off one by one and is difficult to distinguish from the effects of a disease. The only way to separate these symptoms from those of disease is to note that the fish do not respond to treatment, that a disease can not be demonstrated, and that new fish always come down with the same symptoms. If this is the case, it's time to look for a possible cause of subtle poisoning.

Treatment

Obviously, the first step is to find and remove the source of the poisoning. Once again, the value of keeping a note book on aquarium activities is very evident. This will help you track down the time of new introductions, food changes, and other things that may indicate the source of the problem. A good filter cleaning and a water change should put the tank back in shape once the problem has been corrected. Sterilization of the tank is a drastic step and should be a last resort.

Harassment

Harassment can be outright destruction of one or two fish in a tank or subtle repression of a fish into a hole or corner. Most reef dwelling fish require a certain amount of space between themselves and other fish of the same or closely related species. The territory that an individual or a pair establish and protect insures the fish of noncompetitive feeding, shelter, and reproductive areas, and prevents pair bond confusion. This is a most complex and variable aspect of the study of reef fish ecology, and new findings and concepts are frequently published. The study of fish in aquariums can provide insight into fish behavior patterns as long as the artificiality of the environment is understood.

Harassment of one fish by others to the point of death or severe repression most commonly occurs when a new fish is introduced into an aquarium where a fish of the same or closely related species has already established a territory. If that territory includes the entire tank, the new fish is harassed until he is destroyed. In nature, the loser in such an encounter would quickly move on to an unoccupied area to find "lebensraum" or living space. However, in the aquarium there is no place to go, and harassment continues until the intruder is dead. If the tank is large enough for more than one territory for that species, then the new fish may find a scrap of bottom or a hole to call his own. Although the fish can exist in this situation, he takes his life in his own fins when he ventures forth, and is always quickly chased back to his own area.

Territorial defense is usually not as keen in young fish and seems to break down altogether if large numbers of one species are confined in a small space. Intraspecific aggression can develop into harassment in a static tank if a number of young fish are kept until they grow larger and pair bond formation begins. This can happen abruptly or gradually as two fish, usually clownfish or damselfish, begin to repel others of their own or closely related species.

Symptoms

Harassment is usually obvious. In severe instances, the harassed fish is physically damaged with fins frayed and scales lost, and is usually found cowering in an upper corner of the tank respiring rapidly. The aggressor also respires rapidly and moves restlessly about the tank with quick aggressive attacks on the hapless intruder. The behavior of the fish and initial absence of bacterial infection in the wounds, easily distinguishes aggressive interactions from disease.

Treatment

Removal of the harassed fish or partitioning of the tank to separate the fish is the only treatment for incompatible tankmates. After separation, the injured fish should recover on his own unless he is badly chewed up, but watch and make sure that bacterial infection does not set in. It may be necessary to isolate the injured fish in a treatment tank with an antibiotic treatment.

Fungus Diseases

Fungus diseases in fish, especially internal infections, are not uncommon and are very difficult, if not impossible, to cure. Fortunately, fish have natural resistance to fungus disease. If good nutrition and a healthy environment that is low in dissolved organics are provided, fungus infections are rarely a problem. **Internal fungus infections,** Ichthyophonus is the common term, are usually caused by *Ichthyosporidium hoferi,* a parasitic fungus in the class Phycomycetes. This fungus is not detectable until the advanced stage of the disease causes degenerative changes in behavior and appearance. This organism has caused massive death of herring in nature. Feeding the raw flesh of fish infected with *Ichthyosporidium* is the surest way to infect a fish held in a marine aquarium. Unfortunately, there is no positive cure. Many fish seem to be able to contain and control this parasite and evidently live many years with this tiny parasitic time bomb ticking away inside their vital organs. Stress and poor nutrition may weaken the defenses of the fish and release the fungus to destroy the spleen, liver, brain, and other organs.

External fungus infections are usually caused by organisms in the genus *Saprolegnia*. These are visible as cotton-like tufts about the mouth or as a thin whitish coating on the sides of the fish. The appearance of external fungus usually indicates that there is an underlying problem, either nutritional or environmental, that should be corrected.

Symptoms

Symptoms of **internal fungus infections** do not appear until the disease is well advanced. Loss of appetite and listlessness are the first symptoms as the fungus proliferates in the liver and kidneys. Dark nodules under the skin may appear along with areas of upraised scales. The infection soon passes to the nervous system and causes exothalmus (popeye) and loss of equilibrium. The fish swims in random circles often swimming upside down. This gives this disease the common names of staggers disease and whirling disease. The abdomen may also fill with fluid and be distended (dropsy). There is nothing that can be done for a fish in the later stages of this disease.

External fungus infections do not destroy the life function of the fish and are easier to deal with. *Saprolegnia* appears as cottony tufts near the mouth or on the fins, occasionally growth about the mouth is great enough to obstruct feeding and can cause starvation. External fungus also occurs as a thin white coating on the sides of the fish. It can be easily distinguished from *Amyloodinium* because *Amyloodinium* occurs as discrete specks and fungus infections appear as a variable white film with thick and thin areas. Severe cases can erode the skin, introducing secondary bacterial invasion which eventually enters the abdomen and destroys the fish.

Treatment

When it becomes obvious that a fish is infected with either internal or external fungus, there are two important concerns besides the infected fish. These are the health of the other fish in the tank, and the tank environment. Fungus infections are very hard to treat and care must be taken to prevent it from spreading. A water change and, if necessary, a filter cleaning and increased dietary variety are the best preventative steps to take. Also, an effective UV water treatment unit is helpful in preventing the spread to other fishes. Usually only one or two fish show the symptoms of internal fungus disease, and these should be isolated and given good water quality and good food. I know of no really effective medication, and if the fish show no signs of improvement after a few days to a week, it is best to destroy them. Fungus is most often transmitted by healthy fish feeding on an infected dead fish or contaminated fish flesh. Remove dead or dying fish from aquariums immediately and be careful of feeding raw fish flesh. Raw fish flesh and some raw shellfish can introduce internal fungus disease to a marine aquarium.

A persistent case of **external fungus** may be treated by removing the fish from the tank, holding him carefully, and swabbing the fungus area with a cotton ball or a cotton tipped swab soaked in an iodine medication. Copper sulphate solution, malachite green solution, or 2-phenoxyethanol can be applied in the same way, but these are all experimental procedures and could be worse for the fish than the external fungus. Given a good environment and good food, a fish can usually lick a *mild* case of external fungus by himself.

Sporozoa

Sporozoans cause a great many fish diseases including whirling disease of salmonids, boil disease in several species of farmed fish, and what is usually called seahorse disease. There are probably many sporozan diseases that affect marine tropical fish, but few studies have been done on tropical sporozoans. Sporozoan infections may commonly be misdiagonised as internal and/or external fungus disease or piscine TB and, like bacteria, may also often be present in and on fish without causing a life threatening disease. Myxosporidians and microsporidans are sporozoans and identification of species requires sophisicated laboratory techniques and is usually confused and difficult. The microsporidan *Glugea* sp. is most well known and is commonly termed seahorse disease. It causes the formation of well defined, dense white patches over the body of sea horses, pipefish, boxfish, and other fish—usually fish with hard, plate-like scutes covering the body.

It is also possible that a micorsporidian may infect the eggs of clownfish. We had a problem during the very early period of clownfish culture with a white spot disease that developed in clownfish eggs at about day five after spawning. The white infection was located in the yolk of the egg, and the stunted embryo did not develop to hatching. The organisms present in the yolk were tentatitivly identified as microsporidia. Treatment with sulfathiasole and quinine seemed helpful, but many eggs were lost despite treatment. The female eventually stopped spawining infected eggs and produced good eggs for several years thereafter. Formalin baths and/or quinacrine hydrochloride may be a helpful treatment for micorsporidian infections, but little information is available on treatment for this condition in marine tropical fish.

Fish Tuberculosis

Fish tuberculosis, piscine TB, is a wide spread marine fish disease caused by the bacterium *Mycobacteria marinum*. There are a number of species in this genus, including the one that causes TB in man. Although *M. marinum* does not commonly infect people, there are reports of serious skin infections caused by *M. marinum*. In these instances, the aquarists were cleaning tanks that had held TB infected fish and had either an open lesion or suffered a cut while working in the tank. The open lesions developed into abscesses that did not heal, and after several weeks, additional abscesses developed on the hand and arm. These infections did not respond to penicillin, and treatment was not effective until the antitubercular drugs isoniazid and streptomycin were given. This is a very rare human infection, but it can happen; so if you work with an open wound in a marine aquarium, be sure to disinfect the lesion very thoroughly. Penicillin doesn't work on *M. marinum*, so if this does happen to you, tell your doctor that those nodules on your arm may be fish tuberculosis.

Fortunately, fish TB usually hits only one or two fish in a tank, and the course of the disease is slow enough to allow time for treatment. Fish showing symptoms of TB should be isolated immediately, for although it is not highly contagious, it can lead to tank wide mortality. **Contagion is especially likely if fish that die of TB are left in the tank and healthy fish pick at and consume the soft parts of the dead fish.** Feeding raw fish flesh from saltwater fish is another way of introducing this disease to a marine system.

Symptoms

Piscine TB and internal fungus, *Ichthyosporidium*, have similar symptoms and can be confused. However, loss of equilibrium, swimming in circles, sideways, and upside down, is **not** usually a symptom of piscine TB. The first symptoms are loss of appetite and general listlessness. The fish stays hidden and soon has little or no interest in feeding. Rapid respiration is usually noticed about this time also. The fish may remain in this stage of the disease for several weeks. The eyes may become clouded and exothalmus (popeye) usually develops. Another typical symptom is the development of whitish blotches and areas of raised scales. Finally the fins become ragged, the abdomen sunken, and the fish lies on its side on the bottom.

The fish may linger in this state for many days before it dies. The internal organs of affected fish degenerate and small grayish granulomas (tubercles) are found on and in the liver, intestines, spleen, and eyes. One type of piscine TB forms granulomas along the spine of young fish. These can sometimes be seen through the semi transparent flesh as a whitish discoloration along the spine of small fish. Fish can live a long time with piscine TB. Often the fish may appear in good health with no outward sign of the disease for months or years. Only on dissection are the tubercles typical of this disease found in the mesenteries, heart, spleen, liver, and other internal organs.

Treatment

Piscine TB is a difficult disease to treat because it is internal and often chronic, and the effective drugs are not easily obtained and often not very effective. Since there is a strong possibility that the average aquarist will not be able to obtain the proper drugs for treatment, the affected fish should be immediately isolated in a treatment tank to reduce the chances of infecting other fish. At the risk of sounding like a broken record, I must stress that piscine TB is most common in poorly maintained aquaria. A good environment and good nutrition keeps the natural immune system of the fish in top condition and practically eliminates the occurrence, or at least the physical expression, of piscine TB.

If the disease is caught in the early stages, treatment with streptomycin and isoniazid may effect a cure. Kingsford, in his book [which is now out of print] (see reference list) also recommends rifampin and cycloserine, although these two may be difficult to obtain. Streptomycin may be found in some commercial aquarium medications or obtained at drug stores, veterinary supply, and animal feed stores. Isoniazid can be obtained through chemical supply houses and, since it does not seem to affect nitrifying bacteria, it can be used in a tank with an active biological filter. Be sure to turn off all carbon and UV filtration before adding any medication.

Add 40 milligrams per gallon of isoniazid and 40 milligrams per gallon streptomycin to the treatment tank when the fish are transferred. Change water every three days, more often for small tanks and/or large fish, and re-medicate. Add 40 mg per gallon of isoniazid to the display tank to reduce the chance of infection. Soaking the food in streptomycin solution or adding 6 mg of rifampin per 100 grams of food increases the effectiveness of the treatment. If medicated food is prepared, it should be fed to all fish that have been exposed to the disease. Return fish to the display tank when they have apparently recovered. Do not return a fish if there is any question of recovery, for it is best to lose one or two rather than risk all other fish in the tank. If most of the fish in a tank come down with TB, or if the disease persistently occurs in a particular tank, it is best to sterilize the tank and start again. Remember that any fish that was in a tank with TB infected fish is capable of transferring this disease into any tank where it may be placed.

Bacterial Disease

The world is full of bacteria, indeed life as we know it could not exist without the activities of bacteria. Bacteriology has become a very complex discipline involving the most advanced techniques of taxonomy, biochemistry, and microscopy. One of the basic taxonomic tools of bacteriology was developed by the Danish physician Christian Gram in 1884. He discovered that bacteria could be separated into two groups depending on whether they retained (Gram-positive) or lost (Gram-negative) a violet color during a particular staining process. He didn't know it at the time, but this differential staining was caused by fundamental differences in the structure of the cell wall, which also affect the way antibiotics work on bacteria. Most bacteria that cause disease in marine fish are Gram-negative and some antibiotics, including penicillin, streptomycin, and sulfa drugs are not effective. *Pseudomonas* and *Vibrio* are the genera of the principle disease producing bacteria in marine fish. The antibiotics neomycin, chloramphenicol, and secondly erythromycin and tetracycline are usually effective against these bacteria. There are other antibiotics that may be even more effective, but they are also more difficult to obtain. Some of the above antibiotics are frequently found in aquarium pharmaceuticals or in farm animal medications obtainable at feed stores.

Fish have a strong natural resistance to bacteria, so infections caused by *Pseudomonas* and *Vibrio* seldom overrun a fish unless there is a stress and/or weakness already present in the fish. Old age, poor nutrition, poor environment, injury, harassment, fungus infection, etc. can all contribute to the debility that opens the door to bacterial disease. Occasionally, the environment is so poor that bacterial growth can bloom and overrun otherwise healthy fish. Cloudy water of a white, rather than green, hue and persistent sores on the fish are symptoms of this condition.

Symptoms

The most obvious symptoms of bacterial disease are reddened, frayed fins and open sores on the sides, usually near the fins. External ulcers are generally caused by *Pseudomonas sp.* and internal bacterial infections seem to be caused more often by *Vibrio sp. Aeromonas* is another genus of gram negative bacteria that attacks captive marine fish.

Usually only one or two fish in a tank at any one time show symptoms of advanced bacterial infection. If all fish are severely affected, then the aquarium is in bad shape and a major overhaul is required. Common symptoms of bacterial disease are rapid respiration, a grey film over the eyes, bloody scales at the base of the fins, disintegration of the fins, and open sores on the body. Bacterial disease may also cause blindness in fish. Blindness is usually evidenced by cloudy eyes, failure to see their food or movements outside the tank, and lack of response to a net moved slowly toward them. Excessive light alone, if there is such a thing in a marine aquarium, does not cause blindness, although it could increase stress levels in nocturnal fish. The lateral line

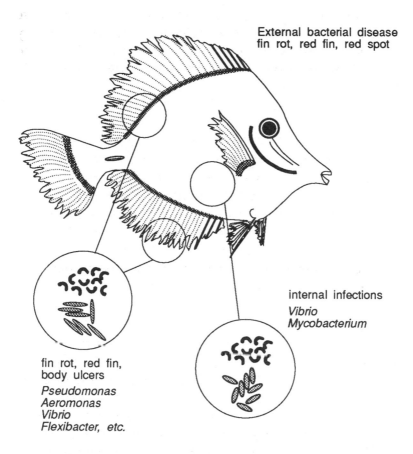

External bacterial disease
fin rot, red fin, red spot

internal infections
Vibrio
Mycobacterium

fin rot, red fin,
body ulcers
Pseudomonas
Aeromonas
Vibrio
Flexibacter, etc.

system, that row of tiny pores extending along the side from head to tail, is the most frequent site of initial external infection. Bacteria can gain entry into a stressed fish through these tiny pores and the soft tissues of the gills. Internal organs are affected as the disease progresses; the fish stops eating, respiration rate increases, and eventually the fish lies on the bottom and dies. Some bacterial diseases may kill the fish in two to four days, but usually, especially in larger fish, the progression of the disease takes one or two weeks.

Treatment

Only the affected fish need be treated if the infection is restricted to one or two fish and the other fish and the environment appear healthy. However, if most of the fish show signs of bacterial infection, it may be best to treat all the fish and sterilize the tank. This will prevent frequent re-occurrences of the same problems during the months to come. The tank cannot be treated with a strong dose of antibiotics without killing the nitrifying bacteria (they are also Gram-negative), so tank sterilization is best in the long run for a severe or persistent bacterial disease problem.

The infected fish should be isolated in a treatment tank. A freshwater bath (see *Amyloodinium* section) on the way to the treatment tank is a good idea in case there is a parasite problem, but it won't do much for a bacterial disease. Reduce light levels on the treatment tank to preserve the activity of the antibiotics and reduce stress on the fish. Add the antibiotic you choose to the treatment tank at the manufacturer's recommended dose. **If there is no listed dose for aquarium fish, use neomycin at 250 mg per gallon, chloramphenicol sodium succinate (Chloromycetin) at 50 mg per gallon, tetracycline at 50 mg per gallon, or erythromycin at 40 to 50 mg per gallon. Positive results should be noted within three to four days if the antibiotic is effective.**

If the treatment is not effective, try another antibiotic. Once the fish gets the upper hand over the infection, with the help of the antibiotic, recovery is rapid. Keep the fish in isolation until recovery is assured. Wait a day or two after ulcers are healed and eyes are no longer filmed before replacing them in the display tank. An effective UV sterilizer on the display tank will be helpful in preventing a build up of dangerous bacteria in the tank water.

If the bacterial disease seem mostly internal, it is a good idea to feed the fish an antibiotic food. If the fish is eating, one can then attack the bacteria directly inside the fish and not just on the external surface of the fish. Some internal antibiotic treatments are commercially available, and one can also put a few drops of an antibiotic solution on a porous food and feed it to the fish. The fish has to take the food quickly, however, to prevent loss of the antibiotic to surrounding water.

Lymphocystis

This is the only viral disease that commonly affects marine tropical fish. It also goes by the name "cauliflower disease" because the appearance of the growth is not unlike that of a miniature cauliflower. The virus invades cells just under the skin of the fish (usually fins or lips are affected),

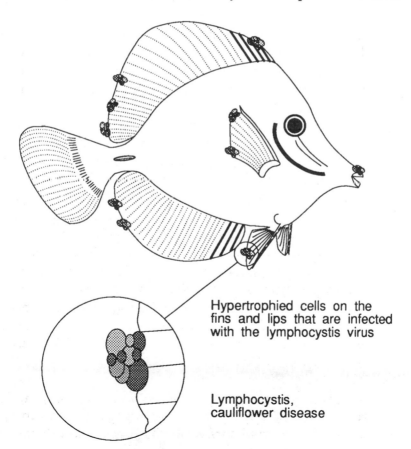

Hypertrophied cells on the fins and lips that are infected with the lymphocystis virus

Lymphocystis, cauliflower disease

and causes these cells to swell greatly (hypertrophy) and form a thickened cell membrane. These enlarged cells proliferate into a small growth with a characteristic form and color. The stress of capture, handling, and closed systems may reduce the resistance of the fish to the virus, thus outbreaks of Lymphocystis are not uncommon on newly captured fish. The virus does not kill the fish directly, although the growths may interfere with feeding or may create a pathway for secondary bacterial infection. In many respects, Lymphocystis is similar to a wart on humans. Given time and no secondary complications, fish will usually recover from Lymphocystis infection on their own.

Symptoms

The fish displays small, discrete, gray or whitish growths on lips and/or fins. These growths may appear all over the body in a severe case. The size of the growths is variable, but most are less than ⅛ inch (3 mm) in diameter. The surface of the growth is smooth and slightly irregular.

Treatment

There is no treatment for lymphocystis, and since the growths disappear in time, no treatment is recommended. However, if the growths interfere greatly with feeding or swimming, they can be removed at the risk of spreading the virus and causing secondary bacterial infection. Use a sterilized curved fingernail scissors or a convex curved or straight toenail clippers to remove the growth at the base. Do this work while holding the fish above a treatment tank to prevent liberating viral material into the display tank. Antibiotic treatment is recommended to control bacterial infection.

Metazoan Parasites

There are numerous parasitic diseases of fish, internal and external, caused by large, relatively speaking, multicellular animals (metazoans) mostly in the categories of worms and crustaceans. Some of these have complicated life cycles involving intermediate hosts and cannot reproduce in the aquarium, in which case they are only a threat to the infected fish. Others have simple life cycles and can, if given the chance, become a major problem. Fortunately, reproduction and growth is much slower than single celled parasites (protozoans) and infestations can be caught fairly early. Two of these larger parasites that occasionally show up in marine aquaria are discussed below and the recommended treatment for these can generally be applied to other metazoan parasites as well.

Tubellarian worms (Black Ich)

The yellow tang, *Zebrasoma flavescens*, is particularly vulnerable to this parasite, but other tangs and sometimes angelfish, butterflyfish, and a number of other species are occasionally infested with parasitic tubellarian flatworms in the genus *Paravortex*. Like *Amyloodinium* and *Cryptocaryon*, these parasitic flatworms can complete their life cycle in closed systems, and left untreated, can destroy fish in small marine aquariums. A tiny free swimming worm first finds and attaches to the skin or gills of a fish host. The tiny flatworm then feeds on the tissues of the host for five or six days, often moving freely about the fish, before dropping off to complete development on the tank bottom. After a few days on the tank bottom, the mature worm splits along the side and releases up to 160 young, free swimming worms that then seek a host fish.

Symptoms

An infected fish displays numerous tiny dark spots, about the size of a period on a printed page or slightly larger, usually on the side of the body just behind the gill opening, and sometimes on the fins. The worms are much easier to see on light colored fish. Infected fish display scratching behavior, are listless, and are not inclined to feed.

Treatment

The best treatment to eliminate this parasite is the formalin treatment as described for *Cryptocaryon*. The bottom of the tank should also be kept very clean during treatment. This removes worms that have fallen off the host fish before the worms can reproduce.

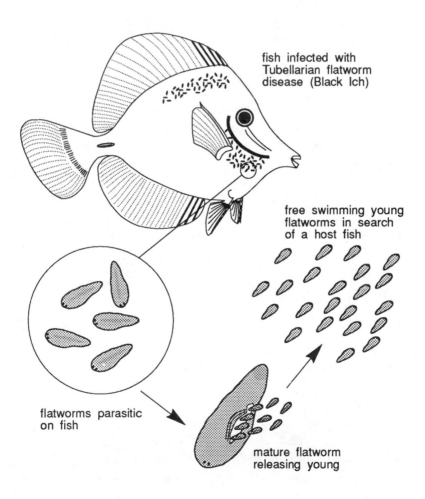

fish infected with Tubellarian flatworm disease (Black Ich)

free swimming young flatworms in search of a host fish

flatworms parasitic on fish

mature flatworm releasing young

Fish Flukes

Benedenia melleni are flattened, almost transparent parasites that attach to the gills and external surfaces of fish. They are usually only about ⅛ inch long, but may reach a length of ½ inch. Their transparency makes them difficult to see, and they are first noticed as numerous small bumps on the side of the fish. They may also infest the gills, but are usually evident on the body at the same time.

Symptoms

Fish that are infested actively scrape and swim against the bottom attempting to dislodge the parasites. Flukes can readily move from one fish to another, although they tend to remain with the same fish. Severe infestations invite bacterial infection by stressing and weakening the fish as well as by breaking through the skin and mucus layers.

Treatment

Benedenia can reproduce in the aquarium, and although each generation takes several weeks instead of days, they can become epidemic. The best immediate treatment is a freshwater bath. Catch the fish as gently as possible, to prevent the parasites from being dislodged, and transfer the fish to a freshwater bath as described under the *Amyloodinium* section. The flukes will turn opaque and drop off the fish very quickly. The fish can be left in the bath, under careful observation, five to eight minutes if necessary if all the flukes do not drop off in two minutes. The freshwater bath can be repeated every day or so whenever the flukes are observed on fish, and the flukes will soon be exterminated—which is fine if you can get fish out of the tank with very little effort. The traditional formalin bath, as described in the *Cryptocaryon* treatment section, is also effective against flukes and fish lice and can be used in conjunction with the freshwater bath. **Make sure that all the flukes are**

eliminated from the net used to catch the infected fish, before placing the net into the same or another tank.

Another rather recently developed treatment for external worm and crustacean parasites is addition of the chemical o,o-dimethyl 2,2,2-trichloro-1-hydroxyethyl phosphorate directly to the tank water. For some strange reason, this chemical is usually referred to only as DTHP. It was developed as an insecticide and was found to be effective against many aquatic fish parasites. This compound is easily removed with activated carbon, does not disturb the activity of a biological filter, and breaks down into harmless compounds within a few weeks. Unfortunately, there is no way the average aquarist can test for the amount of DTHP present in tank water. A concentration of 0.75 to 1.0 mg per liter is an effective dose. This compound is very toxic to crustaceans, and so all shrimp, crabs, lobsters, and, to be on the safe side, all valuable invertebrates should be removed from the tank before treatment. It is compatible with copper medications. DTHP goes under the trade names of Dylox, Dipterex, and Proxol 80 as well as several others. Although DTHP is quite effective against flukes and fish lice and can be added directly to the tank, I recommend the traditional formalin treatment unless you have the laboratory expertise and equipment to calculate and prepare the proper dose for your tank.

Parasite pickers such as small French angelfish, neon gobies, and Pacific cleaner wrasse are helpful in controlling these large parasites. The slow reproduction rate of the parasite allows an active cleaner to defuse the population bomb.

Fish Lice (crustacean parasites)

Argulus is one of a number of genera of marine crustaceans that are parasitic on fishes and go by the general name of fish lice. Their appearance is variable. *Argulus* have flat shield like bodies that help them grip the surface of the fish and the mouth parts are modified into a suction grip and sting. Most *Argulus*, however, are freshwater parasites.

Some parasitic copepods partially embed themselves in the host fish with only the paired, elongated egg sacs noticeably protruding. Others are not permanently attached to the host fish and can move from fish to fish feeding on skin tissues.

It is important to recognize the difference between a parasitic copepod problem and an occasional bloom of free living copepods. Parasitic copepods, especially epidemics of them, are rather rare in marine aquaria. On the other hand, a balanced aquarium with a solid functioning biological filter and good algal growth may frequently experience a

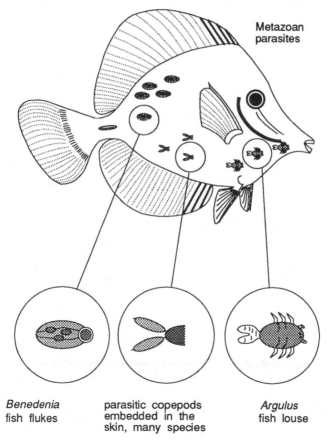

Metazoan parasites

Benedenia fish flukes

parasitic copepods embedded in the skin, many species

Argulus fish louse

bloom of free living tiny copepods. These tiny "bugs" are much smaller than parasitic "bugs" and swarm over the algae covered sides of the aquarium. Occasionally they move over the sides of fish and give rise to fears of parasites. Actually these tiny white copepods, less than a millimeter long, fit very well into the natural food chain of the aquarium. They feed on detritus and algal cells and are in turn fed upon by invertebrates and small fish. Their numbers can be controlled by more frequent filter cleanings, keeping algal growth under control, and by strong filtering action through a UV unit or a small pored mechanical filter. Control measures should be considered only if they are causing the fish obvious discomfort.

Symptoms

Scratching and scraping behavior of the fish indicates irritation from external parasites, and careful observation will reveal the presence of fish lice or other parasite problems. Sometimes these external parasites are almost completely transparent and can barely, if at all, be seen on the fish. They become opaque during a freshwater bath, however, and can be seen to drop off the fish. Do not add the freshwater to any marine tank.

Treatment

Apply the same treatment as described for fish flukes. Embedded parasites may not respond to this treatment and if these are present, it is best to remove them individually with tweezers. Dab the point of removal with an antiseptic solution.

Old Age

Old age is not really one of the "dirty dozen". Fish, as all other animals, must die sometime, and if they bow out from old age in your aquarium, then you've done the best you can for them. A marine fish dying of old age in an aquarium used to be very unusual, so much so that it was seldom considered as a possible cause of death. Marine aquarium keeping has now advanced to the point where keeping a fish one to five years is commonplace, thus old age must now be considered when analyzing fish death. Many fish, for example neon gobies and jawfish, have only a one or two year life expectancy in the wild, and others rarely exceed a five year life span. These fish often exceed their natural life span when kept under good conditions away from natural predators and disease. Marine fish, like all other animals, have immune systems that protect them from disease. The efficiency of this immune system declines with age, as do internal organs and musculature, and the fish become more susceptible to the onslaught of disease. So even if the death of an old fish can be blamed on a specific disease, old age may be the basic cause.

Symptoms

Old age often causes changes in the appearance of fish just as it does in other animals. Fins often get longer, teeth may become more prominent, colors may change, and even the shape of the head and slope of the back may alter. Unlike mammals, fish never stop growing. The rate of growth slows considerably when fish reach maturity, but it never stops, and fish continue to slowly increase in size under normal environmental and nutritional conditions. Large fish usually grow even more slowly in an aquarium, so it often appears that a fish reaches a terminal size in an aquarium, and given the limitations of the artificial environment, this may be the case. Older fish tend to be the larger and heavier individuals; however, considerable variation in growth rate prevents use of size or weight as an accurate index of age.

Treatment

There is no treatment, of course, for old age. Just keep in mind that fish do grow old, sometimes small fish do so quite rapidly, and this may make them more susceptible to common problems.

Please note: If you have to destroy and dispose of sick or dead fish, **NEVER, NEVER** release them in local waters. Although the chance that they will recover and establish a population of non-native fish or that a new disease will be introduced to plague native fish is rather remote, the possibility can not be risked. The best way to dispose of a dead fish is to seal it in a plastic bag and send it out with the garbage, or maybe recycle it as fertilizer in the flower garden.

Tank Sterilization

Sometimes, despite everything, it becomes necessary to "kill" a tank and begin all over again. This could happen because of severe neglect or an extremely persistent parasite or bacterial problem. Sterilization is almost like setting up a tank for the first time, and as far as the life forms in the aquarium are concerned, there is no difference. When the tank is sterilized, **everything** in the tank will be killed, so be sure to remove all animals. Animals removed from the tank may be carrying the bug that caused the problem, so they must be treated and quarantined for several weeks before putting them into other tanks, if one dare risk this.

The agent for sterilization is chlorine (sodium or calcium hypochlorite), the active ingredient in liquid bleach and in the granular bactericidal chlorine used in swimming pools.

You don't have to worry about using too much chlorine (within reasonable limits) to sterilize your tank, but there must be a high enough concentration to do the job. The tank does not have to be dismantled to achieve sterilization. In fact, tearing the tank apart is a waste of time and effort unless the undergravel filter has been disrupted and must be repaired. The first thing to do is to remove all colored plastic ornaments, if there are any, as these may become discolored by the chlorine. Leave rocks and coral in place, as these must be sterilized also. Especially in old aquariums, it is a good idea to remove as much of the accumulated organic matter (detritus) as possible before sterilization. The chlorine must oxidize all organics present, and the less there is, the more thoroughly it can do its job. Also, there is a tendency for foam to form when the chlorine breaks down the organics, and in extreme cases, it is possible for the foam to overflow the tank and cover half the living room. (Someone—wife, husband, mother, or roommate—might never forgive you.)

The easiest way to remove the organics is to scrape the sides and stir the bottom well, then siphon out all the accumulated debris and dirty water. Refill the tank with freshwater—this is cheaper than saltwater and works just as well for this purpose. Put everything else that needs sterilization into the tank including hoses, tank covers (not lights), and cleaning tools. Chlorine is very hard on nets, so it is best just to dip and rinse them well for a few minutes in the chlorine solution, rinse with freshwater, and let them dry completely. Outside filters should be left operating, but their contents must be discarded. Keep the air pump or power filter running and water circulating just as if the tank were in normal operation. Circulating the chlorinated water will sterilize the inside of the tubes, pipes, and containers.

Now add about one tablespoon of dry granular chlorine for each 20 gallons, or a cup of liquid bleach for each 20 gallons. This dose should be enough to sterilize the entire tank. Stir the bottom filter again to eliminate any static areas and let the whole mess cook in its own juices for 12 to 24 hours. After this period, check to make sure that all algae has turned white, if not disintegrated, and that there are no brown or black areas left on the sides or in the filters. If everything is not absolutely white and clean, then add another dose of chlorine and wait another 12 to 24 hours. It would be unusual, though, if the first application did not do the job.

The thing to do next, under some circumstances, is to neutralize the chlorine. It isn't good to put any chlorine into a septic tank, and it won't do the lawn any good either (big, brown dead spots, No, I'm not going to tell you how I know this is so). Add hypo (sodium thiosulfate) or a commercial dechlorinator until the chlorine is gone. You can test for this with an OTO swimming pool test kit, or you can take a sample of the water, a cupful will do, and put in a few drops of food color. When the color of the food coloring doesn't change or bleach out, then there is very little, if any, chlorine left in the water. When the chlorine has been neutralized, the tank should be siphoned again and everything, including the gravel filter, rinsed with one or two changes of freshwater. After the tank has been cleaned and rinsed to your satisfaction, it can be refilled with saltwater and the process of conditioning the filter with nitrifying bacteria can begin again.

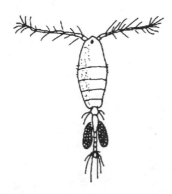

Free living cyclopoid copepod

Summary

As a brief summary, here is a list of treatment do's and treatment don'ts.

Treatment Do's

Do immediately remove dead and dying fish from aquaria.

Do isolate fish for treatment.

Do identify the problem before treatment.

Do change water in the treatment tank every two or three days.

Do keep the bottom of the treatment tank clean.

Do provide shelter for the fish in treatment.

Do keep light levels low in the treatment tank.

Do keep track of ammonia and nitrite levels if the treatment tank has a biological filter.

Do keep fish isolated until the cure is complete.

Do keep aquarium medications out of the reach of children!

Do use medications as directed.

Do monitor copper levels in treatment water every one or two days.

Do rinse any external filters with freshwater and change the media to prevent reinfection of a tank after treatment is complete.

Treatment Don'ts

Don't medicate unless necessary.

Don't continue to add copper without testing the current copper level.

Don't exceed 0.4 ppm copper. No more than 0.25 ppm copper for three weeks is all that should ever be necessary.

Don't use antibiotics in a tank with a biological filter.

Don't use an activated carbon filter with any type of medication unless the object is to quickly remove the medication from the water.

Don't use a UV filter with any type of medication.

Don't release live or dead fish in non-native waters!

Hermissenda, sea slug

Chapter 10

FOODS AND FEEDING
What, When, and How

Feeding marine fish properly is just as essential to their health and well being as providing a good physical and chemical environment. In nature, fish are adapted physiologically and ecologically to certain types of food organisms. These specific foods provide the nutritional requirements of the fish within the specialized "life style" of that species. The same variations in feeding habits found in land animals also exist among fish. Some species, such as the grizzly bear, feed on a wide variety of organisms, and others, like the Everglades kite that feeds only on the *Pomacea* (apple) snail, are very restricted in their diet. Whether broad or restricted, the natural diet provides the amount and balance of proteins, fats, carbohydrates, vitamins, and minerals that each species needs to maintain good health and reproductive capability.

Most marine aquarists do not structure the diet for their fish according to the exact composition, percentage, and origin of the proteins, fats, carbohydrates, and other dietary elements that their fish require. Actually this would be very difficult and very expensive since most marine aquarists are polyculturists, that is they culture or keep a variety of fish that have a variety of dietary requirements. To a monoculturist, on the other hand, this is a very important consideration. He may have 500,763 individuals, more or less, of a single species—catfish, pompano, angelfish, redfish, clownfish, or trout—in his tanks or ponds, and his children's inheritance on the line as well. In this case, it is very important to know exactly the dietary elements that will produce a healthy fish with the characteristics required by the market, and the fish farmer has access to specially formulated diets for each species based on extensive laboratory work and many rearing trials. Most marine aquarists, however, feed their fish commercially prepared diets or a fish food mix they prepare from what is available at the supermarket or seafood shop, and in almost every situation, these sources provide quite adequate nutrition for most marine aquarium fish. The aquarist does not have to know the scientific analysis of the foods fed to his or her fish to keep healthy fish, but one should be familiar with the basics of marine fish nutrition.

This chapter will not go deeply into the science of marine fish nutrition, but will acquaint the aquarist with the essential information. There is a vast scientific literature on the dietary requirements of freshwater and some marine fish, but this literature is almost entirely concerned with food fish species. The advanced or professional aquarist can get a good overview of the science of marine fish nutrition in Steve Spotte's 1992 book, *Captive Seawater Fishes*, which has a comprehensive chapter on marine fish nutrition.

Fish with broad, unspecialized dietary requirements usually adjust easily to the foods and conditions of captivity, while fish with highly specialized diets may have difficulty. However, just because a fish feeds on only one type of organism in nature doesn't necessarily mean that that particular food organism must be available in the aquarium. A fish may be limited by its adaptive behavior patterns to certain food organisms, but still be capable of digesting and utilizing other foods. In other words, a wrasse specially adapted to feeding on certain crustaceans found deep within branching corals can meet its nutritional needs with other crustaceans, such as shrimp, or prepared fish foods when these are made available in an artificial environment.

There are two problems that must be overcome in feeding captive marine fish. The first is to get the fish to accept a substitute for the natural diet, and the second is to provide all the nutritional requirements in the substitute food. Fish that consume a wide variety of foods in nature are usually most adaptable to aquarium fare. This doesn't mean that it is impossible to keep fish with very limited natural diets, such as some of the butterflyfish, but giving these fish an adequate diet requires more care and effort.

Natural Foods

For maximum success with your fish, it is best to select species that are generalized feeders (columns 7 and 10 in Table 7), and feed a good variety of foods. Table 7 is intended as a general guide to the natural food preferences of each major group of fishes. There are many exceptions to these groupings (for example, a few species of snapper are plankton pickers rather than generalized bottom feeders), however, the table will give you an idea of the content and structure of the natural diet of most fishes. Each of the 11 natural food groups from Table 7 is discussed below to provide basic information on natural diets. A possible substitute for each category of natural food is also discussed.

Column 1 — Algae and Seagrasses

The marine algae are generally broken up into two artificial groups, microalgae and macroalgae. The microalgae include all the small species that must be studied under a microscope. They include the one celled, free floating phytoplankton and the tiny filamentous and colonial growths that attach to solid substrate. The macroalgae, however, are large enough to be seen and examined without magnification and range from small thumbnail sized growths to kelp plants 40 feet or more in height. The seagrasses—turtle grass, eel grass, and a few others—are not algae but are true aquatic flowering plants. They often cover vast areas of shallow bottom around coral reefs. Fish, such as parrotfish and surgeonfish, that feed primarily on algae are true herbivores, the browsers and grazers of the sea bottom. These fish can get along for a while on standard aquarium fare, but nutritional deficiencies (sunken stomach, loss of color, inactivity) eventually develop. Marine algae are the best vegetable matter to add to the diet, but leafy vegetables such as spinach, lettuce, romaine lettuce, and even freshwater aquarium plants such as *Riccia fluitans* can be substituted.

Column 2 — Algae

There are many, many species of macroalgae that make up part of the diet of omnivorous fish. Some of these are ingested incidentally as the fish feeds on small crabs, shrimp, and mollusks, and others are deliberately eaten. These algae may make up 10 to 50 percent of the diet of many species, thus vegetable matter should be a basic part of their diet in captivity. Clownfish and batfish, and of course tangs and angelfish, are good examples of fish that normally include a high percentage of algae in their diet.

Column 3 — Algae and Detritus

Detritus is composed of a great variety of organic matter. Bits of algae, organic flocculents, solid wastes from fish and invertebrates, coral slime, bacterial debris, and small worms and crustaceans accumulate in sheltered nooks about the reef. This detritus and the tiny algae and invertebrates associated with it are a food source for many small fish. Some gobies, blennies, and damselfish are among those that utilize this resource. Detritus accumulates in all aquariums, especially in well lighted tanks, and serves, among other things, to supplement the diet of species that normally feed on it. These species do well on normal aquarium foods, but may require old, well established marine aquariums.

Fish Type	Algae and seagrasses 1	Algae 2	Algae and detritus 3	Sponges 4	Plankton pickers 5	Generalized bottom feeders 6	Fish feeders 7	Coral feeders 8	Crustacean feeders 9	Generalized invertebrates 10	Parasite pickers 11
Sharks						√					
Moray eels						√√	√				
Squirrelfishes									√		
Groupers						√					
Hamlets						√					
Grammas					√						
Hawkfish					√	√√					
Cardinalfishes					√	√					
Sweepers					√						
Snappers						√					
Grunts						√					
Porgies										√	
Sea Chubs	√										
Mojarras										√	
Reef drums									√√	√	
Goatfishes										√	
Damselfishes		√	√√		√√					√	
Clownfishes		√			√√					√	
Wrasses						√				√√	√
Parrotfishes	√√							√			
Flounders						√					
Gobies			√√							√	√
Blennies			√√							√	
Jawfishes					√						
Scorpionfishes						√	√√				
Spadefish	√	√	√			√√					
Batfish		√				√√					
Butterflyfishes		√						√√		√	
Angelfishes		√		√√							√
Pompano									√		
Tangs	√		√								
Triggerfishes	√					√				√√	
Filefishes	√							√		√	
Sea robins										√	
Trunkfishes		√		√						√√	
Boxfishes		√		√						√	
Puffers		√		√						√√	
Frogfishes							√				
Sea horses					√						
Pipefishes					√						
Dragonets			√							√	

TABLE 7 Principal food groups of the major types of fishes.

(Two checks indicate the strongest preference.)

Column 4 — Sponge

Sponges are about the simplest of the metazoans (many celled animals) and they exhibit many forms and colors. The typical bath sponge and vase sponge are only two of thousands of types of sponges. A number of species grow in the reef environment and provide homes for many species of small fish and invertebrates. Sponges are incidentally ingested in small volume by most herbivorous fishes as they graze algae, but only adult angelfish consume sponges as the major dietary component. In fact, sponges compose 70 to 97 percent of the adult diet of Atlantic angelfish. Juvenile angelfish feed on small crustaceans and filamentous algae. The diet of sponge feeders cannot be easily provided in captivity, but fortunately the juveniles do well on a varied diet laced with vegetable matter, and adults and sub-adults can get by on the same foods.

Column 5 — Plankton Pickers

Many small fish make all or part of their living by hovering in the water over the reef or burrow and feeding selectively on the planktonic organisms that continually wash over these areas with the currents. Zooplankters—primarily copepods, small shrimp, mysids, and many types of fish and invertebrate larvae—are the usual food items. The proteins of larval forms of fish, shrimp, crabs, etc. are essentially the same as the adults, so these items make good food sources for plankton picking fish. Plankton may form only a part of the diet of some fish, so it's important to also supply some plant food such as algae growths or leafy greens. Almost all larval fish feed on zooplankton, even if the adults are herbivores; so the planktonic pastures are really the foundation for all life in the sea. Plankton pickers in the aquarium do well on bits of shaved shrimp and fish, processed flake food, and other foods that drift about in the water before settling. Many plankton pickers will not take food items once they have landed on the bottom.

Column 6 — Generalized Bottom Feeders

This category is composed mostly of large, non-specific carnivores such as sharks, snappers, and groupers, and includes many groups with juveniles important to the marine aquarist. These fish are opportunistic feeders although they may have a general preference for a specific group of food organisms. In nature, they feed on whatever foods are most abundant and available—vast schools of small fish, shrimp, juvenile lobster, swarms of polychaete worms, almost anything and everything during the season of its abundance. The flexibility of their food requirements make these fish easy to feed in captivity, although some species may have other physiological requirements that make them difficult to keep. Again, a varied diet with emphasis on bits of fresh frozen shrimp, clams, fish, and other seafood will keep these fish healthy and happy until they outgrow the aquarium.

Column 7 — Fish Feeders

Very few marine fish suitable for small home aquariums are totally piscivorous, a fancy name for fish eaters. Some of the scorpionfishes—notably the lionfishes, and the anglerfishes, frog fish, and sargassum fish—come fairly close to being exclusively piscivorous. These fish can be trained to take other foods, but this requires time and patience. Slow moving piscivorous fish are usually so well camouflaged that they appear to be part of the reef. Small fish blunder near them, often attracted by fin modifications that look like small worms or algae growths, and are suddenly engulfed by the monstrous (to them) vacuum cleaner action of the scorpionfish's mouth. These fish are difficult to keep because of their preference for live food and their tendency to eat every other fish in the tank. They are best kept by themselves or with larger fish, and fed small freshwater fish. Guppies and bait minnows live quite long enough to get eaten when dropped into the lionfish's lair, and freshwater fish do not carry parasites that can survive in marine waters. It is possible to train frog fish and lionfish to take dead

minnows and even pieces of fish flesh by loosely attaching
the food to a string, stick, or wire to give it motion.

Column 8 — Coral Feeders

To feed on coral polyps (the soft animal hidden in the
stony coral skeleton), a fish must be able to either crush the
hard coral or reach a tiny mouth into small protected areas
to remove the animals therein. Both of these specialized
modes of feeding can cause problems for the marine aquarist. Unless care and attention is taken in developing a diet
for these fish, they will not be able to obtain proper nourishment. The tiny mouthed butterflyfish are the most difficult
of this category to feed. Bits of shrimp and scallop or live
Tubifex and white worms, *Enchytraeus albidus*, pressed into
coral or irregular rock surfaces often stimulate these fish to
begin feeding. This will also help the butterflyfish find food
in a competitive aquarium situation; however, be sure that
food presented in this manner does not go uneaten and foul
the aquarium.

Column 9 — Crustacean Feeders

These species feed primarily on small crustaceans, but
are not above picking up a worm or clam or two from time
to time. Small shrimps and crabs represent the major part of
their diet, so some crustacean flesh should be a staple part of
their diet in captivity. If fish in nature feed almost exclusively on one type of organism, it is important to include
that general type of food in their diet. Then you can be
reasonably sure that all their required nutritional elements
are available to them. Frozen shrimp or krill is perhaps the
easiest way to get crustacean material into your fish's diet.

Column 10 — Generalized Invertebrates

Many, if not most, small tropical marine fish feed on a
wide variety of small invertebrates with a little bit of algae
included upon occasion. Although one group of organ-

isms—shrimp, snails, clams, worms, crabs, etc.—may be most common in the diet of certain species, a broad variety of small invertebrates are represented. The organism of choice often changes as the fish gains in size and changes its habitat. Since the specific natural diets of most fish at different stages of development are relatively unknown, a variety of foods that includes some item from each basic group of invertebrates is most likely to provide all the basic nutritional needs.

Column 11 — Parasite Pickers

A few popular marine aquarium fishes make part of their living, either as adults or during the juvenile stage, by removing external parasites from large fish. It is not unusual for a diver to watch a huge green moray eel wait patiently with open mouth while a neon goby flits about its head and mouth picking up food debris and small parasites. Large grouper often lean to one side against a coral head and allow small angelfish and gobies to move over its body and gills picking off external parasites, and jacks turn dark and hang over coral heads with open mouths while gobies and wrasses flit over them picking off parasites. This cleaning behavior is quite fascinating and can readily be observed in a home aquarium if neon gobies are kept with larger fish. Cleaner wrasses and even small French angelfish also often display cleaning behavior in aquariums. Obviously, one would not want to provide parasites as a food source in the tank; fortunately, parasite pickers do very well on a varied basic diet when parasites are not available.

Available Aquarium Foods

There is a wide variety of foods available to marine aquarists, most at little cost, that will provide a good diet for almost all marine fish. Many of these foods are listed below, with comment, to help you develop the proper feeding program for your particular needs. There are three main categories listed: **Prepared Diets, Plant Foods, and Animal Foods.** The fish in a traditional community tank should receive two small feedings of a prepared diet each day and one feeding from each of the other two categories once a day, or at least every other day, to keep them in top condition. Most aquarists, however, cannot put this much effort into a feeding regimen for their tank. Even though three or four relatively small feedings of varied foods per day is best, most marine fish can get by nicely on two feedings per day. A good dry flake food feeding in the morning and a feeding of natural animal and plant foods in the evening will keep most fish in good condition. The following information may be more than you need or want to know about foods and feeding; and although you should be able to keep your marine fish healthy and happy with only a few of these options, it's good to know about a broad range of available foods and feeding techniques.

Prepared Diets

The prepared diet specially compounded for marine fish can be a great aid to the marine aquarist; however, total dependence on a prepared diet can cause nutritional problems. Convenience is the most obvious advantage of the prepared diet, but equally important are inclusion of protein variety plus a broad spectrum of trace nutrients including vitamins and minerals. Be careful of using diets compounded for freshwater fish, particularly trout and catfish, because these do not provide the proper nutritional balance for coral reef fishes. They can easily cause problems, such as fatty degeneration of the liver, if fed to excess. Prepared diets can be purchased already compounded, dry flake foods are the most popular form, or they can be made at home in a wide variety of mixtures. Four basic types of prepared diets are discussed below.

Dry flake foods

This is the most widely used, and abused, form of prepared diet. These are relatively inexpensive, considering the small amounts consumed by each fish and the convenience of feeding, and contain a wide variety of nutrients. The flake food you choose should be of high quality, 35 to 45 percent protein, and contain some plant material, hopefully including marine algae and carotene. The flakes should be large and crisp and not smell musty or moldy. Store the well sealed container in a dry, cool place, not next to a hot light

Figure 17 Commercial flake food for tropical fish can be ground into particles suitable for feeding to late larval and post larval marine fish. A mortar and pestle provides good control over the fineness of the grind.

fixture or near the spray of an air lift. Don't buy more than you can use in a month or two, and make sure that the dealer's stock is fresh. There are now a number of dry flake and pellet foods that are compounded just for marine fish. Even though flake food for freshwater fish may be less expensive, marine fish are better off when fed a dry food compounded especially for marine fish, especially if a dry processed food is the major portion of their diet.

Remember that flake food is very dry and compressed, thus contains a lot of food energy in a small space. It's easy to habitually overfeed the stuff. Just think what it would be like to eat all your meals as a dry, highly compressed flake with only a glass of water to wash it down (and saltwater at that!). Coral reef fish do not normally feed on the surface, and when they do take floating food, they may also ingest air bubbles which can cause excessive buoyancy and disturb the digestive process. If this is a problem, soaking the food in a small volume of water before feeding eliminates floating food and surface feeding. Small fish, such as young clownfish, may gorge on dry food and develop a case of the "bloats" as the food expands in their stomach. When this happens, the abdomen of the fish is greatly distended and the fish continually fights to keep from floating at the surface. The cure for this condition is to stop feeding for a day and then feed mostly a wet food mix with only an occasional light feeding of dry food. Don't depend entirely on a dry flake food—fish need fresh plant and animal foods on a regular basis also.

The seafood paste mix

There are many variations of a wet blended diet that you can mix up yourself, and if you have the time and interest, this is a good way to give your fish the best possible diet with the least amount of daily fuss. It will, however, take an hour or two to make up the food for one or two months of feeding—a relatively minor investment of time considering the aesthetic and monetary value of your marine display.

Figure 18 The general purpose shrimp base food mix. Upper left, leafy green *Ulva* algae—Upper right, the red algae *Hypnea*—Lower left, small peeled shrimp—Lower right, frozen cubes of the blended food mix.

Building your own diet for your fish also has the advantage of being able to adjust it for the type of fish you favor. Heavy on the greens for example, if you favor tangs and small angelfish.

The basic ingredient to this mix is fresh frozen shrimp, scallops, clams, fish, lobster (if price is no object) or other crustacean. Animals that break down to a paste-like consistency when blended, such as shrimp, are preferred over those that become watery, like oysters. Clean the meat of all shell, scales, or skin and blend it with a little water to a paste-like consistency. A blender or a food processor works well for this task. If possible, use two or three types of seafood (shrimp, clams, squid, and/or a non-oily fish) to provide a variety of nutrients. Other types of meat can also be added sparingly for additional variety. While this mixture is still in the blender (the average aquarist shouldn't need more than two or three cups of prepared diet at any one time), add about 20 percent by volume of vegetable material. Unless marine algae (*Caulerpa, Ulva, Hypnea,* etc.) are available, use a mixture of greens such as chopped spinach and lettuce. A spoonful or two of dry kelp powder can take the place of some vegetable matter.

Blend the mixture and add either a crushed tablet of a multivitamin mineral complex, or better yet, make up your own dry powder from vitamins A and E (dry powder from a capsule), vitamin C crystals, defatted liver powder (for B vitamins), and for minerals—kelp powder, bonemeal, and dolomite. The egg quality of spawning clownfish is often enhanced by addition of chitin. Make enough of the mixture to fill an ice cube tray, several cups, or as much as you will need for a month or two. The consistency can be controlled by adding water if it's too dense and dry flake food if it's too wet. The mixture is then frozen, either in ice cube trays or in spoonfuls on a wax paper tray. After the mixture is well frozen, the individual cubes can be stored in a plastic bag.

At feeding time, one of the cubes is removed and small pieces of the right size for your fish are snipped off and dropped into the aquarium. A fine stainless steel grater can also be used to provide the tiny pieces that are just right for juvenile fish and plankton pickers. If the mix is the right consistency, it will hold together until consumed by the fish. It isn't good to just toss a chunk into the aquarium and forget it, for it can dissolve into the water if uneaten and add too much too quickly to the organic load of the aquarium. Those with many tanks may wish to use the gelatin mix.

[There are now a number of frozen food formulas commercially available to the marine aquarist. These are considerably more expensive than mixing and freezing your own, but do offer certain advantages. Not the least of these is the convenience of not having to mix up your own formula. There is also the advantage of inclusion of marine animals and algae that the average marine aquarist can't collect on an afternoon's excursion, and having these varied ingredients in the proper balance. Some of these mixes also provide vitamin C in a stabilized form that keeps it available to the fish despite months of frozen storage. Thus, commercially available frozen food mixes offer a lot to marine aquarists, but as with all products, read the label. Also look at the condition of the package. Has it been in the store freezer since the first issue of TFH? Has it been thawed and refrozen a time or two? If it is not a fresh product in good condition, then you're better off making it up yourself, or finding it fresh and good someplace else.]

The gelatin mix

This diet is similar to the seafood paste mix, but is a little more versatile and a little more fuss to make. The ingredients can be quite varied because the whole thing is held together with gelatin instead of the protein paste of the fish or shrimp. The basic ingredients for the seafood mix can be used as the base for the gelatin mix. Many other ingredients such as trout pellets, kelp bits or powder, and algae can be included either ground or whole. Use up to 10 or 15 percent by weight of unflavored animal gelatin and about 50 percent water to make the basic mix. Add a little less water if the basic ingredients are wet. It will probably take a few attempts before you settle on the best formula for your fish, so don't be afraid to experiment if you decide to use the gelatin mix. Dissolve the gelatin in the water at a temperature of 150 to 200°F. Add the melted gelatin to the other ingredients when the temperature falls below 150°F and stir until the mixture is smooth. Now add the vitamin and mineral supplements and, if you wish, a little green or red food coloring. The coloring aids the fish in seeing the food and helps the aquarist to find uneaten food so it can be removed before it decomposes. Pour the completed mix into a tray and chill until set. The mix can then be cut up into cubes and stored in a closed container in the refrigerator or freezer. Bite sized pieces should be cut or grated from the cube at feeding time.

The plaster mix

This mix has certain advantages, but may not be worth the bother of preparation to the average aquarist. "Plaster mix" you may be thinking, "has this guy developed a crack in his think tank? " But no, there is a good basis for a plaster mix. Most of the herbivorous fishes and some coral and sponge eaters spend a great deal of time biting and scraping at the reef to consume the proper amount of coral polyps and algae. Life is much easier in the aquarium, and even if the fish get along on the change of diet, they miss the extensive feeding activity. In fact, in the absence of browsing activity, the dentition of some fish may grow long enough to cause feeding difficulties.

The plaster mix allows these fish to feed under simulated natural conditions and gives them the exercise they need. The basis of the plaster mix is simple, just prepare a small amount of a pure plaster of paris according to directions. Trace nutrients can be added while the mixture is still fluid as can food coloring if desired. Wet ingredients added to the plaster mix often interfere with hardening so the addition of the solid food ingredients must be carefully timed so that they can be folded in just before the plaster hardens. Adding them too soon may affect the hardening of the mix and adding them too late causes a rough, unblended mass. Chopped shrimp and fish, dry trout pellets, dry flake food with algae flakes, chopped spinach, and kelp or marine algae are good inclusions. Make sure all excess water is removed from the ingredients before folding them into the hardening plaster. The food ingredients should only make up 10 to 15 percent of the total volume of the mix.

Store unused mix in the refrigerator or freezer. Even though the food items are encased in plaster, they will still spoil readily, so the uneaten food mix should be removed from the aquarium after four or five hours. This diet is most used by public aquariums that keep large fish, but may be useful to the advanced aquarist who keeps surgeonfishes and parrotfishes, although the average aquarist looking for a simulated natural feeding approach may also wish to experiment with the plaster mix diet. There are plaster feeding blocks commercially available as time delay feeders for freshwater fish. A marine aquarist with a parrot fish or two may want to experiment with something like this before expending the time and effort to create a mini plaster mix.

Animal Foods: Live

Most coral reef fish consume animal food as a major portion of their diet, thus animal foods are most important to the marine aquarist. Fish, like most other wild animals, consume the entire live prey organism when feeding. This gives them access to minerals in hard parts and shells, plus vitamins from internal organs, and proteins and food energy in the flesh and fat. Obviously, a variety of live food organisms is the best possible diet for most fish, and equally obvious, only a most unusual marine aquarist can supply their fish with an exclusive diet of varied live foods. However, there are a number of live foods that can be provided.

Brine shrimp

Brine shrimp are the most common live food marine aquarists offer their fish. They are generally available in small portions as live adults or as dry eggs (cysts) that the aquarist hatches as necessary. Opinions on the value of live, adult brine shrimp differ greatly among marine aquarists. Although live, clean, and well fed adult brine shrimp are generally conceded to be an attractive and nutritious food (but not as an only food) for most marine tropicals, some aquarists fear introduction of bacteria and parasites from unclean cultures of brine shrimp. Adult brine shrimp can also be obtained in frozen and freeze dried forms. Frozen brine shrimp can lose much of their nutritive value (58%

Figure 19 Brine shrimp eggs (cysts). The dried eggs of brine shrimp can be purchased in large cans or in small vials. Once the container is opened, it should be tightly sealed and stored in the refrigerator. It is wise to purchase no more than you can use up in a few months.

protein) if they are not handled properly. Thawing and refreezing, or slow initial freezing, causes ice crystals to form in the tissues. Ice crystals rupture cells and internal organs and cause most of the fluids to leave the shrimp as it is thawed before feeding. Thus the nutritional value of thawed and refrozen brine shrimp is limited to the protein in the exoskeleton.

Adding frozen brine shrimp directly to the tank as a small block and allowing the fish to snap them up as they drift off the block provides the most complete frozen shrimp possible for the fish. However, it also allows all juices and materials frozen in the shrimp block to escape into the tank. Thawing the block in water and straining the shrimp from the accompanying liquid eliminates adding unnecessary organics to the tank, but it may also eliminate much of the food value of the brine shrimp. If the brine shrimp were quick frozen live in clean water, it's best to just drop a small block in the tank and let the fish go to it. However, if the shrimp were frozen after they were dead for awhile, or frozen too slowly, or thawed and refrozen one or more times—it's probably best not to feed them to the fish at all. Thaw a small part of the block in a clear glass and observe the result. If the water turns brown and the shrimp are nothing more than empty shells, it's a good bet the fish will gain little from eating them. Freeze dried brine shrimp have a strong tendency to float since they have no water at all in their tissues. It is best to soak these shrimp in freshwater so that they sink and drift in the currents when introduced into the aquarium.

Ingestion of a large amount of dry food can cause difficulties for marine fish. Newly hatched baby brine shrimp (nauplii) can be very valuable to the marine aquarist. They are easy to hatch, and can be used to feed small plankton feeding fish such as damselfish and jawfish, many filter feeding invertebrates, and young fish of many species. Brine shrimp are very small when they hatch, not much bigger than a comma on a printed page, but even so, you may be amazed at the large size of many fish that eagerly eat them.

Hatching is quite simple. All that is necessary is a gallon jar of full salinity seawater or artificial salt mix (even a straight rock salt mix will do) and an air stone for aeration. Bubble the saltwater and brine shrimp egg mixture vigorously so that the eggs do not accumulate at the surface. The jar should be filled about ¾ full to reduce spray from the bottle. A cap with a hole for the air tubing, or a plug of cotton also reduces spray from the hatching jar. A jug with a narrow neck is good, but it can't be cleaned as easily as a wide mouth jar. One or two teaspoons of eggs should provide plenty of hatchlings for most aquarists. The eggs hatch within 24 hours at temperatures of about 80°F. At temperatures in the low 70's, hatching may take up to 48 hours. Time of hatching and yield of brine shrimp depends greatly on

Figure 20 Two inexpensive, effective brine shrimp hatcheries. The average aquarist and small breeder will seldom need more of a hatchery than a couple of gallon jugs and an air supply. The floss plug in the top of the jug allows air to escape but keeps eggs and spray inside. A larger hatching jar can be made by cutting the bottom off a five gallon plastic water jug and supporting it in a wooden frame or even in a large bucket. Although an inverted cone or pyramid shape makes a more efficient hatchery, the above devices will work well for the home aquarist.

egg quality and the set up of the hatching jar. Keep temperatures above 75°F and allow light, preferably sunlight, to reach the hatching jar.

For about eight hours after hatching, baby brine shrimp sink to the bottom and empty egg shells float at the surface when aeration is removed. A very clean separation can be obtained from good quality eggs at this time. It is an easy matter to insert a small siphon into the jar and draw off the hatchlings from the bottom of the jar. Be sure to wait 15 or 20 minutes to let the shells and the hatchlings separate and break the siphon before the floating egg shells reach the bottom of the jar. Newly hatched brine shrimp are strongly attracted to light and can be concentrated at one spot by a narrow beam of light.

If the hatch goes too long before separation (two or three days), the hatchlings remain mixed with the egg shells at the surface, and separation is difficult. If this occurs, the best method of separation is to use light to concentrate the hatchlings away from the empty shells. An elaborate separation box can be constructed that allows the new hatch to swim from a dark compartment to a lighted compartment under a partial partition that prevents the floating eggs from leaving the darkened compartment. A simpler procedure, but less effective, is to shield the hatching jar with a piece of black paper that has a hole about an inch in diameter. Position the hole a few inches above the bottom of the jar and shine a light on the hole. The light will draw the baby brine shrimp from the surface and cluster them about the light. They can be easily siphoned from the jar after they have had time to gather about the lighted area.

A fine mesh net can be used to separate the hatchlings from the culture water and concentrate them in a small volume for feeding to the fish or invertebrates. Baby brine shrimp have a dense oily yolk sac that gives them an orange or yellow color. It is possible to overfeed young fish on new hatched brine shrimp and cause fatty degeneration of the liver. Thus, feed baby shrimp carefully to young fish and be sure that they do not over feed on this very attractive food. Post larval clownfish about 12 to 20 days old, incidently, can overfeed on baby brine shrimp to the point that their abdomens are so distended they look like they are about to burst. When so overfed, the young clownfish may drift to the bottom and die.

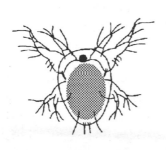

Newly hatched brine shrimp nauplii, 350 to 400 microns in length.

Brine shrimp eggs are properly termed cysts, and they have gone through the early stages of development while still attached to the mother. These cysts (eggs) then drop off the female and drift to the shore of the brine shrimp ponds where, in most species, they must undergo a dry period before complete development and hatching can occur. It is after they are deposited in wind rows along the shore that they are collected, processed, and packaged. The dry eggs are separated from debris and bad eggs by first sieving the shoreside debris to concentrate and recover all the eggs, and then air blowing the eggs in a chimney to blow out all the lighter, unhatchable eggs. The heavier, good eggs can be kept viable for many years when sealed in a vacuum pack.

Brine shrimp eggs can also be put through a process that "decapsulates" the eggs. This process removes the hard, indigestible coating on the eggs and leaves only a soft membrane around the yellow-orange yolk. The eggs go from dark brown, to white, and then to orange during this process. The decapsulated eggs are stored in brine under refrigeration, and are able to complete development and hatch just as untreated eggs. Larval fish are able to eat and digest even the unhatched decapsulated eggs and do not suffer intestinal blockage and death from eating unhatched eggs. Decapsulation is a dangerous process and should not be attempted unless one has some experience in working with dangerous chemicals. The decapsulation process is described in the *Marine Aquarium Reference*.

Live fish

A number of popular marine aquarium fish—lion fish, panther fish, groupers and small snappers, sargassumfish and angler fish—either require or enjoy small live fish in their diet. It is best to feed small freshwater fish because they are less expensive than marine fish, and most important, do not carry marine diseases and parasites. Goldfish, guppies and mollies serve this purpose well, and stay alive long enough in the marine tank to entice the predator to strike.

Some aquarists who keep piscivorous fishes maintain breeding colonies of guppies or mollies as fodder fish for their marine predators. If you do feed small fish from a marine or brackish water source, be sure to give them a two minute freshwater bath before feeding, to remove external parasites.

Small shrimp and other crustaceans

An occasional feeding of live food is one of the best things you can do for the diet of your marine fish. Small live crustaceans are not too difficult to find if you are willing to spend a little time and effort. A fine mesh dip net or seine worked in grass beds in fresh or marine areas will often provide a surprising number of small shrimp, amphipods, crabs, worms, etc., and most of these are excellent live food organisms for your marines. Give the marine organisms a quick dip in freshwater to reduce the possibilities of parasite introduction. The freshwater dip (saltwater dip for freshwater organisms) is a good way to either kill or incapacitate the organisms so that the fish can snap them up before they find shelter in the bottom of the tank. You may be surprised at how much small crustacean life already exists in your marine tank. Fish usually feed only in the daytime, and many small crustaceans are active only at night. Old well established tanks often develop a population of amphipods and copepods that can only be observed crawling about algae covered rocks and tank walls several hours after dark. Examination of the tank by flashlight at some time well into the night may reveal aspects of your aquarium you never knew existed.

Rose coral

Rose coral is a solitary coral found near coral reefs in tropical seas. The common species in Florida waters is *Manicina areolata*. Because it is a solitary coral, rose coral is easily collected, handled, and shipped and most coral polyp eating fish enjoy an occasional treat of fresh coral. Coral does not live long in captivity under the normal aquarium conditions, so be sure it is alive and in good condition before purchase. The flesh embedded in the coral skeleton should be firm and brown or greenish in color. It should not smell putrid or of decomposition when removed from the water and held to the nose. This coral can be frozen and kept fresh for long periods, however it will quickly decompose when fed after being frozen, so do not add more than the fish will eat within a few hours if the coral is not alive.

[Live rose coral can no longer be collected in the Florida Keys, so it is no longer readily available as a specialty food organism for keepers of butterfly and other fish. A shrimp paste or *Tubifex* worms pressed into the matrix of dead and artificial coral (as mentioned below) may be the best presentation for finicky butterflyfish and other coral pickers.]

Tubifex Worms

Tubifex worms have always been popular with freshwater aquarists, but they also have an application in marine aquariums as well. One very useful method of feeding *Tubifex* worms is to press a small ball of worms deeply into a coral skeleton and then place it in the tank. Hard to feed fish such as butterfly fish are often attracted by the movement of the worms and begin to feed actively. Use caution when feeding *Tubifex* worms. They can quickly foul a tank if overfed to marine fish. Be sure to wash the ball of worms very well before feeding and remove all dead worms and decaying organic matter. *Tubifex* worms, like the organisms mentioned below, should not be a major portion of the diet.

Other Possibilities

Some marine aquarists with a background in freshwater fish keeping may wish to experiment with other typical live freshwater fish foods such as whiteworms (*Enchytraeus albidus*), earthworms, and fruit fly larvae. These are good occasional foods and may have some special uses for certain fish, but remember that the proteins and fats are not those that marine fish digestive systems have evolved to handle. A diet rich in these foods will probably cause liver problems for marine fish. Make sure that these foods are cleaned before introducing them to the tank. Wash worms and fly larvae carefully and try to remove all dead organisms before feeding the live ones. Earthworms are a good food, but the intestines carry much soil (the earthworm's natural food) and this soil should be removed before the worm is cut up and fed. Strip the soil from the worm by squeezing the worm between the thumb and index finger and pull the worm between the fingers to eject the contents of the digestive tract.

Animal Foods: Dead

Most marine aquarists cannot feed live foods to their fish on a regular basis, and fortunately, most fish do well on foods that can be stored in the freezer or on the shelf.

Shrimp

Shrimp is one of the best basic foods for marine fish. Crustaceans of one type or another are a major part of the diet of many marine fish, and shrimp, being a common marine crustacean, is a good substitute for the natural diet. Shrimp can be obtained in frozen packages designed as tropical fish food, or as shrimp from the market in either fresh or frozen form, which is also excellent for marine fish.

There are numerous methods for feeding shrimp to marine fish. In almost all instances the shrimp should be peeled and washed to remove the hard exoskeleton and excess fluids. Perhaps the easiest method of handling this basic food is to freeze the washed shrimp into a fist sized ball and keep it in a plastic bag in the freezer. Select a metal grater that shaves particles of the proper size for the fish to consume in one bite. More than one size grater can be used if small and large fish are kept together. The proper portion can be grated from the ball at each feeding time. Thus one preparation of shrimp can last for several weeks, and feeding is quick and simple. It is also possible to grate the entire portion of frozen, peeled shrimp at one time either with the grater wheel of a food processor or with a bit of elbow grease on a manual model. The shrimp bits can then be frozen in portions packed for each feeding, and then feeding for the next few weeks consists only of dropping the pre-measured frozen cubes of shrimp bits into the tank.

Mollusks

After crustaceans, mollusks are one of the most common food items in marine fish diets. Scallops, squid, clams, oysters, and conch are the most commonly encountered mollusks in food, bait, and fish food products. All of the above can be utilized by marine aquarists in the same manner as shrimp. Most mollusks are not as "gelatinous" as shrimp, and although they are readily grated into small pieces when frozen, the pasty, binding quality of shrimp is absent. Alternate one or more of the mollusks with shrimp or mix them together to provide a good mix of marine animal protein.

Processed plankton

Marine plankton is now available as frozen, dried, and freeze dried products. This plankton comes from the nutrient rich cold waters of the Arctic and sub-Arctic regions of the Atlantic and Pacific oceans. It is composed primarily of small euphasid shrimp and/or calanoid copepods and is rich in protein (60 to 70 percent), wax esters, and lipids. Cold water, northern plankton is not a natural food of marine tropicals. However, it is a good, but rich, fish food, and one should be careful not to overfeed, especially with the dry form of the product. This cold water plankton is rich in pigments and lipids and feeding it should enhance the condition and color of your marine fish.

Fish

Ocean fish is another good source of animal protein for your marines. Most small reef fish do not commonly eat fish, as they are not equipped to chase and capture them. However, when an injured or dead fish presents the opportunity, most are quick to partake of their hapless comrade. Boneless fish flesh can be prepared and fed like peeled shrimp. Be careful not to overfeed, because fish seems to have a greater tendency to foul the aquarium water than shrimp or scallop. All fish products, like all marine animal foods, should be hard frozen before feeding, to reduce the possibility of parasite introduction. Fish roe and fish liver are also excellent foods for marines. These foods are best fed by snipping small pieces off a frozen block and feeding them slowly. Fish roe has much oil and shouldn't be fed to excess, but a little bit now and then will provide many of the nutrients and important pigments that may be missing or altered in other foods. Watch the color of your fish improve after feeding fish roe once or twice a week.

Other meats

Lean beef, beef liver, and beef heart are often recommended for feeding to marine and freshwater fish. An occasional feeding of these products is helpful if seafoods just aren't available and the only alternative is a constant dry food diet. If you must feed meat of land animals, rabbit and chicken may be better because there is less fat in their flesh. Defatted beef liver powder is a good source of B vitamins and can be added to the paste mix and does not add much fat to the diet. Remember that fish are cold blooded (poikilothermic) and all digestion reactions take place at 70 to 80 °F, the temperature of the aquarium water. Thus, they may not be able to efficiently digest or use the types of fats present in the flesh of warm blooded animals. They are much better off with the flesh of animals that are similar to their normal prey.

Plant Foods

As mentioned previously, vegetable matter is an important part of the diet of most marine fish. Tropical marine algae, since they are the natural plant foods, are much desired for inclusion in the diet. Broad, thin, green algae such as *Caulerpa* and *Ulva*, and meaty reds and browns such as *Hypnea*, *Gelidium*, and *Dictyota* are commonly found in stomach contents analyses, and are best for feeding. These algae can be added to prepared diets or washed with freshwater and placed in the aquarium as browse for the fish.

Unfortunately, most marine aquarists do not have ready access to tropical marine algae, and one must also be able to identify the desirable types among hundreds of species of unsuitable calcareous and filamentous species. Substitutes for tropical marine algae are available, however. Pacific kelp and other algae are used as a human food supplement and are available in health food, oriental food stores, and grocery stores, usually in dried form. Greens can be supplied by inclusion of chopped spinach and/or turnip greens and an occasional leaf of lettuce. These can be included in the prepared diet or fed as browse in the aquarium. Be sure to remove uneaten greens after a day or two to prevent them from rotting in the tank.

Feeding Invertebrates

Most active invertebrates such as shrimp, octopus, lobsters, and crabs, prefer a chunk of solid food that they can hold and tear apart with their mouth parts. These animals often feed at night and are adept at finding small food particles that the fish may have lost during the day. A few small pieces of frozen shrimp or fish dropped into the tank after lights out, will usually keep these animals well fed since they don't have to compete with the fish after dark.

Good algal growth in the tank keeps most of the slow moving grazers like nudibranchs and sea urchins quite happy. If you live near the sea, a rock heavy with marine growth provides much food for invertebrates and some fish. However, beware of parasite introduction. Unless the "live rock" is put through a quarantine, it may be best to restrict it to an "invertebrate only" tank. Many of the invertebrates now kept are basically plankton feeders such as tube worms, some anemones, corals, and bivalve mollusks. They all have some sort of feeding mechanism that catches or filters out the tiny planktonic organisms that normally surround them. There are two ways to feed these animals with live organisms: introducing the food organisms to the tank or removing the invertebrate from the display tank to place it in a feeding tank. Newly hatched baby brine shrimp are a very good food because they are nutritious, do not foul the aquarium, are easy to produce, and are readily taken by filter feeders. Wild caught live ocean plankton is also very good, but besides being difficult to get, it may also introduce disease organisms.

A baster is a handy tool at feeding time. Concentrate the brine shrimp in a cupful or two of saltwater and use the baster to direct a stream of brine shrimp nauplii into the vicinity of the filter feeding invertebrates. Some animals such as small anemones that are attached to a moveable rock, feather duster worms, small basket stars, some soft corals, and barnacles can be removed from the aquarium and placed in a bucket or small tank with a high concentration of new hatch brine shrimp and good aeration. After several hours they will be well fed, and can be replaced in the display tank.

Caulerpa prolifera

Anemones

Anemones are beautiful animals, but difficult to keep. They require the highest quality water and intense, full spectrum lighting to keep them in good condition. Anemones of the genera *Stoichactis* and *Radianthus*, the typical clownfish anemones, trap and feed on larger invertebrates and fishes as well as planktonic creatures in nature, thus they relish a piece of shrimp or fish once or twice a week. If a clownfish is kept with the anemone, it can often be persuaded to feed its companion by giving the clownfish a morsel of food too big for the fish to swallow. The clown usually carries the food to the anemone and obligingly thrusts it deeply into the tentacles. Fine tentacled anemones also take small planktonic food, so it is good to give them an occasional feeding of live baby brine shrimp. Anemones, like their cousins the corals, also obtain nourishment a third way. Their tissues contain living algal cells called *Zooxanthellae;* and in exchange for a protected place to live, these algal cells produce food through photosynthesis in excess of their needs and supply the anemone with this additional food energy.

Lighting must be intense and close to full spectrum to provide the algal cells buried in the anemone's tissues with enough light for photosynthesis. This is why anemones in captivity so often fade to whiteness and gradually wither away to nothing and die. Once the anemone has turned completely white or cream colored, all the algal cells are gone and the anemone is on a downhill ride that is almost impossible to reverse. It may live another six months or so, but will lose condition, get very much smaller, and eventually die. The only remedy is to insure adequate light while the anemone is still in good condition. A few hours of sunlight every day is very helpful and should be arranged if at all possible. An incandescent bulb, 60 watts or better, can be put in a reflector and placed outside the tank very near the anemone to supplement the normal tank lighting, which should be 40 to 80 watts of full spectrum florescent lighting. The incandescent bulb will provide the right spectrum and increase the total light the anemone receives, but it will also increase the temperature of the aquarium, and this effect must be carefully controlled. The incandescent light can be put on a timer to cycle the light for an exposure time that will not greatly increase the tank temperature.

[The reef tank aquarist now well understands the importance of light to anemones and corals, and provides the marine reef aquarium with the intensity and spectrum of light required to maintain anemones and corals in good heath. In fact reproduction of anemones by splitting and/or egg production is occurring more and more often in hobbyist's tanks. If one wishes to keep anemones, it is really essential to use modern lighting equipment over the tank, for otherwise, the anemone is doomed to a short life, wasting away for lack of light.]

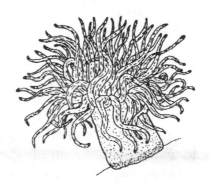

Summary

A marine aquarist can now buy a good quality marine flake food, a good formula frozen food, a marine pellet food for bottom feeders, and some romaine lettuce or spinach leaves for fish with herbivorous leanings—and this will keep most marine fish and invertebrates reasonably happy. Things won't be as good as they could be, but as long as feeding is fairly regular, not too much at one time, and includes as much variety as possible, the tank's inhabitants will be reasonably "happy" and will not resort to buying groceries on the black market from the dog and the canary.

An aquarist can also grow or buy marine macroalgae, (*Caulerpa* and *Ulva* sp.) for herbivorous fish, make up a shrimp based food mix with vitamins B and C every month, add a little iodine and minerals to the food mix (from the health food store), and feed live brine shrimp grown out in a green microalgae culture every two or three days, and really have happy fish.

I have tried to avoid getting too academic in this chapter and discussing such things as the various amino acid building blocks of proteins, and which of these are essential (meaning the fish can't make them themselves) and which aren't (meaning the fish can make them from other amino acids), and, of course, talking about ash residue, and proximate analysis of various food organisms, and undigestible fiber, and the essential ω3 series of fatty acids required by all fish, and the fatty acids not required and not needed by marine fish, and protein quality, and many, many more topics of essential interest to marine fish culturists and nutritionists—simply because the average marine aquarist doesn't use this kind of information, at least not directly. I have tried to talk about things that will help a marine aquarist to understand and supply the basic nutritional needs of marine tropical fish. So it seems fitting that I close this chapter with a list of comments and ideas on foods and feeding, most just common sense, that will help a marine aquarist directly satisfy the nutritional needs of his or her finny aquatic friends. Note that in my other book, *The Marine Aquarium Reference: Systems and Invertebrates*, there is an extensive chapter on food and feeding of marine invertebrates.

1. Strive for variety in foodstuffs. Avoid feeding one food item exclusively over a long period of time. Don't use rancid fats or oils, don't feed seafood items that don't smell good.

2. Avoid too much fats, most marine tropical fish should have 10% or less fat in their diet.

3. Avoid foods compounded for freshwater and cold water fish, especially trout and salmon—too much fat.

4. Avoid large amounts of carbohydrates for carnivorous and omnivorous fish. Carbohydrates should be less then 5% of the diet for most marine tropical fish. Most marine fish also do not need much fiber. Usually about 5% or even less, is apparently enough for most marine fish.

5. Feed high protein foods. The diet of most marine tropical fish should be 40 to 60% protein. Feed protein from various marine animal sources to include all the various essential amino acids for all the different species that are in the tank. (Yeah, I know, 10% fat, 5% carbohydrate, 5% fiber, and 60% protein is only 80%. Don't worry about the other 20% of the diet, the fish will take care of that themselves. These are only rough guidelines, but they should give you some idea of the direction to go in providing food for marine tropical fish.)

6. Supplement the water soluble vitamins C and the B group, especially C. The oil soluble vitamins A, D, E and K are less important to supplement if a good variety of fresh food are fed. A little brewers yeast in the food mix is a good source of B vitamins.

7. Iodine is often lacking in the diet of marine tropical fish and a constant lack of iodine can cause goiter. Supplement iodine if fresh foods are rarely fed.

8. Fish color, especially yellow, orange, and red, is greatly enhanced by the addition of certain pigments to the diet. The most effective pigments are the carotenoids canthaxanthin and astaxanthin. Beta carotene is probably the only carotenoid most aquarists can find, and it is slightly better than none, but fish generally cannot use beta carotene effectively. Astaxanthin on the other hand, with the proper lighting, will brighten up yellow, red, and orange fish remarkably. Look for foods that list canthaxanthin and astaxanthin in the ingredients. Note that some foods designed to enhance color in freshwater fish contain the male hormone testosterone. This is ineffective in enhancing the colors of marine fish that are not breeding colors. A good dose of testosterone, however, will quickly take the wind out of the sails of a breeding female of any fish species.

9. Breeding fish require great attention to diet. Find and supply the natural diet for the species that is to be bred, or a good natural (fresh or frozen) substitute.

10. Raw foods of marine origin provide the best mix of essential nutrients, but also carry the greatest risk of disease and parasite introduction. Feed raw marine foods, but be very careful, and select foods only from fresh and healthy sources. Freezing better preserves the nutrition of marine foods than cooking, but it is not as sure a control of disease contamination as is cooking.

11. Use a turkey baster to squirt small particulate foods or small live foods directly at specific invertebrates or in the vicinity of small fish.

Chapter 11

BREEDING MARINE FISH
The Basic Process

[After reading this chapter over and making a few corrections and additions, I think it is still a good guide for a marine aquarist interested in breeding clownfish. Many hobbyists have successfully spawned and raised clownfish and neon gobies over the last 10 years. I know of about a dozen personally, and some of these aquarists have even been, and are, successful to the point of selling a fair number of young clownfish to shops and wholesalers, and they have said that this chapter was very helpful. So it is possible, now in the 90's, for an aquarist to breed marine fish, but it is not easy, and it requires a lot of experience and dedication. A couple of mandarinfish, *Synchiropus splendidus*, have been reared by a young enterprising marine aquarist, Julian Sprung; and Sea Scope, Volume 7, 1990, reprinted an article by a Dutch aquarist, Herman Wassink, describing the breeding and rearing of the marine comet, *Calloplesiops altivelis*. The popular pygmy angelfish, *Centropyge* sp., has been spawned many times by many aquarists, but rearing these species through the larval stage has not yet happened. The mandarinfish and the pygmy angels reproduce with pelagic eggs and have very small larvae that do not, or with difficulty, begin feeding on rotifers, the standard first food

Figure 21 The "Hijack". A unique fish made possible only by controlled marine fish culture. The mother was a high-hat, *Equetus acuminatus*, and the father was a jackknife fish, *Equetus lanceolatus.* This manmade hybrid does not exist in nature.

of most marine fish larvae. Julian used marine infusoria and copepod nauplii to bring through the mandrinfish. Thus, the door is not shut for marine aquarists to be successful with species other than clownfish and gobies. Sometimes the most important thing is simply for people to be aware that it is possible to do what seemingly can't be done. And when marine aquarists reálly begin to work with the amazing array of marine invertebrates that it is now possible to keep successfully in reef tanks (as discussed at the end of this chapter), the next 10 years should be exciting indeed.]

Not very long ago, as late as the early 70's, it was possible to find authoritative quotes in the aquarium literature stating that marine tropical fish could not be successfully reared in commercial numbers because the particular conditions required by the delicate larvae could not be consistently maintained. This was certainly true up to the late 60's, but at that time increased interest and experimentation in propagation of marine food fish stimulated development of new techniques that could be transferred, with some modifications, to the culture of some marine tropical fish. Propagation of pompano, the gourmet fish of our subtropical waters, was the subject of intense and highly competitive effort by several commercial firms and government laboratories. These efforts, some biologically successful and some not, have all been dropped or redirected due to financial, economic, and technical difficulties. Some individuals involved in these projects, however, have shifted their knowledge and talents to propagation of marine tropicals. Although developing slowly, farming of marine tropical fish has a strong toehold and should continue to expand.

It was soon apparent that the most immediate financial rewards lay not with food fish culture, although the market was vast (as was the capital requirement), but in propagation of marine tropical fish. For even though the market was far smaller than for food fish, the price per unit was far higher. Thus, in late 1972 and early 1973 I began to work at home in my garage on the problems of rearing marine tropical fish, and succeeded in early 1973 in rearing thousands of juvenile "percula" or common clownfish, *Amphiprion ocellaris*, from two spawning pairs. The early part of this work was reported in the March-April 1973 issue of *Salt Water Aquarium Magazine*, Vol. 9, No. 2, published by the late Robert P.L. Straughan. Mr. Straughan contributed greatly to the development of the marine aquarium hobby and was always optimistic about the possibilities of rearing marine tropicals in large numbers. It seemed appropriate that the first account of rearing large numbers of a marine tropical fish should appear in his publication. Since that time there has been much activity and many published articles dealing with marine tropical fish propagation; and many species have been reared through the larval stage, although only a

few in commercial numbers. Aqualife Research first mar-
keted tank reared clownfish and neon gobies in 1973, and
since then, several other companies have begun rearing
clownfish. Thus, because of the increased activity, there
should be a good selection of tank reared marine tropicals
on the market in future years. The basic technology is here,
but in most instances, additional time and effort is required
to bring these species into commercial production. [This
statement is just as true in 1992 as it was in 1982. The only
difference is that, with the opportunities that lie in the culture of live rock and invertebrates as well as fish, there is
even more potential today than there was 10 years ago.
Biology, technology, economics, and dedication, however,
must still come together to make it happen.]

The species of marine tropical fish that have been
spawned and reared to the juvenile stage include, but are
not restricted to, the listing in Table 8.

There are reports of other species being reared, and I
have probably missed a few, but these are the marine "tropicals" that I am sure have been reared into the juvenile stage.
There are many other species that have been spawned and
reared for only a few days into the larval stage, and many
others that have been reared from wild spawned eggs taken
in plankton tows. Also some food and bait species of tropical and subtropical waters not mentioned here have also
been reared very successfully. Thus, the basic technology
exists to rear many important marine aquarium fishes, and
tank reared fish should become a significant part of the
future of the marine aquarium hobby.

[A few additional species have been added to Table 8,
but there have not been many new species of marine tropical aquarium fish spawned and reared over the last 10 years,
and the few new species of marine tropical fish have not
been reared in large numbers. Most of the new species of
marine fish that have been reared are food and sport fish
such as some of the snappers, redfish, seatrout, snook, and a

Common name	Scientific name
Skunk clownfish	*Amphiprion akallopisos*
Orange-fin clownfish	*A. chrysopterus*
Clarkii clownfish	*A. clarkii*
Red saddle clownfish	*A. ephippium*
Tomato clownfish	*A. frenatus*
Cinnamon clownfish	*A. melanopus*
Percula (common) clownfish	*A. ocellaris*
Percula clownfish	*A. percula*
Pink skunk clownfish	*A. perideraion*
Saddleback clownfish	*A. polymnus*
Australian clownfish	*A. rubrocinctus*
Orange skunk clownfish	*A. sandaracinos*
Three-band clownfish	*A. tricinctus*
Maroon clownfish	*Premnas biaculeatus*
Royal gramma	*Gramma loreto*
Hamlet	*Hypoplectrus unicolor*
Comet (Marine betta)	*Calloplesiops altivelis*
Cardinalfish	*Apogon sp.*
Florida pompano	*Trachinotus carolinus*
Grey snapper	*Lutjanus griseus*
Yellowtail snapper	*Ocyurus chrysurus*
Porkfish	*Anisotremus virginicus*
White grunt	*Haemulon plumieri*
High-hat	*Equetus acuminatus*
Jackknife-fish	*E. lanceolatus*
Spotted drum	*E. punctatus*
Atlantic spadefish	*Chaetodipterus faber*
Grey angelfish	*Pomacanthus arcuatus*
French angelfish	*P. paru*
Sargeant major	*Abudefduf saxatilis*
Garibaldi	*Hypsypops rubicundus*
Jewelfish	*Microspathodon chrysurus*
Hogfish	*Lachnolaimus maximus*
Yellowhead jawfish	*Opistognathus aurifrons*
Greenband goby	*Gobiosoma multifasciatum*
Sharknosed goby	*G. evelynae*
Neon goby	*G. oceanops*
Mandarinfish	*Synchiropus splendidus*
Skilletfish	*Gobiesox strumosus*
Lined seahorse	*Hippocampus erectus*
Dwarf seahorse	*H. zosterae*
Northern puffer	*Sphoeroides maculatus*

Table 8 Marine fishes reared from laboratory hatched spawns.

few other species reared in marine labs and universities. Clownfish and gobies are still bred in quantity for the marine aquarium market; but companies and individuals engaged in commercial or semicommercial marine fish rearing are short of the time, people power, and financial investment to branch out toward other species. In 1982, I did think that many more species of marine tropical fish would be in production by this time. The problem now seems not to be the understanding of the biological and environmental requirements, as I expressed in the first edition, but a need for the financial and technical commitment required to grind away at the problems presented by each species until some commercial production is achieved. And there is always the specter that where it may be possible to develop the technology to rear a species in some numbers, it may not be economically feasible to do so commercially under the conditions that prevail at that time.]

Propagation of marine tropical fish has progressed slowly for many reasons; but perhaps the most important of these is the lack of understanding, and the difficulties of creating, the pelagic environment essential for larval survival. Since widespread marine aquarium keeping is a relatively recent development, the basic concepts of aquatic life held by most aquarists relate to freshwater experience. Freshwater fish reproduction usually involves some processes we can readily understand, and that fit in well with our preconceived ideas of terrestrial animal reproduction. Things such as nest making, live birth, baby fish that can be easily seen with the naked eye, baby fish that swim in schools, parental care of eggs, and parental protection of baby fish, and all of the above taking place in a bottom type environment are all basically familiar. It is natural to retain these concepts when we move from freshwater to marine aquariums.

Unfortunately, these freshwater concepts about the nature of the watery world can cause a number of misconceptions about what we see in the marine environment. Marine fish do not care for their young once they have hatched. In fact, since most marine fish spend their larval period as a part of the plankton, plankton feeding fish quickly eat their own young if they happen to drift by. During their time in the plankton, larval fish are totally dependent on planktonic microorganisms for food, and although they can move about within the space of a few feet at most, major movement is dependent on ocean currents during their early larval life.

Reproduction of marine fish can be categorized in four basic patterns:

1. The most common is release of tiny, transparent, free floating (pelagic) eggs with complete absence of parental care. Angelfish, butterflyfish, tangs, groupers, snappers, wrasses, grunts, drums, and parrotfishes are among those with this type of reproductive style.

2. The second most common mode is attachment of the eggs to a secure substrate, usually near the bottom, in a type of nesting behavior. These are termed demersal eggs (in contrast to the free floating pelagic eggs) and the resulting larvae may be large as with clownfish or quite small as with damselfish. Gobies, blennies, damselfish, and clownfish are the common nest building marine tropical fish.

3. A variation on the demersal theme is oral incubation of eggs, or mouth brooding. Instead of attaching the eggs to the bottom, the male retains them in his oral cavity during the period of incubation. Jawfish and cardinalfish are mouth brooders.

4. A very few marine species, such as sea horses, give birth to well developed live young.

Mouth brooders and those fish that lay demersal eggs produce far fewer eggs than fish that spawn pelagic eggs. These species aerate and protect their eggs from predators during early development, thus attain an economy of repro-

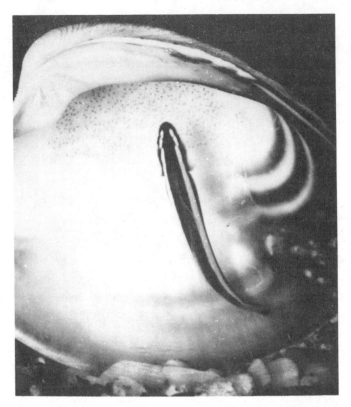

Figure 22 The male neon goby, *Gobiosoma oceanops*, guarding his nest under a clam shell. The male takes on the task of keeping the eggs tended in the secret nest. The eggs are near hatching, and the well developed eyes of the embryos can be seen through the transparent eggs.

ductive energy in exchange for a period of parental care. Nesting and mouth brooding species incubate their eggs from three to ten days depending on the species, and the young are hatched with a small residual yolk sac, fully developed eyes and mouth parts, and the ability to swim with purpose and direction. Their early larval period is passed as a creature of the plankton, but the helpless egg and prolarval stage of a pelagic egg is avoided, and the total larval period is usually shortened.

The spawn of species that protect their eggs varies in number from a low of 50 to 100 to a high of 10 to 15 thou-

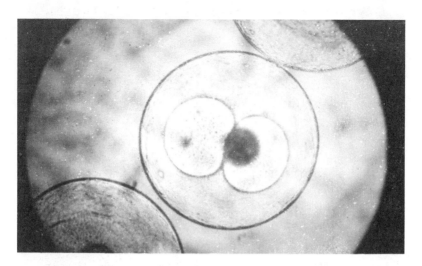

Figure 23 The pelagic egg of the French angelfish. The egg, bounded by the large circle in the center of the photomicrograph, has a diameter of about one millimeter, the thickness of a dime. The two center circles are the first two cells of the developing embryo. They appear about 30 minutes after fertilization and are located at the bottom of the floating egg. The indistinct dark circle in the center of the egg is an oil droplet located at the top that provides the buoyancy to keep the egg floating near the surface.

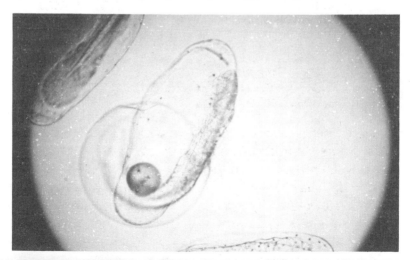

Figure 24 The pelagic prolarva of the French angelfish at the moment of hatching. Hatching occurs about 20 hours after fertilization. The hatchling is in the prolarval stage—little more than a yolk sac and tail—when it breaks out of the flexible egg shell. Two full days must pass before fins, eyes, and gut are developed well enough for the larva to begin to feed.

Figure 25   The circle of development of the French angelfish. The egg hatches in 18 to 22 hours. Development of the organ systems occurs during the prolarval stage, a period of about 72 hours, and the larval fish is then ready to begin feeding. Typical juvenile coloration begins to appear in 12 to 17 days. The larval period is complete when the early juvenile drops out of the water column and begins to live in the bottom environment, a period of 3 to 5 weeks after hatching.

sand, whereas those species that spawn pelagic eggs can produce well over 200 thousand eggs or more per spawn and may spawn on almost a daily basis during the height of the spawning season. Of course small species such as pygmy angelfish spawn fewer eggs, only 300 to 500 per spawn, but these spawns can also occur on a daily basis.

The larvae that hatch from pelagic eggs are completely helpless. They carry a large yolk sac and have not yet formed pigmented eyes, a functional gut, or mouth parts, and the paired fins are still mere buds. Another 72 hours must pass before these larvae develop to the point that the yolk sac is consumed and they can swim and feed on their own.

The popular aquarium literature in recent years has hosted numerous articles on rearing marine tropical fish, and most of these were of some help to aspiring culturists. However, successful rearing of marine fish requires consistent care, detailed observation, some basic knowledge, and a good bit of experience. The printed page cannot supply the dedication and actual experience, but it can give the basic information and some suggestions on technique along with the knowledge that it actually can be done. In this chapter, I will try to summarize the information already available on rearing clownfish in the light of my own experience and present a guide to the basics of rearing clownfish. Clownfish are among the easiest of all marine tropicals to rear, and this information is specifically directed towards them since they give the amateur marine fish breeder the best chance to succeed.

There are a number of other species that the amateur marine breeder may be able to rear as the quintessence of the marine fish keeping experience: neon gobies and other species of gobies and blennies, sea horses, royal grammas, jawfish and other species of clownfish. These fish, except sea horses, are more difficult than clownfish, but are definite future possibilities for the amateur marine breeder.

Spawning

Marine tropical fish are not unlike all other creatures of the earth that depend on sexual reproduction to continue their species. The drive to reproduce is extremely strong, and they will spawn, providing—and this is a crucial "providing"—that the environment and the physical condition of the fish meet the species' minimum requirements for reproduction. The problem, therefore, is to identify and provide the necessary conditions for each species that is to be spawned. There are four basic criteria:

1. Adult fish in good health.

2. Proper nutrition—quality and quantity.

3. Suitable physical environment—light, temperature, and surroundings.

4. Proper chemical environment—water quality.

Obviously, all the proper conditions exist in nature during the spawning season, so we must look to the wild to find clues to the conditions that must be created. The following discussion is directed toward the common or percula clownfish, *Amphiprion ocellaris,* but can apply in principle to other species.

The fish must be adult, that is of the proper size and age for spawning activity, and must be in good physical condition. There must be male and female fish present, in the case of clownfish one of each sex is all that is necessary. In fact, unless the aquarium is quite large, a mated pair will seldom allow others of their species to survive within the tank. Other species, however, such as wrasses and damsels, may need to aggregate in small groups before spawning behavior is stimulated. I have found no sure color markings on percula clownfish that differentiate male and female, but there are size and shape differences between adults. The female is larger and more robust than the male, and when the gonads are active, the abdomen is quite rotund. The adult male is perhaps half to three quarters the size of the full grown female and is slim without the heavy belly of the female. Given a population of adult fish, these size and shape characteristics are sufficient to select sexes with about 90% accuracy. Immature fish and young adults cannot be accurately sexed on appearance—indeed, when young, they are probably all immature males.

Sex reversal has recently been demonstrated in seven species of clownfish. The sex change is protanderous, from

Figure 26   Large species of clownfish such as *Amphiprion clarkii* produce large nests. Some of these nests may have 1500 eggs. Although clownfish usually hide their nests if possible, they occasionally lay them out for all to see. The male guards proudly.

male to female, and is apparently stimulated by changes in the social structure of the group. In the wild, one dominant female, an adult male, and a variable group of subadult fish inhabit the same general area about a host anemone. The smaller fish are repressed in sexual development by the presence of the active pair. They do not mature sexually or grow large in size. If the adult male is lost to a predator, the largest of the immature male fish rapidly matures and becomes the female's mate. If the female is lost, the active male changes relatively quickly into a female and mates with the now maturing young male. Nature thus assures that every host anemone will have a functional pair of clownfish without regard to any predetermined genetic sex distinction.

Since it is often difficult to find adult fish in good condition, it is usually best to grow your own clownfish brood stock. It takes a little patience, 6 to 18 months depending on their size when you begin, but there is the advantage of often winding up with more than one pair. Start with a good established tank of at least 20 gallons, 40 is better, and then purchase 8 to 12 healthy young clownfish. Statistically, you need a minimum of 6 fish to assure that at least one of each sex is present, assuming an equal distribution of sexes and no artificial selection in choice of fish. Statistics also do not allow for sex change, but this phenomenon works to the advantage of the aquarist in the case of clownfish, unless one begins with sexually mature fish.

If you begin with juvenile fish, tank reared clowns are good for the initial breeding stock since they haven't been exposed to treatment or collection chemicals, but wild caught fish should do just as well if they are in good condi-

Figure 27 A breeding pair of maroon clowns, *Premnas biaculeatus*. The large and aggressive female of this species is not afraid to nip the hand of any unwary aquarist that ventures near the nest.

tion. Depending on their age and size, the fish will coexist peacefully for a while until they begin to pair. An anemone, preferably a pacific carpet anemone, will promote natural behavior patterns, and thus is an aid to pairing and spawning.

When a pair forms, the two fish become protective of a territory about the anemone and prevent any other fish of the same or closely related species from entering their area. The territorial imperative is so intense that a strong pair will destroy the hapless fish that cannot flee their boundaries. The new pair, or the other fish, must be removed soon after aggressiveness is first displayed, to prevent loss of the unpaired fish. Other pairs may also form from the unpaired fish after the first pair is removed. The tank may be partitioned to house separate pairs, but the partition should be opaque so the pairs do not visually impinge on each other's territory.

After pairing, the fish are prepared for spawning by maintaining an optimum environment in the aquarium, as per the previous chapters, and providing the best possible nutrition. The daily duration of light and tank temperature are also important. The pituitary gland, which sends hormones that activate the gonads, is stimulated to do so by constant summer day length and warm temperatures. The aquarium light should be set to provide 14 hours of light per day and the temperature should be a constant 80°F. Also, provide rocks, flower pots, slates, tiles, or other hard surfaces near the anemone to give the fish a spawn site. All that is needed from this point on is good aquarium management and patience. The fish will do what comes naturally when they mature.

The behavior of the pair usually gives an indication of impending spawning. The female is the dominant member of the pair since she is larger and seems to be chiefly responsible for defense of the territory. She is the one that attacks the fish, net, or hand that dares to invade their protectorate. The male, on the other hand, is the chief caretaker of the

Figure 28 The common clownfish, *Amphiprion ocellaris, is*
probably the best known of the demersal spawning marine tropical
fish. The nest is usually laid at the base of an anemone and the
male does most of the "babysitting".

eggs and seems to be constantly appeasing the female to
suffer his presence. Evidently there is a behavioral conflict
in the female. She has on one side the stimulus to drive the
male from the territory as she does with other members of
her species and, conflictingly, she must keep him near her to
be successful in reproduction. Obviously, there must be a
frequent exchange of information between them to remind
each other of their respective functions.

When the female attacks the male, he turns the attack
away by head shaking and "chattering" directly in front of
the female, a sort of submissive behavior. Just as the female
must not actually attack the male, he must not actually flee
her presence, or reproduction will not succeed. As the attack
is turned away, the male, and often the female also, engages
in cleaning activity on any nearby hard surface. This is a
displacement activity that turns the fish away from attack
and flee behavior and strengthens the pair bond. To the

casual anthropomorphic eye the fish appear to be "playing tag" and "showing off", however, these are actually ritualized behavior patterns that strengthen the pair bond and prepare the fish for spawning.

Unless you observe the fish carefully and critically each day, the first spawn will probably come as a surprise. As the time for spawning approaches, the fish may display heightened chasing activity and increased substrate biting. The female also becomes notably full in the abdomen. These conditions may persist for several days, especially with a first spawn, and you may think that the fish just don't know what to do. Take heart, though, for it will eventually occur.

Common clownfish almost always spawn in late afternoon or early evening. The female's ovipositor extends early on the day of spawning, and her fullness is quite pronounced. The male's organ is small and almost transparent and appears only shortly before the spawn occurs. The pair select a spawn site an hour or two before the first eggs are

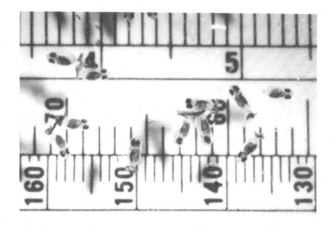

Figure 29 The clownfish egg just before hatching contains a miniature fish bent double inside the transparent membrane. The egg is only 2 mm long and the hatched larva is 4 mm long. The eyes, fins, and gut are fully developed at hatching, and feeding begins within a few hours.

laid and begin to clean the site by biting at the substrate while jerking the head from side to side. This activity becomes very intense as spawning approaches. At the end of the cleaning activity, the female begins to make passes over the cleaned area with her ovipositor lightly touching the hard surface. After several "dry" passes, the first bright orange eggs appear. They slip individually from the ovipositor, touch the substrate at one end and instantly adhere. A mass of very sticky, microscopic filaments attach the egg to the nest site. This is a flexible attachment and allows the eggs great side to side movement. The female leaves behind a single straight line of eggs across the nest site at each pass. Any eggs that do not adhere are quickly eaten by either parent. The female continues to lay a line of eggs at each pass until the patch of tightly packed eggs covers an area of one to four inches in diameter. The female pauses after every few passes and allows the male to fertilize the eggs she has just laid down. The male's motions are more rapid and fluttery than the female's and he seems to cover most of the enlarging patch of eggs each time he is active.

The male is the chief caretaker of the developing eggs. He frequently fans them with his pectoral and caudal fins, which aerates them and stimulates the developing embryo by movement. He also "mouths" the eggs, which consists of gentle biting at the egg patch. Although the parents are said to remove dead and diseased eggs this way, I have never seen them actually select and remove a dead egg. Eggs that die, quickly decompose and are swept off the nest by the general care patterns of the male. Any fallen eggs are usually consumed by one of the parents. The female also takes care of the nest in the same manner as the male, but her attentions are much less frequent.

Complete development to hatching takes place in 6 to 12 days depending primarily on temperature. The average time is 7 to 8 days at the typical temperature of 80 °F. Temperatures below 75 °F greatly delay development and hatching. The bright orange of the new eggs becomes dark brown in about 3 days as the tissues of the developing embryo envelop the yolk. The dark pigment of the eyes becomes noticeable at about day 4 and turn silvery at day 5 or 6 when the light reflecting pigment forms. On the day of hatching, the embryo develops a light violet sheen and the egg almost seems to bulge a little.

Hatching

Normal hatching always occurs at night within two hours of first dark. Usually all the eggs in the nest hatch very quickly, within 15 or 20 minutes. If any eggs do not hatch at this time, chances are that they will wait for the following night to hatch.

Night hatching effectively reduces predation on the newly hatched larvae when they are near the bottom and are most vulnerable to bottom dwelling plankton predators, including their own parents. The adults will seek out and consume every larva at first light if they remain together in the breeding tank. The clownfish larva is doubled up in the egg at hatching, with the tail tucked in just below the head at the tip of the egg. For maximum reproductive economy, the eggs must be small and numerous; but for maximum survival, the larvae must be as large as possible at first feeding. Various species have different methods of resolving these conflicting demands. Most pelagic spawning species carry a large yolk sac in a small egg and hatch very early into an only partly developed prolarval stage. The prolarva then continues development to a significantly larger first feeding larva outside the physical constraints of a small egg.

Pelagic eggs have no parental care, thus are subject to many predators and environmental hazards during their early development. Such species depend on production of vast numbers of eggs for survival. The egg in the mouth brooding jawfish is also small, about a millimeter in diameter, but the larva that hatches is comparatively large, about 4 millimeters long with a head that is almost one millimeter in diameter. This economy of space is achieved by wrapping the body of the larva about the head during development. At hatching, after 5 to 7 days of incubation, the body unwinds from the head and, despite development in a small egg, the larva is a respectable size and is ready to begin feeding almost immediately.

The clownfish egg is one of the largest of marine fish eggs at 1 mm in diameter and about 2 mm in length. Most larval fish hatch from the egg at the head by dissolving the egg shell with a proteolytic enzyme and then thrusting itself head first out of the egg case with tail and body movements. Clownfish are different, however. At hatching, the egg case ruptures at the tail just below the top of the egg. The tail and lower body then fall free, and the larva frees itself from the egg (which is still attached to the substrate) by a few rapid jerks of the tail and body. If the egg does not remain attached to the substrate, the larva is unable to easily free its head from the tip of the egg case, and swims about pushing the egg case before it. This is usually fatal to the larval fish, for it cannot respire normally, nor can it remove its egg case cap. Thus, clownfish eggs should not be removed from the substrate before hatching.

Larval Rearing

Clownfish spend the first two to three weeks of their life as pelagic larvae. In nature, this period is spent in the upper reaches of the sea feeding on the tiny animals that surround them in the plankton. Juvenile coloration develops as early as 8 days and as late as 20 days, and shortly after this metamorphosis they begin life on the bottom. The period of greatest concern to the marine fish breeder is the first two weeks, for this is the stage that is most difficult to maintain and feed.

Since the larvae are immediately pelagic at hatching, the first task is to set up a rearing tank that substitutes for the pelagic environment, and to have it ready when the larvae hatch. This is relatively simple for a small scale operation. An adequate rearing environment can be prepared with a bare (no filter), high sided tank; one or two fine bubble air releasers; and good lighting directly over the tank. Black plastic wrapped around the tank excludes side light and helps the larval fish find the pelagic food organisms. With careful management, about 100 fish can be taken through the larval stage (to about ⅜ of an inch long) in a 10 gallon tank, but greater success can be had more easily in tanks of 30 to 50 gallons.

The first major problem is recovering the larvae since they must be moved from the breeding tank to the rearing tank. There are three basic methods to achieve this transfer.

First, and perhaps most feasible for the amateur marine breeder, is to remove as many of the newly hatched larvae from the breeding tank as possible. The larvae are strongly attracted to a light source after hatching, probably an adaptation to assure their movement into the upper water strata. Because of this trait, it is an easy task to concentrate them with a flashlight in one corner of the aquarium. Darkening the tank a few hours early on the day of hatch will bring them off earlier in the evening and hopefully prevent late night activity on the part of the aquarist. When the larvae have accumulated in one area of the tank, they can be removed for transfer to the rearing tank by either siphoning them from the tank into a bucket or by capturing them with a cup or glass. The cup method is more time consuming and frustrating, but the chance of injury is less than that with the siphon. Of course, a net should never be used, for the larvae cannot withstand the physical abrasion at this early age.

The second method consists of removal and transfer of that part of the substrate containing the nest to the larval rearing tank, and artificial hatching of the eggs. The eggs can be kept in good condition until hatching with an even curtain of bubbles gently rolling over the entire nest. Darkening the tank at the proper time causes the eggs to hatch.

The third method requires a more elaborate set up with the breeding tank mounted directly over the larval tank and a constant water flow between the two tanks. This way the hatched larvae are automatically siphoned down to the rearing tanks and the two water masses (breeding and rearing) do not differ in quality. The intake from the rearing tank to the pumped return to the breeding tank must be well protected by a large surface area of fine mesh screen to prevent loss of larvae, and the flow must be discontinued or greatly diminished to prevent loss of the larval fish food when the young fish begin to feed. Only those amateur breeders strongly inclined toward systems engineering will find it necessary to build such a unit.

Once the larvae have been transferred from the breeding tank to water of the same temperature and pH in the rearing tank, the real problems begin—to provide the proper type and abundance of food organisms for the larval fish. There is a very good reason for the fantastic reproductive potential of most marine fish. This is that very, very few, one out of millions, survive the larval and juvenile stages in nature. Thus a great many potential lives must be launched to assure survival of a few and continuance of the species.

These tiny larvae have little stored food and must begin feeding very soon after their systems are mature enough to capture food organisms. Even if the available food organisms are compatible with their nutritional and behavioral requirements, they must be abundant enough to provide energy for both movement and growth. Most attempts at rearing marine fish larvae fail for one or more of three reasons:

1. Improper physical and/or chemical environment.

2. Lack of an acceptable first food organism.

3. Lack of sufficient numbers of food organisms.

The proper physical and chemical rearing environment has already been discussed, and it remains only to say that the tank bottom must be cleaned every day or two, and if possible, a partial water change effected with each cleaning. One water change of 50 to 80% once a week for the two to three week rearing period is all that is really necessary if a 10 to 20% change is not accomplished every two days. The more larvae that are reared in the tank, of course, the more important water changes become. Bottom cleaning is best done with a small siphon that picks up sediment without endangering larvae higher in the water column.

Don't be alarmed if a green algal bloom develops in the rearing tank. This is actually good for the rearing environment as it provides nutrition for the food organisms present (usually rotifers) and takes up some of the metabolites produced by the animals in the tank. A white bloom, however, may be caused by bacteria and is usually detrimental to the larvae. Too many larvae, too many food organisms, lack of bottom cleaning, too much turbulence, and introduction of too much scuzzy water from the food organism (rotifer) rearing tanks can all contribute to conditions that foster excessive bacterial growth. A thorough cleaning and water change with subsequent restocking of food organisms may save the larvae if a bacterial bloom is caught in the early stages. It is important to note that it is possible to rear limited numbers of clownfish in small tanks without any significant water changes over a three week period if care is taken to keep food organism populations at just the right levels.

Marine fish can be reared scientifically by precise measurement of water quality and food organism density, which is the best way to achieve reproducible results; or the aquarist can develop a "feel" for the requirements of the larvae and know from trial and error what will and what will not work. In actual practice, a blending of the two approaches seems to produce the best results. Perhaps the most important consideration—aside from the basics of tank, water, air and light—is to have the proper abundance of an acceptable food organism, usually rotifers or wild plankton. Three to eight food organisms per ml is a good level, although clownfish can survive on less, especially if there are only a few larvae to feed. If you can't make an actual count of the number of food organisms by looking at a prepared sample in a counting chamber under a microscope, you'll have to use simpler techniques or even just go by visual estimate. With a little experience, it's possible to get to the point of looking into the tank and immediately knowing if the food levels are adequate.

Five food organisms per ml translates to about 150 per ounce, so a shot glass of rearing tank water should contain over 150 food organisms. At this level there are 25 to 30 food organisms per teaspoon, an easy enough number to count. The best way to get an estimate of the actual level of food organisms in the tank is to count the number in each of four or five sample teaspoons, and when the average count is between 25 and 30, there will be enough food organisms for good larval survival. Placing the sample in a shallow glass dish and examining it over a black background with a low power hand lens will facilitate the count. Maintaining the food organisms at this level will assure survival of most of the larvae.

Even though clownfish are about the largest and best developed of marine fish larvae when they begin feeding, new hatch brine shrimp are still too large for a first food. Of all the possible first foods that the aquarist can work with, there are four that give a good chance of success:

1. Wild plankton

2. Cultured marine rotifers

3. Fresh frozen rotifers

4. Cultured marine ciliates

Other organisms and methods may also be successful, but these are ones that have actually worked. It may also be possible to rear a few clownfish with pulverized dry foods as a first offering and then a quick switch to new hatch brine

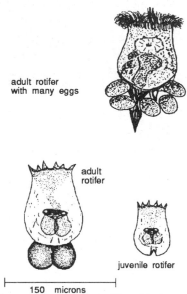

adult rotifer
with many eggs

adult
rotifer

juvenile rotifer

|— 150 microns —|

Figure 30   The marine rotifer, *Brachionus plicatilis,* adult and juvenile. This tiny marine animal is easy to culture and makes an excellent first food for many marine fish larvae. The adult female (left) carries 2 to 8 eggs on her tail when conditions for growth and reproduction are good. The eggs hatch into juvenile female rotifers (right) that become egg bearing adults in 24 hours. Such rapid reproduction allows phenomenal population growth, and rotifer cultures must be carefully tended to keep population levels and culture conditions within proper bounds. Males appear in the population when temperature and/or food conditions are not favorable. Females and males produce a resting stage egg that survives even if the population dies. These eggs hatch when conditions improve, and the rotifer population blooms again.

shrimp as soon as the larvae are large enough to take them. This later method would require frequent tank cleanings and water changes, and would be worth trying if the only other thing available was determination. A good quality dry flake food pulverized in a mortar and pestle, dry egg yolk, and freshwater fish fry food are all possible dead food particles. If dry, pulverized food is used, the water turbulence controlled by the air release should be kept as high as possible to keep the food in suspension as long as possible. It should not be so high, however, that the larvae cannot control their own movements. Feeding should also be very frequent to keep food levels high enough in the tank water long enough for the larval fish to get adequate nutrition. This also necessitates frequent siphoning of the tank bottom.

For those aquarists living near the coast, one of the easiest larval foods to obtain will be wild plankton. The relative ease or difficulty of collecting wild plankton every day for 10 to 15 days will determine for each individual case whether to culture a food organism or rely on plankton collection. The very smallest zooplankters are not needed by the relatively large clownfish larvae, so it is possible to get by with a homemade plankton net, and access to the tidal flow of ocean or bay. Wild plankton, although an excellent food for larval fish, has the drawbacks of great variability in quality, and the possibility of introduction of planktonic

Figure 31 An inexpensive outdoor rotifer culture. A large population of rotifers can be grown and maintained for several weeks in a child's wading pool with a capacity of 100 to 300 gallons. Rotifers grown in the summer in such cultures can be frozen and stored for winter use.

Figure 32 Sorting sieves for rotifers and plankton sizing can be made from short pieces of four and six inch diameter PVC pipe. Industrial nylon and polyester fabrics in the range of 35 to 300 microns are attached to the pipe ends with PVC glue (be careful not to get the glue on the center of the sieve).

predators and parasites, primarily *Amyloodinium*. These problems, however, can be controlled by straining the plankton before feeding, to eliminate organisms larger than 300 microns, and through judicious use of light copper treatment. A light copper treatment (0.05 to 0.1 ppm) placed in the collected plankton for a half hour before feeding (and then removed when the plankton is sieved) will kill *Amyloodinium* and meduse that would otherwise mature and infect the larval fish in a week or two.

A half meter plankton net of a 50 to 75 micron mesh can be purchased at most oceanic research supply houses and will do nicely to collect the necessary wild plankton. Professional plankton nets are expensive, so a handy aquarist may wish to make one instead. Finding a material that will catch the smaller zooplankter and still pass enough water is the most difficult part of the project. A worn bed sheet may do

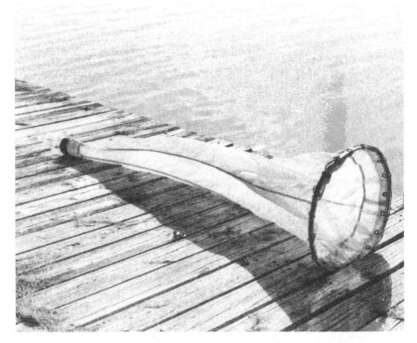

Figure 33   A standard 0.5 meter plankton net with a quart collecting jar at the cod (posterior) end. The rim is made of 0.25 inch thick bar aluminum bent to the proper diameter and bolted together with stainless steel bolts. The net can be towed by a small boat or fished from a bridge in a tidal current.

the trick, but some experimentation is going to be required. Depending on the situation (quality of plankton, size of the rearing tank, and number of larvae), one collection of plankton per day for the first three or four days may be adequate, but two may make for better success.

Most wild plankton can survive for several hours in a bucket under light aeration, so feeding can be spread out from one collection. The best chance of success will be had by combining wild plankton with cultured rotifers, although either one alone is adequate. Observe the larval fish carefully to make sure that they are feeding. Actively feeding larvae frequently flex their body into an S shaped curve and then snap forward suddenly to capture the prey immediately before them. The gut area will also become rounded with ingested food and take on a whitish color from plankton or rotifers. It is important to get them on new hatch brine shrimp as soon as possible, for this will enhance their growth rate considerably. Add new hatch brine shrimp early, but in small quantities. Three to four days after feeding begins is about right. The color of the gut will change from whitish to a pink or orange color when they begin to take the baby brine shrimp.

Post larval clownfish seem reluctant to take non-living foods until after they take on adult coloration. At this point, somewhere between 10 and 20 days, they will take blended shrimp or scallop and pulverized dry flake food. Go easy on the dry flake food, for it can cause the gut of young fish to bloat if it is overfed. Also keep the tank bottom clean once the switch to dry foods is begun. In fact, in a small rearing situation it is best to move the young fish to a tank with an established undergravel or trickle filter as soon as all have taken on adult coloration and begin to stay near the tank side or bottom.

Be careful not to overfeed baby brine shrimp at this point. The little fish seem not to have any mechanism that tells them to stop feeding when they have eaten enough, and they can continue to feed on brine shrimp until they look like little footballs, and then fall to the bottom and die.

Marine fish culturists have looked long and hard for a good first food organism for marine fish larvae. Baby brine shrimp, although an excellent and readily available food, were of limited value because they are just too large for most marine fish larvae. What was needed was a small organism, about half the size or less of baby brine shrimp, that was easy to culture in large numbers, and that would be readily taken by the fish larvae and provide their first nutritional needs. The National Marine Fisheries Service at the Fishery-Oceanography Center in La Jolla, California, was working with the culture of the northern anchovy and gulf croaker in 1969 and 70 and reported good success using cultures of the marine rotifer, *Brachionus plicatilis*. A starter culture of this organism was sent to our Florida pompano culture program

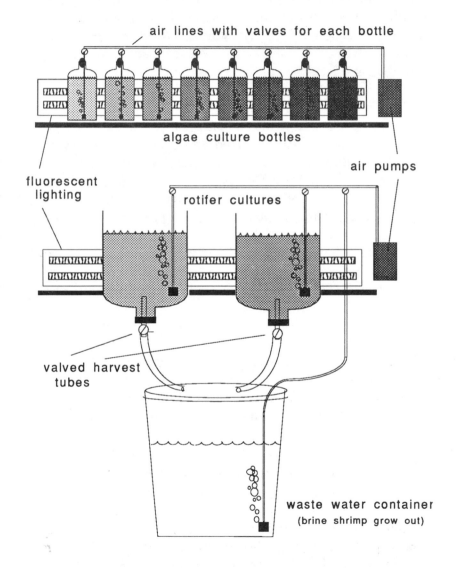

Figure 34 A small, two shelf microalgae and rotifer culture system
(from *The Marine Aquarium Reference*).

in December 1970, and proved to be a successful first food for pompano, spot fin pinfish, sea trout, redfish, and other species at our laboratory. This organism is now widely used in fish culture throughout the world and is available from many fish culture laboratories and several private companies. It was a short hop from food fish to tropical fish culture, and B. plicatilis is probably used to some extent in all marine tropical fish culture operations.

B. plicatilis is not difficult to culture, but it does require daily care by the aquarist. The strongest and most nutritive rotifer cultures are those fed on one celled marine algae; however, cultures can also be grown on dry activated yeast. There are many methodologies and techniques for culturing marine one celled algae and rotifers, and I can only present a few general principles and outline one simple culture method in this chapter.

The best algae to use are Dunaliella, Isochrysis, Monochrysis, and Chlorella as these are easy for the rotifers to eat and provide good nutrition. The algae should be grown under conditions of constant illumination in one to five gallon containers and at temperatures of 75 to 80°F. There should be no way that rotifers can get back to the algae cultures, for these hungry little beasts will quickly wipe out the algae if they do. Feed the algae with a basic nutrient mix: sea water enriched with nitrate, phosphate, and iron. One of the liquid, total element plant foods now on the market may do well for this purpose. Algae and rotifer culture requires use of considerable new saltwater or great economy and reuse of a well filtered, reservoir stock.

Small cultures of algae and rotifers are dynamic—they reproduce and grow fiercely in the excellent conditions provided—and when the limits of growth are reached, they crash quickly into death and decay. Therefore each culture has to be harvested and renewed regularly to keep it in the constant growth phase. The growth of the rotifer cultures can be controlled somewhat by the amount of algae fed. Feeding can be increased several days before a hatch is due, thus stepping up production of rotifers for when they are most needed. The rotifer cultures are harvested by passing the culture through a fine screen (25 to 50 microns) and collecting the concentrated rotifers on top of the screen for feeding to the rearing tank.

It is possible—not better, but possible—to rear rotifers for larval fish without the problems of algae culture. Dry activated yeast, the kind used in baking bread, can be fed in light suspension to rotifer cultures, resulting in good growth. Yeast suspensions have been used for decades to feed small aquatic organisms. This is best done outside under sunlight since the yeast method encourages bacterial growth and sunlight helps control it. Rotifers can be grown in small volumes by the yeast method, 15 to 40 gallons, but do better in larger volumes of 90 to 200 gallons. A plastic kiddie pool about one foot deep and five feet across in partial shade with several air stones for turbulence makes a very good culture vessel. Low temperatures, below 70°F, depress rotifer reproduction, so accommodation must be made for winter conditions.

The yeast for feeding to the rotifers is prepared by dissolving about a tablespoon of the dry yeast in a pint of warm water. The resulting milky suspension can be kept in the refrigerator for several days and fed to the cultures as required. The rotifer cultures should be fed the yeast solution once a day for maintenance and low harvest rate and twice a day for maximum harvest. The bottom of small volume cultures should be siphoned every day, and any water loss made up with clean saltwater. The proper amount of the yeast suspension to feed is that amount that keeps the culture water slightly milky for a few hours after feeding. It is wise to have several such cultures, for yeast fed rotifer cultures are far more precarious then algae fed cultures. **Note that without culturing, there is no way to develop the numbers of rotifers necessary for even a small clownfish rearing experiment.**

It is also possible to rear clownfish larvae solely on frozen rotifers as a first food. The rotifers are taken from dense cultures, strained and washed, and then frozen in saltwater in small blocks. The frozen blocks are thawed in a cup or two of saltwater just before feeding, and then fed to the rearing tank. The rotifers are dead, of course, but if tank turbulence is adequate, they do not immediately settle out. They remain in the water column long enough for the clownfish larvae to obtain adequate food. They do settle fairly quickly, however, and the bottom must be siphoned daily if frozen rotifers are used. Also, more than one feeding per day is necessary since the rotifers are not continuously available to the larval fish. Two and perhaps three feedings are necessary each day depending on tank conditions. This technique makes it possible to rear large amounts of rotifers in summer, when culture conditions are good outdoors, and then save them for winter rearing runs. New hatched brine shrimp must be provided as soon as possible for best success when frozen rotifers are used as a first larval food.

Marine ciliates in the genus *Euplotes* have been used successfully to rear limited numbers of clownfish larvae at the Wilhelma Aquarium in Germany. However, the most successful trials with *Euplotes* also included a low density of various other zooplankters produced by a tank rich with invertebrate populations. *Euplotes* are smaller and apparently less nutritious for larval fish than rotifers, but they can bridge the gap from first feeding to baby brine shrimp for some larvae. Living *Euplotes* cultures can be obtained from some scientific supply houses and can be cultured with yeast suspensions as described for rotifers. Potato water, algal cultures, and decomposing meat can also create rich cultures of *Euplotes*.

Juvenile Growth

When the young clownfish are fully colored and about ¼ to ½ inch long, they should be moved to a tank with an established filter. They will grow faster and stronger in a bottom environment after this stage of development is attained. Gradually wean them from dependence on baby brine shrimp to standard marine tropical fish foods.

Other species

The amateur marine fish breeder must concentrate on those species that will reproduce readily in the aquaria and that have hardy eggs and/or early larvae that allow recovery. The neon goby and the royal gramma are two species that fill these requirements. Both species can be paired by the same basic method as described for clownfish, for a mated pair will not tolerate other individuals in their tank space. Despite this similarity, there are many biological differences between them. The male is usually the larger of the pair in both neon gobies and royal grammas, and the abdominal fullness of the active female is the prominent sexual difference.

Neon gobies attach their eggs to the substrate very much like clownfish, but their nests are more secretive. They place their eggs under shells and rocks, and the presence of the nest is seldom known until the tank is suddenly filled with tiny, transparent hatchlings. Hatching usually takes place at night, but it is not uncommon for a nest to hatch in the daytime. The male is in charge of the nest and spends much time working over the eggs. The presence of a nest can be suspected if the male is observed entering and leaving the same small opening with great frequency.

Royal grammas have only recently been spawned and reared successfully. Their reproductive mode has been little known up to this point. Because their relatives, the sea basses, produce planktonic eggs, it was thought that the grammas may also release free floating eggs. Tank spawns, however, have demonstrated that royal grammas are secretive nest builders. The male selects a nest site hidden deep in some crevice or under a rock. He actively cleans this hidden area of stones and shells until the nest site meets his specifications. He then brings algal strands into the nest area until

Figure 35   Royal gramma, *Gramma loreto,* are secretive spawners. These eggs were laid in a nest of *Entromorpha* algae carefully built by the male several days before the spawn. The eggs have small "pimples" on their surface, each with several long sticky threads that bind the eggs to each other and the strands of algae. Each egg contains several oil droplets, perhaps left over from an ancient time when the eggs were pelagic.

it appears filled, with only a small entry hole visible. The female is enticed into the nest at about this point, the male also enters, and up to 30 minutes may pass before either of them leave the nest. During this period, the female lays from 20 to 100 large eggs that have numerous long, sticky filaments extending from their surface that serve to bind the eggs to each other and to the surrounding algal mass.

The eggs are relatively large, about one millimeter in diameter, and have six or more small oil droplets. They are not transparent, but have a yellowish, translucent appearance. The female may enter the nest every day or two for a month or more, and repeat the performance each time. The male cares for the eggs in the nest periodically, but the eggs do not seem to require the nearly constant care a male clownfish gives to his nest. The eggs develop slowly (5 to 7 days from fertilization to hatching) and hatch in the daily sequence that they were laid. Thus, only a few are ready to hatch each night.

The constant daily hatch of larvae may be an adaptation to constantly release larvae throughout the spawning season, to take advantage of conditions favorable for survival whenever they may occur. The larvae are relatively large and hardy, but recovery is complicated by the hatch and release of only a few per night. They somehow find their way out of the nest site and into the upper water column after hatching. Hatching always takes place within a few hours after dark, similar to clownfish hatching. The male is in the nest at hatching, but does not seem to aid the hatchlings in their journey to the plankton rich, upper water levels. The small transparent larvae are ready to feed on the day after hatching and grow very fast under the right conditions.

[I have no idea how the tiny larvae get from the hatched egg, entwined deep in the nest with other eggs and multitudinous algae filaments, to the open waters of the tank, but they do. Perhaps the male helps, although I have not observed this. I have, however, seen a male neon goby appear at the entrance of his nest, open his mouth, and then release a tiny, new hatched larvae that then swam up in to the water column. Not once, but twice did I see this!]

Although not totally comprehensive, this chapter on marine fish breeding is a new addition to books on marine aquariums. It is a sign of the changes developing in the hobby and an indication of new directions. We know relatively little of the biology of many of the creatures that find their way into our marine aquariums. Reports of observations and breeding attempts by amateur marine aquarists, even those published in local society newsletters, add much to our knowledge, understanding, and enjoyment of the ocean life within our homes. So be encouraged to observe, think, and share your findings with fellow marine aquarists.

Invertebrate culture

[Over the last few years, marine aquarists have learned to keep a great many species of invertebrates that are capable of a variety of reproductive modes in addition to production of microscopic, free floating eggs with long-lived, pelagic larvae. Ten years ago, keeping hard and soft corals and other animals that depend on symbiotic algal cells within their tissues was considered almost impossible. Even anemones seldom survived long in the typical marine aquarium. Now an advanced marine aquarist can not only keep many of these animals alive and healthy, but many species reproduce naturally in good reef tank systems.

The Porifera (the sponges), the Cnidaria (the corals and anemones), and some of the Annelids (the polychaete worms) are the animals that are most easy to propagate naturally in reef systems. Mollusks (clams, oysters, snails, and octopus), Arthropods (mainly the crustaceans—crabs, lobsters, and shrimp), and Echinoderms (starfish, sea urchins, brittle stars, and sea cucumbers) are more difficult, since most of these reproduce with pelagic larvae and require great care during the tiny, pelagic larval stage. Some of these difficult-to-rear invertebrates are almost impossible. Take the spiny lobster for example. We worked for several years trying to rear the Caribbean spiny lobster, *Panulirus argus*, in our laboratory in the Florida Keys. The period of larval life in nature is six to nine months long, and the tiny larvae go through about eleven different larval stages. We managed to bring them through seven stages in 81 days, but were not able to rear them completely though the larval stage. Japanese biologists have recently been able to rear a few specimens of the Japanese spiny lobster, *Panulirus japonicus*, through to the juvenile stage, but this required 340 to 403 days in the larval stages. Detailed accounts of our rearing experiments are included in my recent book, *Lobsters: Florida • Bahamas • the Caribbean,* and this would be helpful to an aquarist interested in rearing crustaceans.

Most of these invertebrate organisms require low nutrient water, high intensity lighting of the proper spectral quality, oxygen levels at or near saturation, control of dissolved carbon dioxide, low levels of dissolved organics, proper management of trace elements, and active water flows. Given these environmental conditions, many of these organisms can reproduce through colonial proliferation (new polyps forming in a stony, colonial matrix), fission (splitting apart), budding (small polyps forming at the base of large, single animals), actual physical separation of healthy colonies, production of benthic eggs and larvae, and/or production of short term pelagic larvae. These are all reproductive modes that may adapt to a "set it up and let it run" production system. A marine aquarist may be able to reproduce certain marine organisms in such systems on a care and maintenance schedule that allows for dinner out and a movie once a week or so, and maybe even a free Saturday afternoon once a month. As time goes on, I think we will see more than a few marine aquarists producing some species of corals, sponges, marine worms, and mollusks for their own satisfaction and for small, localized markets. These invertebrates may reproduce from their own spawns, controlled and reared by the aquarist, or by actual physical separation of colonial organisms by the aquarists. A sterile razor blade can be used to separate coral colonies into smaller colonies that will grow again into large colonies.

Unfortunately, a simple "set it up and let it run" methodology is seldom routinely successful when dealing with marine systems, especially when reproduction is the goal. Organisms may die (or fail to thrive and grow) for no apparent reason, and after dozens of failures, punctuated by a few equally mysterious successful trials, the aquarist is reduced to seeking success by playing Mozart in the fish room and placing candles in circles drawn on the floor. A lot of mysterious failure in the past was caused by mismanagement of the physical and chemical parameters of marine aquarium systems—things like high nutrient levels, improper lighting, low pH, lack of specific trace elements, etc. Now that serious marine aquarists have a better understanding of what is required (see *The Marine Aquarium Reference*), and access to the equipment that can provide good marine environments for many invertebrates, a lot of the more mysterious problems that we encounter are probably caused by bacteria.

Wet, warm, and wonderfully organic tropical marine aquarium systems are Hog Heavens for thousands of species of bacteria, some helpful, some harmful, and many unpredictable in growth patterns and effects. Almost all modern marine aquarists are well aware of the essential need for healthy colonies of nitrifying and heterotrophic (decay) bacteria in all closed system aquaria, but the development and effects of disease causing and toxin producing bacteria and viruses are variable and not well known. Even professional aquaculturists and aquarists—who harbor a healthy fear and respect for harmful bacteria and even have microscopes—are often mystified by the activities of various "bugs" in their systems. It usually takes a long time, and a lot of intelligence and equipment, to identify and correct a problem caused by an unknown or previously unencountered bacteria or virus in a commercial aquaculture facility—sometimes driving the business to the brink of bankruptcy. Marine hobbyists and small commercial operations seldom have the capability of positively identifying bacteria and/or viruses, and then providing exactly the right treatment. They usually develop ways of working around such problems; suspecting the cause, but never investing the money and time to actually tie it down if an end run around the problem is successful.

At this point, I want to briefly describe a few unrelated observations, reports, and research results. Some are from my own experience, some related by other marine culturists, and some are comments culled from a few published articles and books. I haven't tried to search the literature or interview marine aquaculturists. These examples have sort of popped out at me over the years, and I'm sure that if I really tried to accumulate information on mysterious problems in marine culture systems that may be caused by bacteria and viruses, it would be quite a book.

1. I started breeding marine clownfish in 1972 in my garage with homemade equipment. One very limiting problem that we quickly ran into was what we called the "toxic tank syndrome" (see Chapter 9). Whenever we had a fairly large number of small clownfish or neon gobies in a closed system aquarium (50 to 500 small fish in tanks ranging from 30 to 100 gallons), we would very often encounter a toxic condition that would kill all the fish in the tank within 24 hours. Experimentation revealed that the cause of this toxin originated in the biological filter, presumably generated by bacterial populations within the filter. Moving the fish to a different system when the first symptoms appeared (shimmying and swimming together into the current), reversed the symptoms and saved the fish. No treatment we tried could save fish left in the original tank. We had to establish the commercial facility with open flow grow-out systems because the toxic tank syndrome occurred so often. Note that we were working with very primitive closed systems at the time, and this problem may be more manageable in more modern systems.

2. We moved to the Florida Keys and began experimental rearing of French and grey angelfish. We found that larval and juvenile angelfish of these species were extremely susceptible to the "toxic tank syndrome", which we believed was the development of toxins from bacterial populations in filters and on substrates (tank bottoms and walls) within the rearing tanks. We could not successfully rear marine angelfish through the larval stage until we experimented and developed an antibiotic mix that, when it was added to the rearing water, allowed the larval angelfish to survive. Larval angelfish would also not survive when fed microorganisms (rotifers and copepod nauplii) that we cultured in large tanks.

3. A friend, Syd Kraul, who reared marine larval fish at the Waikiki Aquarium in Honolulu, Hawaii, mentioned that larval tangs and other delicate fish larvae would not survive if fed copepod nauplii (*Euterpina acutifrons*, a semi-pelagic harpacticoid copepod) from tank cultures that were over three days old. Only

copepod nauplii hatched from female copepods that were transferred to a clean, sterile tank, and harvested within three days, allowed delicate larval fish to survive.

4. Tom Capo runs the Aplysia Resource Facility at the University of Miami. He has been rearing sea hares, *Aplysia*, breeding them for scientific research labs for many years. Results were always unpredictable until he learned first that *Vibrio* bacteria were invading the developing egg masses, and second, how to control this bacteria. Treating the egg masses with an iodine solution and moving them to newly sterilized tanks resulted in production of predictable, large scale culture of *Aplysia*. Like many other breakthroughs in aquaculture, the procedure was simple, and the results spectacular. But until bacterial control in the rearing process was developed, the problem presented an almost insurmountable barrier.

5. Charles D'Asaro and Henry Chen worked with the culture of the marine lugworm, *Arenicola cristata*, to develop a technology for production of marine baitworms in northern Florida in the mid 1970's (D'Asaro and Chen, 1976, Lugworm Aquaculture, Florida Sea Grant Report number 16). When developing the hatchery techniques, they found that the egg masses must be kept in closed, aerated, noncirculating systems, and that the water must be treated with streptomycin sulfate at 30 ppm. If this antibiotic was not used, then, in their words: "Larvae are highly susceptible to an unidentified pathogen which destroys all exposed individuals in seven to ten days."

6. Terry Fairfield published a short article in FAMA (FAMA, 1991, Vol. 14; no. 1). Terry experienced the occurrence of "marine sudden death syndrome" in a 55 gallon tank containing various marine fish and invertebrates, an event not unknown to many marine aquarists. Terry, however, had the knowledge, expertise, curiosity, and equipment (an unusual combination) to actually find out what happened. It started with a diseased fish that happened to be introduced into his tank and died within six hours. A Pacific blue tang was next affected and soon died, although there were no obvious indications of bacterial infection such as any external or extensive internal lesions or hypertrophy of internal organs. The other fish were saved by moving them to another tank. Using standard bacteriological procedures, Terry identified

an aggressive strain of *Vibrio anguillarum* in the tank and on the external surface of the tang. Cultures of this *Vibrio* rapidly overgrew all other bacterial colonies on the culture plates. Thanks to Terry's work, *Vibrio anguillarum* is strongly implicated as the causative organism in the rapid death syndrome of fish in marine aquarium systems, at least in my opinion. There is a lot of other research that points out how nasty *V. anguillarum* can be, but Terry's quick study sort of brings it all home to roost.

7. Austin and Austin, in their book *Bacterial Fish Pathogens : Disease in Farmed and Wild Fish* (1987, John Wiley & Sons), present a good review of the scientific work done with *Vibrio anguillarum*. Among the interesting research work they summarize are a couple of studies that report extensive mortality of goldfish following injection of filter-sterilized supernatant obtained from 24 hour broth cultures of *V. anguillarum*, which indicate that a toxin produced by this bacteria, and not necessarily the activity of the bacteria itself, can cause death in fish. They also report on some studies that show that the presence of heavy metals, notably copper, contribute to an exacerbation of vibriosis. Evidently the bacteria is capable of using copper to enhance its growth. This observation is of significance to marine aquarists that rely on copper to control infestations of the parasite *Amyloodinium* (saltwater ich, coral fish disease). A case of vibriosis could very well follow a copper treatment for this parasite, especially if the symptoms of a marginal occurrence of a mild strain of vibriosis is mistaken for an *Amyloodinium* infestation. The damage caused to the fish by *V. anguillarum* involves destruction of blood cells and proteins, and causes anemia and reduction of osmolarity (loss of ability to regulate water levels in blood and tissue).

Note also that vaccines are now available to commercial culturists for *V. anguillarum*. These vaccines are mostly for salmon and trout. Three experimental projects discussed by Austin and Austin reported mortality of vaccine injected fish to unvaccinated controls at 1.4% to 33.8%, 0% to 52%, and 7% to 100%. Thus it is probably possible to protect expensive marine tropical fish against vibriosis, but development of the vaccine will require some experimental work. This would be worthwhile, however, for fish vaccinated against vibriosis exhibit better all-round health and growth than unvaccinated fish.

So what does all this have to do with the breeding and reproduction of marine fish and invertebrates in small, closed, marine aquarium systems? Well, serious efforts at reproduction of marine invertebrates will require a marine aquarium system designed expressly for that purpose, and this section will provide some ideas along these lines. It should be obvious at this point that controlled breeding of marine organisms in closed marine aquarium systems intrinsically includes close control of bacterial populations within the system. To keep, and of course to breed, marine animals, one has to have bacteria. It must be good bacteria, nitrifying bacteria that will break down and nitrify waste organics, and denitrifying bacteria that will change nitrate back into nitrogen gas. In other words, good biological filtration is an essential requirement.

The biological filter would probably best be a trickle type filter, although a live rock tank may provide more complete biological filtration by adding a natural denitrification process to the system. Live rock may provide excellent biological filtration by supporting a well balanced bacteria population, or it may serve as a dangerous reservoir for harmful bacteria within the breeding system. Experimentation will be required.

Of course, other types of filtration in addition to biological filtration, i.e., protein skimming including careful ozone use, chemical filtration, good gas exchange, mechanical filtration, and perhaps a good algal filter, would be included in the filter side of the system. Each rearing chamber, however, has to be designed for easy cleaning and sterilization, and easy separation from the water flows in the rest of the system when necessary. The system sump tank must also be large enough to hold the extra volume of one or two rearing chambers so that the chambers can be emptied and cleaned without sending the chamber water to waste unless it is necessary.

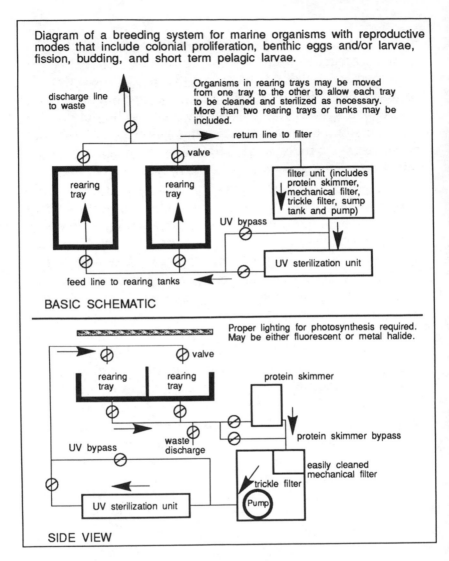

Figure 36 Experimental invertebrate rearing system.

Although bacterial colonies are necessary for biological filtration, the organisms under culture will need protection from *Vibrio* and other detrimental bacteria, and there must be a way to shift from an old, contaminated rearing chamber to a new, sterile chamber with a minimum of fuss, bother, and stress to the organism involved. Obviously, there has to be a sterile barrier between the filter and each of the rearing chambers, and a good UV sterilization unit will do this job very well. Be sure to ground the saltwater in the system to avoid any effect that stray electrical charges might have on organisms in the system. Two or more chambers, trays, or tanks that are fed from the water line after the UV unit will serve as interchangeable rearing chambers so that rapid movement of the eggs, larvae, and/or growing colonies to a new, clean, sterile environment can be easily accomplished. Each rearing chamber can also be isolated from the system water flows for separate treatment with antibiotics or other medications if necessary.

The accompanying diagram, Figure 36, is an experimental design for a marine invertebrate breeding/rearing system. It will also work for rearing the larvae of marine fish, but the rearing chambers should then be high sided tanks rather than shallow trays. High sided tanks will substitute for the pelagic environment, while shallow trays will provide a well lit, bottom type environment for benthic invertebrates and/or eggs and larvae. The design is simple at this point, but if you want to work with propagation of marine invertebrates or even fish, you may want to consider a similar type of setup.]

Oculina, bush coral

Selected References

This is by no means a complete listing, there are many books available that deal with tropical marine fishes and invertebrates, marine aquariums, and things of the sea. The books listed below, however, have been of value and interest to me and they should also benefit other marine aquarists.

[Now, 10 years later, there are many, many more books and articles to list. Of course, I can't list them all, in fact, not even a major portion of them. I have expanded the list considerably, however, to give the reader a good representation of the literature that is available and that is of interest to marine aquarists. I have included a few highly technical, academic publications because an advanced aquarist may wish to consult these foundation works, but for the most part, the list is composed of popular or general works that the average marine aquarist will find informative, useful, and not too difficult to find. Most of the popular books on marine aquariums cover the same basic information, but often in different ways and with different perspectives. Collecting and reading a variety of books makes a good marine aquarist a better marine aquarist.

In an academic or serious book or article, an author always cites the source of important information so that the reader can consult the original work if necessary. I did not do this in this book since it is a basic introductory text. I did cite references in the *Marine Aquarium Reference*, however, since that book is more advanced. The reference citations in that book refer directly to the scientific literature and specific popular articles relevant to the subject discussed. A serious aquarist will find the reference section of that book to be a helpful guide to recent marine aquarium literature.

Most of these books are available at libraries, bookstores, and aquarium shops. Aquarium societies often have excellent collections that members may use as a lending library, but please, be sure to return the books you borrow. I have also listed some out-of-print books since even these are often available in libraries and society collections. The popular aquarium magazines and many aquarium society newsletters are also excellent sources of topical information. A marine aquarist may discard Time and Newsweek after a month or so, but back issues of aquarium magazines are gold mines of information and are rarely put out on the curb. The references listed below will give you an idea of what is available (remember, there is much, much more than just this little list) and help you get started in browsing through the wonderful world of marine aquarium literature. A couple of computer programs and videos are also listed to make the aquarist aware of the various types of media with valuable information that are now available.]

Adey, W.H. and K. Loveland. 1991. **Dynamic Aquaria.** Academic Press. San Diego, CA. USA. 643 p.

Allen, Gerald R. 1980. **Butterfly and Angelfishes of the World. Vol. 2: Atlantic Ocean, Caribbean Sea, Red Sea, Indo-Pacific.** Wiley-Interscience, New York, N.Y. 352 pp.

Allen, Gerald R. 1980. **Anemonefishes of the World: Species, Care, and Breeding.** Aquarium Systems, Mentor, Ohio 104 pp.

Allen, Gerald R. 1975. **The Anemonefishes: Their Classification and Biology. (2nd Edition)** T.F.H. Publications, Inc., Neptune, N.J. 352 pp.

Atz, James W. and Douglas Faulkner 1971. **Aquarium Fishes: Their Beauty, History and Care.** The Viking Press. New York, N.Y. 112 pp.

Banister, K and A. Campbell (Editors). 1986. **The Encyclopedia of Aquatic Life.** Facts on File Publications. New York, NY. 349 pp.

Bellomy, Mildred D. 1969. **Encyclopedia of Sea Horses.** T.F.H. Publications, Inc. Neptune, N.J

Blasiola, G.C. 1991. **The New Saltwater Aquarium Handbook.** Barron's Educational Series, Inc., Hauppauge, NY. 134 pp.

Bohlke, James E. and Charles C. Chaplin 1968. **Fishes of the Bahamas and Adjacent Tropical Waters** Livingston Publishing Co. Wynnewood, Pa. 771 pp. (out of print)

Bower, C.E. 1983. **The Basic Marine Aquarium.** Charles C. Thomas, Publisher, Springfield, IL: 269 pp.

Breder, Charles M. Jr. and Donn E. Rosen 1966. **Modes of Reproduction in Fishes.** T.F.H. Publications, Inc. Neptune, N.J.

Burgess, W.E. 1987. **A Complete Introduction to Marine Aquariums.** TFH Publications. Neptune City, NJ. 128 pp.

Burgess, W. 1989. **Dr. Burgess's Atlas of Marine Aquarium Fishes.** TFH Publications. Neptune City, NJ 736 pp.

Chaplin, Charles C.G. 1972. **Fishwatchers Guide to West Atlantic Coral Reefs.** Livingston Publishing Co., Wynnewood, Pa.

Colin, Patrick 1975. **The Neon Gobies.** T.F.H. Publications, Inc. Neptune, N.J. 304 pp.

Colin, P.L. 1978. **Caribbean Reef Invertebrates and Plants.** T.F.H. Publications, Inc., Neptune City, NJ, USA. 512 pp.

Dawes, C. J. 1981. **Marine Botany.** John Wiley & Sons, New York, NY, USA. 628 pp.

Dawson, E. Y. 1956. **How to Know the Seaweeds.** WM. C. Brown Co., Dubuque, IA, USA. 197 pp.

de Graaf, F. 1973. **Marine Aquarium Guide, (English translation, Dr. J. Spiekerman).** The Pet Library, LTD., Harrison, NJ 284 pp.

Debelius, H. 1984. **Armoured Knights of the Sea.** Quality Marine (English Edition), Los Angles, CA, USA. 120 pp.

Debelius. 1989. **Fishes for the Invertebrate Aquarium.** (3rd ed., English). Aquarium Systems, Mentor. OH. 160 p.

de Graaf, Frank 1973. **Marine Aquarium Guide.** The Pet Library, Ltd. London, England, 284 pp

Dewey, D. (Editor) 1986. **For What It's Worth, Vol. 1.** *FAMA Anthology Lib. Ser.* R/C Modeler Corp. Sierra Madre, CA, USA 271 pp.

Emmens, C.W. 1990. **Marine Aquaria and Minature Reefs.** TFH Publications, Inc. Neptune City, NJ

Florida Aqua Farms. 1987. **Plankton Culture Manual.** Fla. Aqua Farms, Dade City, FL, USA. 53 pp.

Friese, U. E. 1972. **Sea Anemones.** T.F.H. Publications, Inc., Neptune City, NJ, USA. 128 pp.

George, David and Jennifer. 1979. **Marine Life. An Illustrated Encyclopedia of Invertebrate Life in the Sea.** John Wiley & Sons, New York, NY, USA. 288 p.

Gosner, K.L. 1978. **Atlantic Seashore : Invertebrates and Seaweeds of the Atlantic Coast from the Bay of Fundy to Cape Hatteras.** The Easton Press. Norwalk, C.T. 329 pp.

Herald, E.S. 1961. **Living Fishes of the World.** Doubleday and Co., Garden City, N.Y. 304 pp

Haywood, M. and S. Wells. 1989. **The Manual of Marine Invertebrates.** Tetra Press, Morris Plains, NJ, USA. 208 p.

Hess, Deb and John Stevely 1981. **The Biology of Marine Aquarium Fishes Collected in Monroe County, Florida.** NOAA Technical Memorandum, NMFS-SEFC - 59. pp 26-83.

Kaplan, E.G. 1988. **A Field Guide to Southeastern and Caribbean Seashores.** Houghton Mifflin Co., Boston, MA, USA. 425 pp.

Kaplan, E. G. 1982. **A Field Guide to Coral Reefs, Caribbean and Florida.** Houghton Mifflin Company, Boston, MA, USA. 289 pp.

Keeley, D, and T. Evans. 1987. **The Encyclopedia of the Marine Aquarium.** Cresent Books, New York, N.Y. 208 pp.

Keenleyside, Miles H.A. 1979. **Diversity and Adaptation in Fish Behavior.** Springer-Verlag, New York, N.Y. 208 pp.

Kingsford, Edward 1979. **Marine Aquarium Compatibility Guide.** Palmetto Publishing Company, St. Petersburg, Fla. 70 pp.(out of print)

Kingsford, Edward 1975. **Treatment of Exotic Marine Fish Diseases.** Palmetto Publishing Co., St.Petersburg, Fla. 92 pp. (out of print)

cek, Rodger and John Kolman 1976. **Marines (The Fishes).** Marine Hobbyist News Publications, Bloomington, IL. 144 pp. (out of print)

Littler, D. S., M. Littler, K. E. Bucher, and J. N. Norris. 1989. **Marine Plants of the Caribbean.** Smithsonian Institution Press. Washington, D.C. 263 pp.

Lundegaard, G. 1985. **Keeping Marine Fish.** Blandford Press, Dorset, England. 94 pp.

Melzak, M. 1984. **The Marine Aquarium Manual.** ARCO Publishing, New York, NY, USA. 175 pp.

Miner, R.W. 1950. **Field Book of Seashore Life.** G. P. Putnam's Sons, New York, NY, USA. 888 pp.

Moe, M.A. Jr. 1989, 1992. (revised, 1992) **The Marine Aquarium Reference: Systems and Invertebrates.** Green Turtle Publications. Plantation, FL, USA. 512 pp.

Needham, James G., F.E. Lutz, P.S. Welch and P.S. Galtsoff, Ed. 1937. **Culture Methods for Invertebrate Animals.** Comstock Publishing Company. Dover Edition 1959. Dover Publications, New York, N.Y. 590 pp.

Palko, Barbara J. 1981. **A Balanced Marine Aquarium.** NOAA Technical Memorandum, NMFSSEFC - 59. pp 1-25. (out of print)

Quick, Joe A. Jr. 1977. **Marine Disease Primer: Book One, A guide to disease prevention in aquarium fishes and invertebrates.** Marine Hobbyist News Publications. Bloomington, Ill. 47 pp. (out of print)

Randall, John E. 1965. **Food Habits of Reef Fishes of the West Indies.** *In* Studies in Tropical Oceanography, Vol. 5. pp 665-840.

Randall, John E. 1968. **Caribbean Reef Fishes.** T.F.H. Publications, Neptune, N.J. 318 pp.

Reichenbach-Klinke, HJ.-H. (1972) **Fish Pathology. English translation, Christa Ahrens.** TFH Publications. Neptune City, N.J. 512 pp.

Robins, C.R., G. C. Ray, J. Douglass and E. Freund. 1986. **A Field Guide to the Atlantic Coast Fishes of North America.** Houghton Mifflen Co., Boston MA. 354pp.

Sefton, N. and S.K. Webster. 1986. **Caribbean Reef Invertebrates.** Sea Challengers, Monterey, CA. 112 pp.

Spotte, S. 1970. **Fish and Invertebrate Culture: Water Management in Closed Systems.** John Wiley & Sons. NY, USA. 145 pp.

Spotte, S. 1973. **Marine Aquarium Keeping.** John Wiley & Sons. NY, USA. 171 pp.

Spotte, S. 1979. **Seawater Aquariums, The Captive Environment.** John Wiley & Sons. NY, USA. 413 pp.

Spotte, S. 1992. **Captive Seawater Fishes : Science and Technology.** John Wiley & Sons, Inc., New York, USA. 942 pp.

Steene, R. 1990. **Coral Reefs : Nature's Richest Realm.** Mallard Press, New York, NY. 336 pp.

Sterrer, W. 1986. Editor. **Marine Fauna and Flora of Bermuda. A Systematic Guide to the Identification of Marine Organisms.** John Wiley & Sons. NY, USA. 742 pp.

Steene, Rodger C. 1979. **Butterfly and Angelfishes of the World. Vol. I: Australia.** Wiley Interscience. New York, N.Y 144 pp.

Straughan, Robert P.L. 1970. **The Salt Water Aquarium in the Home.** A.S. Barnes and Company. Cranbury, N.J. 360 pp. (out of print)

Thiel, A. 1988. **The Marine Fish and Invert Reef Aquarium.** Aardvark Press, Bridgeport, CT, USA. 278 p.

Thiel, A. 1989a. **Advanced Reef Keeping I.** Aardvark Press. Bridgeport, CT, USA. 440 p.

Thiel, A. 1989b. **Small Reef Aquarium Basics.** Aardvark Press, Las Cruces, NM, USA. 175 p.

Thiel, A. 1992 (in press) **Advanced Reef Keeping II.** Aardvark Press. Las Cruces, NM, USA.

Thresher, Ronald E. 1980. **Reef Fish: Behavior and Ecology on the Reef and in the Aquarium.** Palmetto Publishing Company, St. Petersburg, Fla. 171 pp. (out of print)

Thresher, R. E. 1984. **Reproduction in Reef Fishes.** TFH Publications. Neptune City, N.J. 399 pp.

Tullock, J. 1990. **The Reef Tank Owner's Manual.** Arrdvark Press. Las Cruces, NM, USA. 272 p.

Vine, P. 1986. **Red Sea Invertebrates.** Immel Publishing. London, England. 224 pp.

Voss, G. L. 1976. **Seashore Life of Florida and the Caribbean.** Banyan Books, Inc., Miami, FL, USA. 199 p.

Voss, G.L. 1988. **Coral Reefs of Florida.** Pineapple Press, Sarasota, FL 80 pp.

Wilkens, P. 1973. **The Saltwater Aquarium for Tropical Marine Invertebrates. 2nd Extended Edition. (English Translation).** Engelbert Pfriem, Wuppertal-Elberfeld, Germany. 216 pp.

Wood, E.M., 1983. **Reef Corals of the World: Biology and Field Guide.** T.F.H. Publications, Inc. Neptune City, NJ, USA. 256 pp.

Wrobel, D. 1989. **The Living Reef Aquarium Manual.** BioLogic Aquarium Products. Salinas, CA, USA. 58 pp.

Walls, J.G. (Ed.) 1982. **Encyclopedia of Marine Invertebrates.** T.F.H. Publications, Inc., Neptune City, NJ, USA. 736 pp.

Walls, Jerry G. 1975. **Fishes of the Northern Gulf of Mexico.** T.F.H. Publications, Inc. Neptune, N.J.

Periodicals

Aquarium Fish Magazine
Fancy Publications, Inc. 3 Burroughs, Irvine, CA. 92718
Freshwater and Marine Aquarium
R/C Modeler Corp. P.O. Box 487, Sierra Madre, CA. 91024
Journal of Aquariculture and Aquatic Sciences
The Written Word. 7601 E. Forest Lakes Dr. NW, Parkville, MO. 64152
Marine Fish Monthly
Publishing Concepts Corp. Main Street, Luttrell, TN. 37779
Sea Scope (a quarterly publication free to hobbyists)
Aquarium Systems, Inc. 8141 Tyler Blvd, Mentor OH 44060
Today's Aquarist Newsletter
Pisces Publishing Co., Suite 2-155, 548 Naugatuck Ave., Devon CT 06460
Tropical Fish Hobbyist
T.F.H. Publications, Inc. One TFH Plaza, Neptune City, NJ. 07753

Special organizations

International Marinelife Alliance (IMA U.S.)
(Publishers of *Sea Wind*, the bulletin of the IMA)
201 W. Stassney, Suite 408
Austin Texas 78745-3156
The International Oceanographic Foundation
(Publishers of *Sea Frontiers*)
3979 Rickenbacker Causeway
Virgina Key, Miami, FL 33149
National Audubon Society
P.O. Box 2666
Boulder, CO 80322

Computer programs

Professor Fish: A computerized, practical guide to Fish Care and Disease Management, Marine Version. Written by Prof. Terry Seigel and Dr. Douglas Robbins. Oddbirds, 220 Willoughby Ave. Brooklyn, NY 11205

Sandpoint Aquarium Manager: Data Logging and Analysis Software. Tracks and logs data needed for aquarium management. A valuable interface between aquarium management and computer analysis. Sandpoint Aquarium Products, 1365-B, Interior St., Eugene, OR 97402

Videos

An Introduction to the Hobby of Reef Keeping. by Julian Sprung. Two Little Fishies, Inc. 4016 Prado Blvd., Coconut Grove, FL 33133

Eye of the Diver. Volume 1, The Florida Keys. 2654 East Oakland Park Blvd. Suite 24, Ft. Lauderdale, FL 33306

There are many videos now available on diving, reef keeping, collecting marine organisms, marine aquarium setup, fish identification, and many other topics. Most of these videos are produced by manufacturers and suppliers and have a commercial intent beyond just dissemination of information. This understood, however, there is also good information in many of these videos, and some are well worth watching. Many aquarium societies also make video tapes of speakers and programs and keep these available for members to borrow. Video can be a dynamic medium and I'm sure that aquarists will find many worthwhile videos available now, and more in the future.

Marine Aquarium Societies

Check your local aquarium shop for the names and addresses of local aquarium societies and clubs. Freshwater societies often have internal marine groups. If you have no local society, join a society in a nearby city or start a new society with a few like minded friends. Individual societies often have speakers, programs, tank shows, auctions, field trips, and other events for local aquarists; as well as providing a forum for the exchange of ideas, experiences, equipment, fish, invertebrates and plants. There are also two international/national aquarium societies that promise to be very helpful to the hobby and science of keeping marine aquariums.

Marine Aquarium Society of North America
MASNA, P.O. Box 9401, Columbia, SC 29209 USA

International Marine Aquarist Association
IMAA, P. O. Box 7, Ilminster, Somerset, TA19 9BY
England

The marine aquarium societies of North America have worked together since 1989 to sponser a Marine Aquarium Conference of North America (MACNA) each year. The fourth annual MACNA will be hosted by the Florida Marine Aquarium Society, Museum of Science, 3280 South Miami, Ave., Miami, FL 33129, and will be held September 19 and 20, 1992. Past conferences have been held in Toronto, Cleveland, and Newark. Consult local aquarium societies and current periodicals for information on future MACNA events.

Symbols, Measures, and Conversions

Abbreviations

Selected chemical symbols

Aluminum	Al	Hydrogen	H	Rubidium	Rb
Arsenic	As	Iodine	I	Potassium	K
Barium	Ba	Iron	Fe	Silicon	Si
Boron	B	Lead	Pb	Silver	Ag
Bromine	Br	Magnesium	Mg	Sodium	Na
Calcium	Ca	Manganese	Mn	Strontium	Sr
Carbon	C	Molybdenum	Mo	Sulphur	S
Chlorine	Cl	Mercury	Hg	Tin	Sn
Cobalt	Co	Nitrogen	N	Vanadium	V
Copper	Cu	Oxygen	O	Zinc	Zn
Fluorine	F	Phosphorus	P		

Selected chemical compounds

Ammonia, NH_3

Ammonium, NH_4^+

Bicarbonate, HCO_3^-

Calcium carbonate, $CaCO_3$
(chalk, calcite, aragonite)

Calcium chloride, $CaCl_{2)}$

Calcium hydroxide, $Ca(OH)_2$
(*Kalkwasser*, limewater)

Carbon dioxide, CO_2

Carbonate, CO_3^{2-}

Carbonic acid, H_2CO_3

Hydrogen sulfide, H_2S

Magnesium carbonate, $MgCO_3$

Nitrate, NO_3^-

Nitrite, NO_2^-

Sodium bicarbonate, $NaHCO_3$
(baking soda, bicarbonate of soda)

Sodium carbonate, dry, Na_2CO_3
(soda ash)

Sodium carbonate, crystalline, $NaHCO_3$ (washing soda, sal soda)

Sodium chloride, NaCl
(table salt, rock salt)

Sodium thiosulfate, $Na_2S_2O_3, 5H_2O$
(hypo, dechlorinator)

Light

1 foot-candle = 1 lumen
1 candlepower = 12.56 foot-candles
1 Lux = 0.0929 foot-candles (or lumens)
1 lumen = 10.76 Lux
1 nanometer (nm) = 10 Angstroms (Å)

Temperature

Fahrenheit scale (°F): water freezes 32 °F, water boils 212 °F.
Centigrade (Celsius) scale (°C): water freezes 0 °C, water boils 100 °C.
Kelvin (Absolute) scale (°K): water freezes 273 °K, water boils 373 °K.
To convert °F to °C: (°F - 32) divided by 1.8 = °C
To convert °C to °F: (°C x 1.8) + 32 = °F

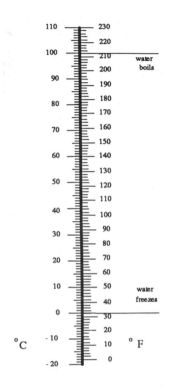

U K (British Imperial measure) conversions
(Courtesy of John Pointon)

US gallons   times 0.833 equals UK gallons
UK gallons   times 1.201 equals US gallons
UK pints   times 0.568 equals liters (Litres)
UK gallons   times 4.546 equals liters (Litres)
US gallons   times 3.785 equals liters (Litres)
liters (Litres)   times 61.024 equals cu. inches
liters (Litres)   times 0.035 equals cu. feet
liters (Litres)   times 2.113 equals US pints
liters (Litres)   times 0.264 equals US gallons
liters (Litres)   times 1.756 equals UK pints
liters (Litres)   times 0.220 equals UK gallons
one cu. foot seawater equals 6.228 UK gallons

UK gallons in a rectangular or square tank:
Length X Width X Height in inches and
divide by 277.42

UK gallons in a cylindrical tank:
diameter squared X 0.8 X height in inches
and divide by 277.42

One UK gallon seawater equals 10.2 lbs,
4.63 k, 277.42 cu. inches

Liquid measure
1 cubic centimeter (cc) = 1 ml, approximately 20 drops
1 milliliter (ml) = 1 cc, 1/1000 l
1 liter (l) = 1000 ml, 1.06 qt, 2.1 pt
20 large drops or 25 small drops = approximately 1 ml
1 teaspoon (tsp) = 5 ml, 1/6 fl oz
1 tablespoon (tbsp) = 3 tsp, 1/2 fl oz, 15 ml
1 fluid ounce (fl oz) = 2 tbsp, 6 tsp, 29.6 ml
1 cup = 8 fl oz, 236.8 ml
1 quart (qt) = 32 fl oz, 2 pt, 946.3 ml, 0.95 l
1 gallon (gal) 128 fl oz, 8 pt, 4 qt, 3.8 l, 231 in^3
1 part per million (ppm) = 1 ml or mg per l (ml/l), 3.78 mg/gal

Length
1 micron (μ) = 1/1000 mm
1 millimeter (mm) = 1/10 cm, 1000 microns, 0.039 in
1 centimeter (cm) = 10 mm, 0.39 in
1 meter (m) = 1000 mm, 100 cm, 39.37 in, 3.28 ft
1 inch (in) = 25.4 mm, 2.54 cm
1 foot (ft) = 12 in, 30.48 cm, 0.3 m
1 yard (yd) = 3 ft, 91.44 cm, 0.91 m

Weight

1 milligram (mg) = 1/1000 g
1 gram (g) = 1000 mg, 15.4 gr, 0.035 oz
1 kilogram (kg) = 1000 g, 35 oz, 2.2 lbs, one l pure water
1 grain (gr) = 0.65 g
1 ounce (oz) = 28.35 g
1 pound (lb) = 16 oz, 454 g, 0.45 k

Surface area (square measure, length X width)

1 square centimeter (cm^2) = 0.155 in^2
1 square meter (m^2) = 10,000 cm^2, 10.764 ft^2, 1555 in^2
1 square inch (in^2) = 0.007 ft^2, 6.45 cm^2
1 square foot (ft^2) = 144 in^2, 929.03 cm^2
1 square yard (yd^2) = 1296 in^2

Volume (cubic measure, length X width X height)

1 cubic centimeter (cm^3) = 0.061 in^3
1 cubic meter (m^3) = 11.77 ft^3, 1.31 yd^3
1 cubic inch (in^3) = 0.00058 ft^3, 16.387 cm^3
1 cubic foot (ft^3) = 1728 in^3, 0.765 m^3
1 gallon = 231 in^3

Formulas and data

1 ft^3 of seawater = 64 lbs, 29.02 k, 7.5 gal, 28.4 l, 1728 in^3, 3785.4 cc

1 gallon of seawater = 8.5 lbs, 3.86 k, 231 in^3

To find the number of US gallons in a rectangular or square tank
Multiply length X width X height in inches and divide by 231.

To find the number of US gallons in a cylindrical tank
Multiply the diameter squared X 0.8 X the height in inches and divide by 231.

To find the number of US gallons in a hexagon, octagon, or other multi-sided tank with sides of equal width, measure the total perimeter and multiply by the width of a single side. Then divide by 2, multiply by the height in inches, and divide by 231 to get the number of gallons.

To find the number of US gallons in a spherical tank, measure the radius (distance from the center to the edge of the sphere) in inches and cube this measurement (times itself by 3). Multiply this figure by 3.1416 (pi) and multiply the result by 1.33. Divide by 231 to get the volume of a sphere and again by 2 to get the volume of half a sphere.

Full salinity seawater contains 35 to 37 parts per thousand (ppt, ‰) salt. This is 35 to 37 grams per kilogram or liter, 4.7 to 5 oz per gal, and 2.9 to 3.1 lbs per 10 gal. *Approximately* 2.7 to 3 lbs of artificial sea salts make up 10 gal of full salinity seawater.

True specific gravity (sg) of full strength seawater (35 ‰) is 1.0260.
A standard hydrometer calibrated at 59 °F (15 °C) reads 1.0234 sg at 77 °F (25 °C). Seawater at a salinity of 30 ‰ has a true specific gravity of 1.0222. At 30 ‰, a standard hydrometer reads 1.096 sg at 77 °F.

Index

About the Author

Martin A. Moe Jr. has been a marine biologist since 1960. He holds a masters degree from the University of South Florida and has worked as a fishery biologist, marine biologist, ichthyologist, and commercial marine fish culturist for over 30 years. His scientific and popular articles and books date back to 1962 when he began his career as a marine biologist for the State of Florida. He entered the private sector in 1969 and developed the basic technology for breeding Florida pompano in 1970. He accomplished the first commercial culture of marine tropical fish (clownfish and neon gobies) in a garage in 1972, and over the years has reared over 30 species of marine tropical fish, including spawning, rearing, and even hybridizing French and grey Atlantic angelfish. Moe is the author of a definitive book on tropical Atlantic lobsters, *Lobsters : Florida • Bahamas • the Caribbean*, as well as his popular and best selling marine aquarium books, *The Marine Aquarium Handbook : Beginner to Breeder* and *The Marine Aquarium Reference: Systems and Invertebrates*. He founded Aqualife Research Corporation in 1972 and Green Turtle Publications in 1982. He and his wife Barbara now write and publish books on marine life and aquarium topics, and work with experimental keeping and rearing of aquatic organisms.

Books by Martin Moe

The Marine Aquarium Handbook :
Beginner to Breeder

A practical handbook on the theory and methods of keeping and breeding marine tropical fish. Everything you need to know to set up and maintain a successful saltwater aquarium. New edition revised and expanded in 1992.

320 pages
ISBN 0-939960-07-9   **$16.95**

The Marine Aquarium Reference :
Systems and Invertebrates

A major reference for the modern aquarist. This book contains 512 pages of text, tables, figures, and drawings that clearly and simply explain the techniques and technology of modern marine aquarium systems, including reef systems. *The Reference* clearly explains and integrates the new marine aquarium technology, trickle filters, high intensity lighting, gas reactors, denitrifying filters, protein foam skimmers, and many other advances with the traditional, established techniques of keeping marine aquariums. It also introduces the aquarist to the latest classification of invertebrates and other living organisms, with expanded discussions of the invertebrate groups most important to marine aquarists. This book is a companion volume to *The Marine Aquarium Handbook* and contains new (not duplicated) information.

Fourth printing, revised January 1992.

512 pages.
LC CIP 89-7554
ISBN 0-939960-05-2   **$21.95**

obsters : Florida • Bahamas • the Caribbean

The Caribbean or Florida spiny lobster, *Panulirus argus*, is one of the most important marine natural resources throughout the western, tropical Atlantic Ocean. This is a comprehensive reference to the natural history, evolution, morphology, taxonomy, care and culture, and the recreational and commercial fisheries of the Caribbean spiny lobster. It includes a detailed description of larval rearing attempts on the the spiny lobster in Florida Keys and a synopsis of the world wide literature on rearing and farming of spiny lobsters. Anyone interested in the ecology of coral reefs, the natural history and the fisheries for spiny lobsters, and the care and culture of marine crustaceans in aquarium systems will find this book an educational and entertaining reference.

512 pages.
LC CIP 91-23948
ISBN 0-939960-06-0   **$22.95**

You can borrow these books from your local library. You can purchase them at your local book store, aquarium shop, and at many public aquariums. If you can not find them locally, send your order to the address below.

Green Turtle Publications
P.O. Box 17925
Plantation, FL 33318

Please include $2 for shipping. Florida residents also please include the appropriate sales tax.

Marine Aquarium Log Sheet (1)

From - The Marine Aquarium Handbook: Beginner to Breeder, by Martin A. Moe, Jr.

Each marine aquarium system should have a log sheet to record setup, maintenance, changing conditions, and live stock data. This form may suit your needs. You may remove it from the book and make as many copies as you wish. (An enlarged copy will make the form easier to use.)

Tank Designation _____ Tank size _____

Setup date_____ filter run-in date_____ actual gallons _____

freshwater treatment _____ salt (brand and amount) _____

_____   _____

filter run-in method and data _____
_____ starting salinity
(ppt or S.G.) _____

Run-in and Maintenance Testing

Date	salinity	temp.	pH	NH₃	NO₂	NO₃	Cu	ORP	CO₂	O₂	PO₄	Fe	Ca	Carb. KH

Columns grouped as: basic data (pH, NH₃, NO₂, NO₃, Cu); Redox (ORP); reef tank data (CO₂, O₂, PO₄, Fe, Ca); Carb. KH

General Service (enter date)	cleaning	changes	addition
water			
top off (evap.)			
filter media			
tank (sides & bottom)			
carbon			
trace elements			
light bulbs			
other			

(Keep additional dated comments and photographs in a plain notebook.)

Marine Aquarium Log Sheet (2)

From - The Marine Aquarium Handbook:
Beginner to Breeder, by Martin A. Moe, Jr.

Tank Designation _____

Foods and Feeding (record changes and additions)

type and/or composition	frequency fed

Medication and Treatment History
(copper, vitamins, trace supplements, antibiotics, medications, etc.)

treatment	date	dosage	dates retreated	date removed	comments

Live Stock History

species	date of introduction	date of loss or removal	comments